Beyond Smart Cities

The promise of competitiveness and economic growth in so-called smart cities is widely advertised in Europe and the US. The promise is focused on global talent and knowledge economies and not on learning and innovation. But really to achieve smart cities—that is, to create the conditions of continuous learning and innovation—this book argues that there is a need to understand what is below the surface and to examine the mechanisms which affect the way cities learn and then connect together. This book draws on quantitative and qualitative data with concrete case studies to show how networks already operating in cities are used to foster and strengthen connections in order to achieve breakthroughs in learning and innovation. Going beyond smart cities means understanding how cities construct, convert and manipulate relationships that grow in urban environments. Cities discussed in this book—Amman, Barcelona, Bilbao, Charlotte, Curitiba, Juárez, Portland, Seattle and Turin—illuminate a blind spot in the literature. Each of these cities has achieved important transformations, and learning has played a key role, one that has been largely ignored in academic circles and practice concerning competitiveness and innovation.

Tim Campbell has worked for more than 35 years in urban development with experience in scores of countries and hundreds of cities in Latin America, South and East Asia, Eastern Europe, and Africa. His areas of expertise include strategic urban planning, city development strategies, decentralization, urban policy, and social and poverty impact of urban development. He is chairman of the Urban Age Institute, which fosters leadership and innovation between and among cities in areas of strategic urban planning, urban policy and management, sustainable environmental planning, and poverty reduction. Campbell retired from the World Bank in December 2005 after more than 17 years working in various capacities in the urban sector. Before joining the Bank, he worked for over 13 years as a private consultant and university professor. His consulting clients included private sector firms, governments, and international organizations. He taught at Stanford University and the University of California at Berkeley. He has also lived in rural and small town Costa Rica for two years as a Peace Corps volunteer.

Praise for this book

"This is a strikingly original piece of work that is unlike previous efforts to understand city development. Although there is a long history of the study of networks of influence in sociology, most recently by Manuel Castells, it has never been connected to city innovation and learning in the way that Campbell does here."

Michael Teitz, Emeritus Professor, University of California, Berkeley

"Perfectly timed for this moment in history, when more of mankind is urban than rural, this incisive book shows that profound urban transformations now underway in cities are being led by innovators—formal and informal leaders—who are harnessing the power of shared learnings to convert information and knowledge into innovation, both in policy and in practice. Campbell offers a practical approach to understanding urbanization through a distinctive lens."

Wim Elfrink, Executive Vice President and Chief Globalization Officer, Cisco

"At last someone has unravelled the complexity of urban networks that lead to learning and help drive a city's creativity and innovation. These are issues that so far nobody has addressed in this comprehensive way. Only a person with Tim Campbell's immense global experience could have achieved this."

Charles Landry, author of *The Creative City*

"A 'flaneur' of the modern global city, Campbell perceives new features, like 'clouds of trust,' in the collective learning of cities. His unexpected findings will compel cities and city associations to rethink their strategies about learning and global city networks."

Josep Roig, Secretary General, United Cities and Local Governments

Beyond Smart Cities

How Cities Network, Learn and Innovate

Tim Campbell

publishing for a sustainable future

London • New York

First published 2012
by Earthscan
2 Park Square, Milton Park, Abingdon, Oxon OX14 4RN

Simultaneously published in the USA and Canada
by Earthscan
711 Third Avenue, New York, NY 10017

Earthscan is an imprint of the Taylor & Francis Group, an
informa business

British Library Cataloguing in Publication Data
A catalogue record for this book is available from the British Library

Library of Congress Cataloging-in-Publication Data
Campbell, Tim, 1943–
Beyond smart cities : how cities network, learn and innovate /
   Tim Campbell.
      p. cm.
   Includes bibliographical references and index.
   1. City planning—Case studies. 2. Cities and towns—Growth—
   Case studies. I. Title.
   HT166.C25 2012
   307.1'216—dc23   2011031183

ISBN: 978-1-84971-425-9 (hbk)
ISBN: 978-1-84971-426-6 (pbk)
ISBN: 978-0-20313-768-0 (ebk)

Typeset in Frutiger
by Keystroke, Station Road, Codsall, Wolverhampton
Printed by Bell & Bain Ltd., Glasgow

Contents

List of figures and tables

Figures

Tables

Foreword

Dr Joan Clos

United Nations Under Secretary and Executive Director, UN-HABITAT

By now the world is well aware that the planet has become urbanized. Policy makers are not always so cognizant that this long-running historical process is unfolding unevenly. Africa is the fastest urbanizing continent on the globe, and poverty is shifting to cities. At the same time, cities everywhere share needs in the core areas of urban development.

One of the natural consequences of an urbanized planet is the rise of inter-actions among cities as they grow. Only 50 years ago, most cities in the developing world were the weak and dependent creatures of subnational governments or mere agents of central authorities. Even then, cities were often blamed for failures to correct glaring problems that for the most part were not of their own making. Today, cities are beginning to see, and many of them to act upon, the latent potential they hold as vehicles for change.

This urban transition over half a century has been accompanied by a largely unseen but open process of learning at two levels. Individual cities have engaged in collective learning by key leaders in public, private and civic realms. Importantly also, cities are engaging increasingly in an exchange of ideas and best practice. Indications are that investment in city learning and exchange has been growing rapidly over the past two decades. Knowledge exchange can help the 4000 cities and towns around the globe to overcome past deficits.

In 2001, UN-Habitat published some of the first documents calling attention to horizontal assistance as a vehicle to advance urban development. Today, UN-Habitat is sharpening its focus on key areas that affect all cities: planning; urban institutions, and governance; and economics, job creation, and finance. New attention is given to issues such as urban mobility and energy supply as key elements of the prosperity of cities. Harnessing the spontaneous exchanges taking place between cities can serve both the normative objectives of UN-Habitat and the operational needs of its most important stakeholders.

Tim Campbell's exploration into "learning cities" deepens our understanding about how the learning process works. His key observation is that although several kinds of learning systems can be observed, the process of learning may be as important as the product in contributing to sustainable outcomes. Outside knowledge is only part of the solution. The critical limits are often internal. He suggests that the policy environment—local, national, and international—can help facilitate, even accelerate, learning, and enhance the richness of a city's collective thinking.

Foreword

Wim Elfrink

Executive Vice President and Chief Globalization Officer, Cisco

Over the past several decades, leading members of the corporate sector, academic community, governments and organized civil society have been turning their attention to solving long-standing urban problems with the new tools of advanced technology. It is ironic in a way that the signature features of cities—density and high levels of interaction—have become the target for innovation by the very technologies that grew out of urban settings in the first place. Today we are crossing the threshold to put internet-based tools to work in cities. This signifies a new urban age, one that makes much greater use of technology—networks, sensors, and the analytics—to tie cities together. Now and in the future, practically any object at both the personal and the household level—objects that will soon number in the trillions—will have an accessible address over the internet.

Cisco's Smart+Connected Communities initiative has taken a leading role, utilizing the network as the service delivery platform to transform physical communities to connected communities. This approach helps community leaders in the public and private sector redefine the way public information and services are delivered. Through smart and seamless connections, individuals, communities, and cities can realize significant pay-offs: working arrangements without a commute; transit without the burden of large carbon footprints; health care virtually from the home or a public location; the operation of public facilities opti-mized; and economic development. For all of this to work well and at scale, the city itself—its leaders, both public and private—must understand and agree on pathways forward.

Tim Campbell's book invites us to look deeper into the fabric that makes cities work in a seamless manner. This book reminds us of several principles that are important to making cities more livable, economically, socially and environmentally sustainable, and congenial. One is that technological devices are merely tools that can make our lives better only if they are put in the hands of users who understand and can make the most of them. The great sociologist Peter Marris observed that matches and firearms were taken up quickly by many groups because the receiving societies understood that new technologies could advance their purposes. In the complexities of cities, identifying a city's purpose and learning about new options takes on an entirely new order of effort, one that must engage a wide spectrum of formal and informal leaders in the city. Campbell points out that the tissue of trust between and among groups is a magic ingredient in achieving a coherence of effort.

A second feature of this book, one that Cisco understands and supports, is the sharing of learnings from one place to the next about how to make things work. Campbell documents for the first time the active trade in ideas that is taking place among cities around the globe. Part of the inter-connectedness of the new urban age is that cities by the thousands all around the globe are increasingly exchanging ideas between and among themselves. Indeed, Cisco, like many other corporate players, is forming partnerships with the many actors in the urban arena, seeking to facilitate the exchange of good ideas, the hastening of implementation and the continued innovation that must follow.

The Cisco Smart+Connected Communities initiative brings together a broad portfolio of partnerships, products, services, and solutions to address this significant emerging opportunity that the network offers as medium of exchange. It will change the way cities, towns, and villages are designed, built, managed, and renewed to achieve economic, social, and environmental sustainability. *Beyond Smart Cities* helps us balance the equation in our quest for progress. The book opens a new window to learning and shows us how cities take into account both the technological and the human elements needed to solve urban problems.

Preface and acknowledgments

Over five decades working in urban development, first as a consultant from Berkeley and later at the World Bank in Washington, I grew increasingly cognizant of a fatal flaw in the approach taken by development institutions towards cities. While Bank lending was both welcome and productive support for infrastructure that is so critical to urban and national development, managing local public choice and investment decisions are equally critical, yet far less diligently pursued in lending. Generalizing broadly, and perhaps unfairly for some agencies, development institutions have not met their responsibilities on the software and management side of urban development. Capacity building takes time; it is tortuous and fraught with headwinds and reversals, like frequent regime change at the local level and capricious policy shifts nationally.

I observed this somewhat schizophrenic approach to development over many years. The hardware of infrastructure moved ahead at a reasonable pace while the software of urban management was left all too often to the whims of fate after World Bank missions had departed the country.

With the waves of decentralization in the 1980s and 1990s, a subtle but now unmistakable change became visible. Nations and cities remained far apart in terms of priorities and policy coordination. But cities began to recognize the many similarities that bound them together, and this common ground became the agora for learning and exchange. Cities of a certain size anywhere on the globe began to realize that often they had more in common with each other than with smaller cities in their own country.

It is hard to say exactly when an inflection point appeared in the history of city-to-city exchange, but the 1976 UN-Habitat Conference in Vancouver is a convenient reference point. This book explores learning in cities that began to take off sometime afterward; certainly horizontal exchange was running much more heavily by the 1996 UN-Habitat Conference in Istanbul. The potential of this phenomenon is still only beginning to be recognized in policy and academic circles.

The book is written for the practitioner, policy maker and scholar. Although I believe the material poses some intriguing questions that need further research, I hope that elected city leaders, members of civil society, and corporate citizens alike will find both resonance with and stimulation from the ideas expressed here.

Of course, ideas about learning in organizations go back a long way, and I am cognizant of the duty to acknowledge all that have come before me. I will occasionally redefine terms or concepts developed by thinkers who have trodden this path before, including the many practitioners of sister and twinning cities: Janice Perlman and her MegaCities, who saw the transfer of knowledge as an important policy and developmental tool long ago; Jochen Eigen and his colleagues at UN-Habitat; Josep Roig at Metropolis; Bill Stafford at Trade Department Alliance; Tim Honey at Sister Cities International; and many more. I hope they have been done no injustice by the licenses I take in the chapters ahead.

Acknowledgments are also due to many who have helped me shape and improve the chapters contained here. Gordon Feller has been unfailingly supportive and imaginative; Mozart Vitor and Maria Teresa Serra provided ideas and insight from the very earliest drafts. I am indebted also to the German Marshal Fund and especially to the city coordinators—Brian Collier in Charlotte, Mike Wetter in Portland, and Elisa Rosso and Judith Trinchero in Turin.

Gratitude also goes to Michael Teitz for urging me to move ahead; K. C. Sivaramakrishnan and Prod Laquian, Neal Peirce, Paul van Lindert and Marike Bontenbal for reading early versions and providing valuable comment; David Leipziger for helping to manage data and providing excellent draft material; Yang Yu for help with graphics; and Nicki Dennis at Earthscan for helpful advice all along the way. Thanks too to the staff of the Library of Congress where I spent uncountable and pleasurable afternoons doing research.

Finally, special thanks to the family—wife Linda, who unfailingly provided fresh perspective and new insight, and daughter Alana, who helped me work through logical arguments and provided statistical expertise. Thanks also to Kathryn and Eric, for being understanding and supportive over the many months of production.

Tim Campbell
Chevy Chase, MD, USA
August 2011

Part I

The changing place of cities in the urban age

1 Overview

> "Why did you spend US$25,000 apiece on those two 28-year-olds to come here to visit Shanghai?" I asked the Vice President of Boeing about the youngsters on the study tour from Seattle. The VP didn't bat an eye. "It's the best training money can buy. They get to know their customers, the Chinese, and we get to know ourselves, the Seattleites. When we get back to Seattle, we can pick up a phone to call the city or county or Microsoft, and the person on the line is someone we have a relationship with."

Do cities learn?

The vignette about Seattleites in Shanghai contains an important kernel of truth about urban development. It suggests that learning takes place in the heads of people who care about and take action to affect the cities where they live. This is the essence of city learning. The central concept to be explored extensively in this book is unlike organizational learning where new knowledge is captured, recorded and shared in line with mission goals and often a corporate bottom line. The nature of city learning is more closely akin to collective learning, but, as recognized in the substantial bodies of literature built up over the post-war period in both organizational and collective learning, cities are places that are more open, more loosely organized, and more riven with cross-currents of social, economic and political interests than most firms, knowledge-intensive organizations and even associations with broadly shared goals.

And yet, the most successful of cities, the innovators, reformers and survivors in the competitive race for talent and economic power, exhibit a pattern of deliberate and systematic acquisition of knowledge. Good practices in successful cities offer short-cuts. Cape Town and Buenos Aires drew on the waterfront renewal experience of Baltimore and London. Da Nang took lessons from Japan in conversion and regulation of urban land. Regional centers in Rajasthan in the north of India are following lessons of infrastructure expansion and business readiness that peer cities developed in central and southern India. Amman, Jordan is studying the many experiments in decentralized governance from other parts of the world, even outside the Middle East. These examples arise from direct city exchange.

We shall see that the most active of learning cities also develop mechanisms to store, spread and verify newly acquired ideas and apply them to solve local problems. How do they get into these circumstances? Are all learning cities successful and all successful cities learners? This book explores these and other questions that are now arising as cities emerge in this century more prominent in global trade and national standing.

We cannot go very far either without asking, what is learning? In its simplest form, learning is acquiring new knowledge. This book makes the point that cities learn as part of their governance function, but often learning is informal or technical and sometimes even off the governance radar screen altogether. Learning and knowledge acquisition come about almost as a by-product of running a city. Yet learning is qualitatively different from urban governance.

Learning can be straightforwardly linear and mystifyingly complex. In one recent configuration, MacFarlane's idea of "assemblages," groups of like-minded individuals, like slum dweller advocates, share an ethos that is bundled up in one city and transferred elsewhere by dedicated slum advocates working in other cities (MacFarlane, 2010). Practitioners internalize the ethos and apply it to their own city. Janice Perlman's core idea of mega-cities represents another point on a spectrum of learning where knowledgeable practitioners share and develop ideas of best practice (Perlman, 1987). These are both useful and important kinds of learning, but not the kind explored in this book.

The learning of cities is also to be distinguished from the emerging consensus about cities and urbanization that we receive from such influential thinkers as Geddes, Mumford, Castells, Hall and Glaeser. Our focus is how cities learn, as collective units, not on what is received wisdom about cities and policies that are then synthesized and adopted by a wider community of scholars and practitioners.

Learning cities depend upon clusters of people in close exchange of ideas. This is one of the mechanisms that produced the *Triumph of the City* (2011) so eloquently articulated by Edward Glaeser. But while Glaeser highlights the chains of innovative entrepreneurs embedded in cities, *Beyond Smart Cities* focuses on collective learning across public, private and civic networks that function as public goods. Because they provide the context for these networks, cities are the fulcrum upon which policies can help to leverage learning to achieve innovation and change. But most cities have been lethargic about the machinery of learning, merely providing a passive matrix in which exchanges take place. Cities could play a more proactive and productive role in encouraging and expanding networks, filling in key gaps, identifying weak spots, and most of all mobilizing new membership from the ranks of young talent, both native and global.

This book sees city learning as a collective process, which always starts with discovery by individuals. The critical distinction is that individuals begin to learn together. The collective process involves subjective exchanges of values and perceptions, leading to validation and eventual adoption of new ideas by wider groups, such as NGOs, neighborhoods, business communities, public officials, and many more. In contrast to MacFarlane's packaged ethos, learning cities create a common understanding rooted in widely shared values. Thus learning takes place on several levels. On one level is the superficial acquisition of new ideas by a businessman, a city official, a neighborhood activist, picked up by observing the way something works in a city. At another level, learning involves the willing sharing of values that get internalized on the basis of trust. Later in the book, the idea of a milieu of trust will be used to describe environments where this learning takes place.

We shall see also that transmission of ideas, and the values behind them, occurs close to or nearly simultaneously with innovation. The acceptance of the idea itself in learning is a form of innovation. When this is accomplished at city level— in the way taxation is applied, or commercial interests are incorporated into development plans, or a parking meter system is adopted, or neighborhood preferences are heard—breakthroughs are made in policy or in the innovative application of a practice or technology.

Smart cities and learning

The popular literature and current trends in Europe and the US about global talent and knowledge economies advertise the promise of competitiveness and economic growth in so-called smart cities. Yet some smart cities succeed better than others; some cities low down on the IQ list achieve great things. Building up a knowledge economy of highly educated talent, high-tech industries and pervasive electronic connections are only the trappings of smartness and cannot guarantee the outcomes that policy makers hope to achieve. Though global talent and seamless connections are important, they can also amount only to the dressing of a pauper in prince's clothing.

To achieve the real promise of smart cities—that is, to create the conditions of continuous learning and innovation that has led cities like Seattle, Barcelona, Bilbao and Curitiba to keep pace with economic change—cities need something more. This book aims to understand what is below the surface in these places, to examine the mechanisms which are effective in the way open institutions like cities learn, to identify different levels (I will call them "orders") of learning, and to explore ways to connect knowledge communities together to accelerate change.

Learning far and near

In a recent presentation about New York's PlaNYC, Mayor Bloomberg stated that his team

> drew on the experiences of Berlin for our renewable energy and green-roof policies: from Hong Kong, Shanghai and Delhi for our transit improvements; from Copenhagen for our pedestrian and cycling upgrades; from Bogota for our plans for Bus Rapid Transit; and from Los Angeles and Chicago for our plan to plant one million trees.
>
> (United Cities and Local Governments, 2010: 1)

New York is not alone. Seattle has been visiting other cities every year since 1993 to benchmark, build relationships, and capture best practice. Seattle's Trade Development Alliance, born out of the Chamber of Commerce, is a dedicated agency to keep Seattle at the cutting edge. But the real secret of Seattle's learning is not just finding new ideas. The productive secret, as the Boeing executive recounted, is forming relationships that are conducive to collective learning.

Though Seattle is a recognized leader in learning, hundreds of cities around the world are now engaged in the learning process. Large cities everywhere stand astride the most critical arenas in this century. On a global plane, cities are a platform where the fortunes of nations are decided in a globally competitive environment. More and more, the products of city economies are tradeable, meaning that back-office services like hospital accounts in Manchester or design coding for Texas Instruments are handled on the other side of the globe.

These examples represent shifts in the locus of production and a sharp increase everywhere in the stakes for cities to win a race for investments and global talent. These shifts also mean that cities know they must understand their competitors and outperform them in order to move ahead. The exchange of knowledge between cities is part of this understanding and is now taking off in leaps and bounds. Cities can get new knowledge in dozens of ways. Some of the most important are commercial, internal development and exchange with other cities.

Buy it

Some cities, like Bogota, San Salvador and Amman, have turned to a commercial source of knowledge that is developed from international practice, complemented with local data, adapted to local circumstances and packaged for city customers, often the chamber of commerce or more specialized business group. The Monitor Group, McKinsey, Bearing Point, and many other consulting firms offer these services. The analytical work is useful and often of high quality. Some firms aim to be inclusive in the process, taking pains to expose clients to the assumptions and analytical exercise. But often the process is divorced from the day–to-day business of the intended beneficiaries. Key players who must understand and implement the many parts of a typical plan are not involved in working through the strategy.

Worse still, many parts of what must become a functioning whole—that is, the core leadership of a city—are not engaged in working through the discovery. Regulatory bodies, issue-oriented neighborhood groups, local investors and businesses and public officials all have to be a part of uncovering new truth. The Monitor product for Bogota included high-quality data and useful analysis, but ended up with many familiar recommendations in support of clusters in such well-known and already established industries as floristry, electronics, health care and tourism. The knowledge packaging includes recommendations which are also predictable, such as relaxing the regulatory process, streamlining decision making, setting up dedicated agencies to cut transaction costs and urging a marketing of the city brand. And while these may be analytically correct, they cannot themselves produce a magic sauce that results in a wholesale transformation. Without involvement of key stakeholders in the discovery, the creation, the deep and sometimes intensely personal exchange of values, analytics and recommendations often remain only artifacts, having objective truth but not personal conviction.

Invent it at home

Many cities have found ways to innovate by applying already known, locally found or invented techniques to improve an existing process, say taxation or licensing for businesses, or delivery of a new service, like web-based transactions in public business. Curitiba is perhaps one of the early leaders in local invention. A bus rapid transit system was built up on the basis of a social convention about controlling the automobile in the city. A local institutional genius was born in Curitiba. The main elements of the bus system were conceived in Curitiba's planning institute. From the beginning, decades before other cities caught on, while most cities were still stuck on underground metros, the planners in Curitiba aimed to run their system like a surface metro on tires.

Local planners in Curitiba, many with experience in Europe and other international cities, contributed their sometimes exotic knowledge to innovative applications, including the layout of rights of way, dedicated lanes, building densities along the bus routes, revenue sharing of operators, and a host of other clever ideas that make Curitiba a working laboratory of innovation. The learning underlying these innovations was derived from local experts applying knowledge gained from work and travel abroad, and the climate that helped incubate new ideas and nurture them to fruition is a critical part of Curitiba's success.

"Foreign exchange"

Seattle has created a process of learning that ventures out to other cities in an organized exploration of best practice and benchmarking for lessons that can be brought back home. The study missions of Seattle are elaborate, highly organized, dedicated visits organized on a yearly basis by the Trade Development Alliance, a dependency of the Greater Seattle Chamber of Commerce. The study missions engage up to 100 business and civic leaders in the greater Seattle area. Their objectives are many, but one key overarching objective made explicit in the ethos of Seattle is to build relationships internally. As participants visit peer cities, they broaden their understanding of the position of Seattle vis-à-vis the visited city, its region and state, and indeed, increasingly, the entire global context of urban economies.

Participants on the missions include the top leadership figures of the city and county along with utilities, ports, universities, private firms, and NGOs. Not all of the delegates are senior officials, as indicated by the high-level Boeing executive whose vignette opens this chapter.

The heart of the learning experience takes place during the many opportunities where participants are together; in plenary sessions, in working groups, at meals, on the bus, when delegates sit for the post-action meeting on the last day, and even after they have returned home. During these gatherings, they question and digest what they have seen and heard and exchange perceptions and opinions with each other. They are able to gain perspective and insight on their own issues back home.

Above all, the interactive learning style of Seattle's study missions creates a personal bond of shared experiences. Participants often spoke long afterwards, back in Seattle, of the benefits of having participated in a mission. Back home, when placing a phone call to a government agency or business, the advantage of having had this shared experience and knowing the face of the "person on the other end of the call" greatly facilitated understanding and the speed of doing business (Trade Development Alliance, 2001).

The rise of city learning

At a global level, cities are forming a thick and growing web-work of ties that constitutes an underground economy of knowledge. A survey conducted in preparation for this book shows that city-to-city exchanges—i.e., technical visits of professional practitioners seeking new knowledge and best practice—reach thousands, perhaps tens of thousands, of visits each year across the globe.

In both global and local arenas, proactive cities are developing a dynamic of internal leadership that involves acquiring outside knowledge, building an internal capacity to learn, and exchanging ideas about policies and practices in order to validate present performance, benchmark against others, and shape long-term strategic change.

It is not surprising that cities should be entering a global hunt for knowledge. It can be (and has been) argued that the very *raison d'être* of cities is that they facilitate exchange of all kinds. More to the point, in a globalized economy where knowledge plays an increasing role, cities are the crucibles where linkages are made. In turn, linkages are the channels of learning, and learning is a key not only to good practice, but also to creating wealth and reducing poverty among the poorest.

The intermediate position of cities puts them between their citizens and the outside world, mother nation-states and other cities around the globe. In the coming decades, cities will become increasingly important players in the implementation of policy, dissemination of knowledge, and creation of wealth. But while cities have long been seen as central to innovation, they have not been plumbed for their knowledge-exchange properties until now.

City learning: blind spot in urban innovation and governance

In-depth studies developed for this volume document recurrent patterns in making modern transformations. Dozens of cities discussed in this book—from Barcelona, Spain to San Fernando, Philippines—illuminate a blind spot in conventional approaches to urban development as well as in the bulk of scholarly literature. Each of the cities scrutinized in this book has sought best practice abroad and most have achieved important transformations based in part on what they have learned from others.

Bilbao launched its pursuit of the Guggenheim Museum only 10 years after city leaders had pondered lessons from other cities around the world about industrial restructuring. Key leaders in Lima, Peru, long embattled over the role of private developers, saw in London the magic of private sector contributions—it wasn't the money; it was the incentives to partner in public goods. The secret: the public sector structures a framework for mutually beneficial returns for both public and private players. That lesson broke a logjam in Lima's deliberations over large pieces of infrastructure needed in the city's metropolitan development. Though these new configurations didn't come easily to Bilbao or Lima, the key insights came in a collective learning process. In these and many other cases, learning has played a key role, one that has been largely ignored in academic settings, policy circles and by professional practitioners concerned with competitiveness and innovation.

Indeed, few cities have given serious and systematic thought to both *what* and *how* they learn. A dozen different approaches to urban development, from regime theory to economic geography, cover pieces of this story. But no one approach has viewed the modern metropolis as a learning entity, active in acquiring and processing new knowledge as a part of its governance mechanism. Not only do cities not pay much attention to learning, their leading agencies often do not bother to measure their own progress, to evaluate the effectiveness of visits and other forms of learning, to ask whether knowledge or technology transfer is meeting city objectives, and to explore whether and how city leadership and innovation can be improved to meet the many challenges facing the city.

Research for this book over the past five years has developed quantitative data to address these questions. The findings reveal new patterns about learning and innovation. For one thing, learning cities tend to be innovative places and vice versa. They devote more time and resources to acquiring new knowledge and validating it for application at home. Second, they exhibit patterns in the way they learn, in acquisition of new knowledge from "external" sources as well as in internal processing and adaptation of knowledge to local circumstances. Cities that are serious about learning invent civic processes that facilitate the conversion of tacit to explicit knowledge. Successful cities like Seattle create opportunities for internal bonding; for instance, by involving civic and business leadership in a continuing program of study tours. In doing so, Seattle achieves internal bonding—as with those young professionals from Boeing—as it harvests a rich crop of data and best practice.

Patterns are also found in how cities internalize new knowledge. My research uncovers signature styles of trust and collaboration that characterize a city, particularly in the shape and features of internal networks. These attributes are critical to converting knowledge to innovations and are important for understanding how to accelerate learning and make knowledge more useful.

Clouds of trust in the machinery of learning

This book shows that the vital factors for smart cities are informal leadership networks that I call "clouds of trust." These are ties of trusted links between and among key actors in the community. Elected leaders come and go, but business, civic and youth leaders who are incorporated into ongoing "thinking" about the city represent an important form of social capital, not just because they bridge gaps in connectedness or reinforce social norms, as Burt and others suggest (Burt, 2001). They also provide a platform for learning and sustain the threads of continuity in a place over time.

Qualitative and quantitative data gathered during five years of research from cities around the world illustrate the mechanisms and the policies that enable cities to be smart, i.e., to create dense "clouds of trust" to exchange knowledge, to store it for wider and longer term use, and to convert learning to innovation. Clouds of trust pervade the machinery of learning (see Figure 1.1).

Later chapters will explore each of four elements that compose the learning city. *Trusting milieu* refers to the "ba" atmosphere of which clouds of trust are emblematic. *Institutional process* refers to documentation, deliberation, and discussion of knowledge which is gathered by internal and external mechanisms. *Agency* refers to a central office or responsible unit for managing and recording knowledge. *Knowledge gathering* is the activity of harvesting ideas from internal and external sources for adaptation as innovations in the city. Networks of confidence have a direct or indirect impact in each element.

We shall see, for example, that Portland and Turin, two of numerous in-depth cases explored in later chapters, show intriguing variation in key features of trust

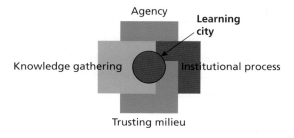

Figure 1.1 Schematic diagram of the machinery of city learning

networks—shape, "tightness" and the dynamics of network growth. The under-lying theory of networks—along with ideas of embeddedness, of weak and strong ties and frequency of exchange, of coherence and speed of information—throw new light on civic action and innovation in cities. Portland and Turin each have to cope with the advantages and disadvantages of their particular style, one with the speed but limited bridging of tight homogeneity in membership, the other with the slow vagaries but rich access to ideas from a diverse membership. This approach to learning opens a new vista onto the world of competitiveness and innovation.

Smart cities and beyond

Because they provide the context for these networks, cities are the fulcrum upon which policies can help to leverage learning, and foster innovation and change. But most cities have been lethargic about the machinery of learning, merely providing a passive matrix in which exchanges take place. Cities could play a more proactive and productive role in encouraging and expanding networks, filling in key gaps, identifying weak spots, and most of all mobilizing new membership from the ranks of young talent, both native and global.

On the other side of the coin, we examine counter-factual cases of cities that have learned but then faltered or that have failed to learn at all. It is rare to find a city that has not glowed with any particular features of learning and still man-aged to be innovative. These cases serve to underscore several points. The first is that the learning process itself is not the be all and end all, not the magic ingredient of city success that for some reason has been overlooked. Rather, the message in this book is that the process itself can be ragged. Progress takes place in fits and starts and sometimes it happens by good fortune. Even strong learners have run aground for a while. But the evidence of data and the examples in this book make a strong case for paying attention to learning as a new tool in the process of urban governance and development.

In this respect, *Beyond Smart Cities* penetrates a deeper level of the social and business networks described by Safford (Safford, 2009). Rather than merely mapping presence on boards and clubs as Safford did brilliantly in the cases of Youngstown and Allentown (and as many others have done to map different forms of ties—corporate department members, research teams, email linkages), the case analysis drills down to the level of confidential trust among individual players in the planning elites. The resulting data portray fresh pictures of city coherence. These data add detail to our understanding of how city elites interact, with consequences for policy to foster competitiveness strategies or recovery after seismic shifts in the economic landscape.

This book shows how networks already operating in most cities are used—and sometimes misused—to foster and strengthen connections, to achieve breakthroughs, and to catalyze and convert information and knowledge into a high-value richness of innovation. Going beyond smart cities means understanding how cities construct, convert and manipulate the matrix of relationships that grow naturally in urban environments.

Unlike Woolcock and others who remind us of complex interactions between macro and micro forms of social capital, the material in this book illustrates the formation of networks horizontally and in minute detail, and the challenges and opportunities of shaping and using them in different contexts (Woolcock, 1998). To achieve smart cities is not merely a matter of improving markets, prices or incentives. Nor is it a radical alteration in the prevailing ideological schema. The key step is to facilitate exchange in cities, internally and externally, but above all to create an atmosphere of trust involving a wide swath of stakeholders. Although the rest might not take care of itself, with the right policies cities and citizens in them hungry for new knowledge can speed up the exchange and make it more efficient.

Policy relevance—why don't cities learn?

A number of cities in the developing world have implemented innovations over the past few decades drawing on systematic learning; i.e., deliberate and continuing acquisition of knowledge often gained from outside sources on topics such as bus rapid transit, historic preservation downtown, participatory planning, and neighborhood upgrading. Cities in OECD countries have also achieved major transformations, including economic turnarounds and whole new identities. Scores if not hundreds of other innovations and achievements are recorded in such places as the UN-Habitat Best Practice awards.[1] But very many large cities, the vast majority of the roughly 1000 cities on the planet that have populations of more than a quarter of a million, lag behind or are bogged down. Why do the few successes not spread more rapidly? Why don't cities learn?

The book explores a half dozen reasons why cities do not learn—small city size, adverse policy and phase changes, to name a few—and suggests what can be done to expand and speed up learning. For instance, getting the most out of networks is a matter of managing tight and loose bonds and fostering intersections, for instance the public and private, the marginal and civic. But management is not just a matter of public policy. It is also a matter of private will, of businesses and corporations as well as marginal communities together with local policy makers recognizing mutual self-interest and joining a wider circle of stakeholders to engage in trusting relationships that are the gold standard of learning cities. The larger institutional task is a matter of growing a learning environment. This line of inquiry is now all the more important as cities begin to take on more important roles in the global economy.

Significance

These questions are important and indeed are arising in part because urbanization on the planet has not only completed a demographic transition, but also because big and intermediate-size cities now number around 1000. These places are likely to play an increasingly significant role in climate change, sustainable development, and poverty alleviation. Most local governments are involved in construction, land use and local transit regulations—all important determinants of sustainable development and greenhouse gases. Cities are the most immediate point of contact for more than a billion people living in slums.

Furthermore, Polese and Freire (Polese and Freire, 2003) have shown that improvements on service delivery in cities can lead to 10 to 20 percent increases in city economic output. Since city economies typically account for 40 percent of national GDP, any improvement in efficiency can have beneficial impacts at the national as well as the local level. A better understanding of how cities learn promises to open new pathways to speed up innovation and reform.

The story ahead

The material ahead is organized in four parts. The first sets the stage by reviewing the present and recent past of urban development on the planet. The key message here is about the stirring among cities following a long history of gradual experimentation with horizontal cooperation. Chapter 3 turns to published record as a rich source of clues about learning, creativity and innovation, particularly as collective endeavors. The literature helps sharpen the focus on creating a climate for innovation.

In Part II we take stock of how much exchange is now going on between cities and how this segment of the knowledge economy relates to the growing body of academic and practitioner literature on innovation and learning. Chapter 4 maps out some of the modalities cities employ in order to learn. A typology developed in earlier work helps to single out features of proactive learners. Chapter 5 widens the field of view with data from 50 cities, showing cities "on the prowl" for knowledge. The survey data also reveal the surprising extent to which cities invest in learning, financing thousands of city-to-city study tours every year.

Part III drills down to specific cases of proactive learners. These are the focus of our inquiry: cities that dedicate substantial time, resources, and organizational structure to acquire new ideas, store knowledge for future use, and convert knowledge into innovative change. Three groups of proactive cities are explored, each group exhibiting a slightly different way of going about learning. A signal idea introduced in this discussion is "clouds of trust," a characteristic feature of learning cities that implies a range of behavioral differences in the civic life of each place.

The common features and qualities that emerge in these cases, along with recommendations to foster learning and innovation, are discussed in Part IV, which covers secrets of learning. The evidence and analysis in the previous sections are richly suggestive of policy directions for nations and cities, along with research areas for further academic work.

As cities take their place as centers of economic regions, defined in terms of economic and social interests, they will be the centers that drive global development in the next century. The opening chapters point to the evidence for this planetary change. Although it is hard to express the exact balances of national and regional powers, there is no doubt that the proportions are changing. Cities are the most rapidly evolving part of a new equation, and their growing importance in world development will have far-reaching consequences for international relations and national policy on a whole range of issues.

Data methods and sources

Data sources for this volume arise from many quarters. Extensive and repeated visits over 30 years have formed a knowledge base about many aspects of urban development. Extended stays in key cities like Barcelona, Curitiba and Seattle, plus interviews with leading figures in Amman, Juárez and Bilbao, provided more focused observations about the role of learning in capacity building. I will also draw upon information and data from additional cities from past professional work and from previously published and unpublished articles.

Web-based surveys conducted in 2008 and 2009 produced data on city-to-city visits as well as insights into the strong demand for learning, the preferences for learning modalities, and priorities among practitioners for further knowledge in topical and management areas. A second web-based survey in Seattle provided hard data and policy insight into the design and impact of peer learning in Seattle's city visit program.

Research during 2009 as a Senior Fellow for the German Marshall Fund drilled down into specific practices of four cities—Barcelona, Charlotte, Portland and Turin, generating quantitative and qualitative detail about the mechanics of learning, and produced insight into the importance of trust networks.

Note

1   See, for instance, the Dubai International Award for Best Practice, established in 1995. http://www.unhabitat.org/content.asp?typeid=19&catid=34&cid=160

References

Burt, R. (2001). "Structural holes versus network closure as social capital," *Social capital: theory and research*, in N. Lin, K. Cook and R. S. Burt, *Social capital: theory and research* (sociology and economics: controversy and integration series), Aldine de Gruyter, New York, pp. 31–56.

Glaeser, E. (2011). *Triumph of the city. How our greatest invention makes us richer, smarter, greener, healthier and happier*, Penguin, New York.

MacFarlane, C. (2010). *Learning the city: translocal assemblage and urban politics,* Wiley-Blackwell, London.

Perlman, J. (1987). "Mega cities and innovative technologies," *CITIES: The International Journal of Urban Policy*, 4 (May), pp. 128–186.

Polese, M. and M. Freire (2003). *Connecting cities to macroeconomic concerns. The missing link,* World Bank and National Institute of Economic Research, Washington, DC.

Safford, S. (2009). *Why the garden club couldn't save Youngstown,* Harvard University Press, Cambridge, MA.

Trade Development Alliance (2001). *Crossroads 10!* (pamphlet), Trade Development Alliance of Greater Seattle, Seattle.

United Cities and Local Governments (2010). "Michael R. Bloomberg: the importance of learning from other cities," *United Cities*, 1, p. 1.

Woolcock, M. (1998). "Social capital and economic development: toward a theoretical synthesis and policy framework," *Theory and Society*, 27, pp. 151–208.

World War II and redefining municipal cooperation

Leading up to and during World War II, there was a lull in the city-to-city inter-action of municipal organizations. After the war, the IGCTPA (International Garden City and Town Planning Association) congresses marked attempts for city-to-city relationships to "restore and strengthen links between nations" (Hardy, 1991: 197). The role of cities assumed a strong undercurrent of universal brother-hood and humanity as revived municipal networks led reconstruction efforts while post-war international politics stumbled slowly to its feet. France and Germany were particularly active in reaching out across borders and between municipalities. The Union Internationale des Maires (UIM) was founded in 1947 to foster recon-ciliation between them. The municipal movement's pre-war community, based around sharing technical expertise and municipal governance, became swept up in a post-war movement for cultural exchange and understanding.

Seas changing—1950 to the present

The post-war environment was fertile ground for city-to-city exchange for many reasons, demographic, economic and technological. Before continuing with a nar-rative on city–to-city relationships, we turn to examine increasingly global forces that impinge on cities and their need to know.

First in chronology and importance in this brief retrospective is the global demographic transition, that is, the massive movement of populations from rural to urban areas, especially in the global South. In fact, urbanization is best seen in two phases. The completion of this urban transition has been advertised for nearly a decade, but the pure growth in city size is only one aspect of demographic change. A very important corollary is usually overlooked, the increase in the *number* of large cities. Among other things, the increase of large cities brings the urban global North and South closer together, as big cities often have more in common with each other than with other cities in their mother countries. We turn first to the flow of migrants to cities and look at the large city implications later.

The onset of large urban migrations in the modern era came into full swing in the late 1950s and early 1960s. Migration pressures would come to push newly independent states to breaking point. The post-war environment brought a global demand for commodities and booming economies in the US and Europe. Peace-time trade in commodities and manufactures created demand for labor in cities around the world. Job opportunities opening up in cities in the 1950s and 1960s provided early evidence that would begin to demolish the idealistic propositions of self-sufficient smallholders living in rural areas. Importantly, to cope with these pressures, it was central, not local, authorities that took on the task of designers and providers of solutions.

Though urbanization was changing at very different rates in the major regions of the world, on the whole urban population doubled between 1950 and 1975 (Table 2.1), overwhelming the capacities of nations, much more so cities, to keep up with demand for shelter, infrastructure and services. The demographic shifts were most intense in Latin America. The growth rate of some cities exceeded 7 percent, doubling the populations of many neighborhoods and some whole cities in a decade. In the end, city populations increased by 100 million people during this 20-year period.

The focus of policy and development was less on cities than on the role of national governments, which were, in the words of Urban Development Timeline, "the main architects and implementers of development in both rural and urban areas."[6] An early and persistent developmental image was rooted in the Gandhian notion of a dignified and self-reliant populace spinning cotton and tilling a largely rural landscape, an image that is reflected in greater and lesser degrees by national leaders in other emerging states of the Third World, like Mexico, China, Egypt, (the then) Tanganyika and elsewhere.

Grand schemes fostered by national ministries sought to demonstrate with iconic projects like Brasilia in Brazil and Chandigarh in India that national responses were up to the challenges posed by mushrooming cities. The cities themselves were plaintive bystanders in this demographic transformation. Even though many tried vainly to address the growing pressures of population increase,

Table 2.1 Urban population size and growth by region

Region	Mid-year population (millions)				Growth rate (percent)		
	1950	1975	2000	2030	1950–1955	1975–1980	2000–2005
World total	751	1543	2862	4899	3.12	2.56	1.92
High-income countries	359	562	697	1036	2.35	1.37	0.68
Middle- and low-income countries	392	981	2165	3863	4.17	3.64	2.40

Source: UNDESA, 2010

the control of power remained at the national level. More to the point, cities were not only bystanders, they were also not engaged in any process of institutional growth and expanding capacity that might have put them in good stead to deal with continuing migration.

In 1957, J. F. C. Turner, a young architect from London, was working on low-cost housing design in Lima. He traveled by car and on foot into the dusty eastern flanks of the city and saw the front edges of sprawl in the metropolis that still can be observed today. The shacks housing residents there have now become the archetypes of self-built shelter around the world. Accompanied by Housing Ministry officials, Turner was told that the *barriadas* he was being shown were growing into the major problem of the city. The solution took the form of homogeneous rows of sterile public housing located further out in cheap government land. Turner famously observed that the problems he was shown, the *barriadas*, were the solutions, and the solutions, public housing, were really the problems.

The Lima anecdote illustrates many things. Foremost, for the present purposes, it illustrates that the city had not been cast as a protagonist in the drama. The Lima squatters whom Turner observed represent perhaps the clearest starting line in a decades-long struggle over shelter policy, a fight that has been focused on cities around the world, but for a long time cities have been out of the picture. Many decades passed before city and neighborhood players were brought into the formation and implementation of policy solutions. Neighborhoods and cities feel the pinch, and often they squawked, but property rights have long been the domain of nations, at least up to the last couple of decades.

Ironically, cities were often blamed as the locus of growing problems. They were held in scorn as the pace of population growth continually overwhelmed each generation of policy. National policy in most countries has either ignored cities, or worse, in developing countries, has long been leery and suspicious of them. Playing into this dynamic, cities and their leaders were very frequently the bulwarks of political opposition to the central state. The truth is that central governments were overwhelmed as well, but for reasons of political power and the relative weakness of local governments, nations continued to be the principal providers of solutions and the main sources of knowledge about policy and practice.

In the late 1970s, foundations, non-governmental organizations and universities were beginning to build a capacity to address urban problems. The Ford Foundation launched its urban program in the late 1960s. Korea and Thailand launched research and development institutes patterned after think tanks in the US and Europe. Major universities either formed urban studies programs or added development programs to existing ones. In the developed world, horizontal exchanges began to appear through specialized city-based organizations.

Organizations like the IULA, United Towns, and Sister Cities began to play more of a role, but found it hard to keep up with demand for technical assistance. Local government associations and their federations formed a significant part of NGO growth from the 1970s onward. Not counting religious and inter-governmental organizations, the number of NGOs rose precipitously from around 1000 in the early 1970s to more than 26,000 by 1999 (Union of International Associations, 2011). They were filling a perceived need for mutual assistance and support. Furthermore, few countries had established national urban strategies to cope with problems of city growth. A 1974 study found that many early sister-city relationships formed out of the post World War II aid programs to Western Europe. The relationships that endured, however, were based on cultural or educational dimensions that created lasting friendships.

International development assistance organizations began to bring cities as consultative partners into large-scale projects, but the structure of national power and Cold War interests in the developing world kept these exchanges at modest levels in the developed countries. The point is, direct city exchange of the kind fostered by the IULA, Sister Cities and United Towns operated at a low level of intensity, often through a single city twinning with another.

Environmental change

The compression of populations in cities inevitably brought environmental change right into policy makers' backyards. Though numerous issues were emerging at once in crowded cities, a rapid and visible decrease in environmental quality was one of the broadest in scope and most influential in alerting the public to a need for change. For example, researchers in Asia began to measure the impact of wood- and coal-fired stoves on indoor air quality and sounded the first alarm about indoor air pollution. These concerns then opened eyes to a half-dozen other issues and have evolved today into sustainability, natural hazards preparation, carbon footprint and climate change.

The case of Curitiba has acquired fame partly because it was among the first to address environmental issues, largely on its own. Curitiba's early steps toward bus rapid transit and its green spaces were based on environmental grounds. In many cities, poor water quality was the recognized culprit in millions of child deaths every year. Environmental health arguments added weight to the policy justification for addressing a wider scope of environmental health issues in drainage, solid waste and sewerage. But for the most part, despite the fact that environmental change hit the ground in cities, cities had neither the full range of powers nor the resources to protect the health of citizens, even though in many cases cities had the legal obligation to do so.

In the US, clean water and clean air legislation corresponded with the growing awareness of environmental health and sanitation in the developing world. The global alert sounded by such works as Rachel Carson's *Silent Spring* (1962) and Meadows and colleagues' *Limits to Growth* (1972) had an impact on leaders around the world. These works suggested that even the middle and upper classes in cities could not escape pervasive environmental change by hiding behind gated communities.

The institutional lags in this story were a telltale indication of the slow and muddling response to the problems of the great migrations. Just as cities were burgeoning toward mega-proportions, the World Bank was busy doubling lending in agriculture. Its president, McNamara, saw rural poverty as a major problem not being addressed, but did not see that rural to urban migration would, in a sense, take care of it even before agricultural output could be increased. To be fair, McNamara also launched the World Bank's first urban project, in Dakar in 1972, and followed it with many more. But the Achilles' heel of international developmental assistance was that, because of charter mandates, banks cannot easily lend directly to cities. Central governments were borrowers, in line with bank charters that were bound to observe national sovereignty and limits on market risk.

Stockholm and Vancouver

Beginning in 1972, concerns about the environment and cities gave birth to two landmark events, the Stockholm Conference on the Human Environment in 1972 and the Vancouver UN Habitat Conference on cities in 1976. Urban pressures became more palpable both for national policy makers and for local city politicians and managers. The Stockholm conference foresaw a need not just to address issues of decline in the quality and availability of natural resources, but also in cultural issues and developmental strategies. Most notably for cities, the Stockholm conference produced a recommendation that a UN agency on cities be established to address the many issues that had emerged from two decades of post-war urban growth. Four years later, the first UN Conference on Human Settlements in Vancouver set a waypoint on the timeline of policy and institutional action to deal with urban problems.

Vancouver also contained the seeds of what we might call self-help, city-centric actions. In the developing world, cities were slowly being brought into shelter and infrastructure programs. In the developed countries, urban renewal and regional strategies began to appear, supported by new tools of intergovernmental finance such as community development block grants and community development corporations in the US.

Box 2.1 *C2C Timeline*

1891 – Fabian Municipal Program
1904 – First International Garden City Congress
1904 – Formation of the British Committee for the Study of Municipal Institutions
1913 – First congress of the IGCTPA
1913 – First congress of the IULA/IUV (Union Internationale des Villes) in Ghent

WWI

1919 – League of Nations founded
1920 – First town twinning[7]: Keighley, West Yorkshire, UK and Poix du Nord, France
1932 – Height of IULA membership

WWII

1947 – UIM created
1951 – CEM (Council of European Municipalities) created
1951 – Monde Bilingue created
1956 – Sister Cities program created
1957 – United Towns Organization (UTO) founded under auspices of Monde Bilingue
1967 – Sister Cities International founded
1971 – UN General Assembly resolution on "city twinnings as a means of international cooperation"[8]
1972 – UN Conference on the Human Environment in Stockholm
1976 – First Habitat Conference in Vancouver
1980s – Regional city networks founded (EUROCITIES, FLACMA)
1989 – Formation of the Municipal Development Program in Africa (World Bank and Government of Italy, Porreta Terme, Italy)
1990 – CEMR (formerly CEM) folded into IULA; Lomé Convention and "decentralized cooperation"
1992 – Rio Earth Summit and UN-Habitat's "Localizing Agenda 21" program launched
1994 – CITYNET founded
1996 – UN Istanbul meeting: WACLAC (World Association of Cities and

Local Authorities Coordination) formed (IULA and UTO are both
members)

1999 – Cities Alliance (a "learning alliance")

2000 – First Africities Conference

2001 – UN Istanbul +5 meeting

2002 – Summit on Sustainable Development in Johannesburg

2004 – IULA merges with FMCU-UTO and Metropolis to form United Cties
and Local Governments (UCLG)

2005 – Centre for C2C Cooperation founded in Seville by UN-Habitat; C40
founded

2010 – Global Urban Forum, Rio de Janeiro

Demographic and political mega-shifts

If environmental change was not a wake-up call for national policy makers, the
leviathan trinity of decentralization/democratization, metropolitanization and
globalization have together produced a thorough transformation in political and
institutional relationships over the last two decades. Many scores of countries
around the globe launched wholesale changes in governmental arrangements,
abrogating significant powers and handing them over to local governments
within the space of a single decade.

These swift changes in institutional responsibilities brought powerful incentives for cities to acquire new knowledge. Cities were suddenly propelled into a
more open environment. They became aware of pressing needs for knowledge
to be able to hold position or shoot ahead to become more competitive.

More cities, more metropolises

The completion of the urban transition on the planet brings with it a corollary—
the creation of more and larger cities. Though noticed less or not at all by many
policy makers, the number of large cities is of equal if not greater significance
than the mere fact that the planet is now urban.

Since 1995, the number of cities with a half-million to a million in population—
so-called "intermediate-size cities"—in developing countries will have increased
by 75 percent to 388. By 2025 they will easily double the 1995 number (Table
2.2) to 531. The same is true for their larger counterparts, those cities in the one

Table 2.2 Number of cities of various population sizes: 1995–2025

Size range (millions)	World total			Less developed			Developed		
	1995	2010	2025	1995	2010	2025	1995	2010	2025
>10	13	21	29	9	15	22	4	6	7
5 to 10	19	33	46	14	26	36	5	7	10
1 to 5	263	385	502	170	282	393	93	103	109
0.5 to 1	337	512	664	222	388	531	115	124	133
0.1 to 0.5	2507	2717	2741	1614	1783	1769	893	934	972
Total	3139	3668	3982	2029	2494	2751	1110	1174	1231

Source: United Nations, Department of Economic and Social Affairs, Population Division (2010). *World Urbanization Prospects: The 2009 Revision*, New York: United Nations

million to five million range. The upshot is that nearly 300 cities have moved into the intermediate and large-city range in the last 15 years, and another 250 will have been added by 2025. By that year, the global total will be closing in on 1200 cities.

The growth in the number of cities and the physical form they appear to be taking have many ramifications. For one thing, growing political pressure will be exerted on nation-states to cope with urban problems. The rising population in middle-ranking cities exerts political pressure across a wider spectrum of cities and voting constituencies. This pattern was noted as one of the many factors that triggered a rise of support for decentralization in Latin America in the late 1980s and 1990s (Campbell, 2003). Many hundreds of new executives and city stakeholders—in the private sector, neighborhoods, communities of interest— will be entering the political spheres of battle to win greater national resources and attention.

The form of urban growth makes matters more difficult. Angel's calculations show a decline in densities in virtually all of the 120 cities sampled in this inter-mediate size range, highlighting an apparent trend toward increased physical separation of settlements and rising service costs (Angel *et al.*, 2011). Also, virtually all of the intermediate and large cities are surrounded by many distinct municipal administrations, creating clusters of cities whose governance and management systems were designed for the most part to service a core cluster, not a spreading network of municipalities. Governance arrangements represent a topic of interest everywhere.

And yet the intermediate size cities may be setting trends for economic growth and consumer demand. McKinsey & Company sees the "middle weight" cities with populations of around 400,000 to 600,000 as driving a significant fraction of global GDP growth in the next 20 years (Dobbs *et al.*, 2011). A growing middle class in these cities will begin to exert economic and political pressure to meet health and housing needs for the very young, coming from newly formed families, and the very old. The growing number and qualitative changes in cities are not the only reasons that cities need help. Other global shifts are also at play.

Decentralization and democratization

Most countries around the globe are engaged in some form of decentralization, meaning that subnational units of government are sharing in powers to make decisions, administer government or spend revenues. Nearly 25 republics in Latin America accomplished this change during the 1990s. Dozens of other countries in Asia and Africa as well as Eastern Europe are also going through the trans-formation of political power, increasing the importance of cities in the conduct of public business. Often accompanied by democratization, these shifts mean that city leadership—mayors, elected officials, the private sector, civic leaders—are playing a more important role for their nations. They are also required to answer to a distinct constituency, one from below. This puts extra weight on local leaders to organize the direction of growth, shape public choices, engage the public and decision-making process, and implement decisions that are made.

Among the more frequently mentioned drivers of these changes are the exhaustion of the central-state model after the collapse of the Soviet Union, and the realization of the need for alternatives to central state-led growth, particularly alternatives that draw on a broader-based pyramid of legitimacy and state presence. Meanwhile in Europe, the process of regionalization encouraged by the European Union as well as scores of countries outside Europe is confronting the emergence of regionalist demands (Spain, Italy, Scotland, Northern Ireland). At virtually the same time, and for similar reasons, the spread of democracy was a palpable form of reconnecting citizens and governments, and many actors and grass-roots movements pushed for deeper democratization in countries of Africa, Asia and Latin America (United Cities and Local Governments, 2008).

Going global

In a related sphere, and about the same time, liberalization of trade and the dramatically increased velocity of global transactions suddenly thrust states into a more vulnerable, more competitive environment, as compared to earlier decades (Amin and Tomaney, 1995). One consequence of the globalized economy has been the rise of cross-state corporate connections. As national borders began to lose their importance as markers of comparative advantage, regions and cities became the next distinguishing feature on the economic landscape (Harris, 2003; Beaverstock *et al.*, 1999). Accordingly, a regional perspective on economic development began to assume an important place in both the process and the outcome of decentralization.

Cities are particularly ready to address these intertwined issues of growth and the environment as they set about creating strategies to retain or advance their position in the global marketplace. In the face of new global competition, cities and regions are discovering that the old approaches and tools are obsolete. Models of growth developed over the past 50 years—in import substitution, for instance—are obsolete in a globalized economy. Cities in which industry and manufacturing were once protected are now more vulnerable to competitive pressures. With the protective shells of trade barriers stripped away and reduced protection from national boundaries, cities, given new spending and decision-making powers, are doubly exposed and looking for answers.

Independent sources of thought emerge

Universities, foundations and NGOs succeeded in establishing a new edge in understanding the dynamics and emerging challenges in urban development. Decentralization itself was one major topic of interest. The Friedrich Ebert Foundation, the Ford Foundation, the Konrad Adenauer Foundation, and the Friedrich Naumann Foundation all launched programs addressing issues related to decentralization. These foundations and bilateral donors found it easy to increase emphasis on democratic decision making as the influences of state reform and decentralization began to spread across the world.

Countries also began to influence one another. Exchanges between and among various national and subnational governments were important in framing issues, formulating approaches, and designing legislation and institutions. For example, the Commonwealth of Local Governments was active in spreading best practices about management. Cities began to be involved in these exchanges. Authorities and policy makers in (unitary) states, such as Peru and Bolivia to cite two examples, were intrigued with the promulgation of Colombia's first laws on competencies and resources in 1986. Various decentralization laws in Colombia accorded powers to cities and regions that approximated those normally given to states in federated republics, much as Spain had done to strengthen the autonomy of its regions. Nearly all nations learned from—and, certainly, policy makers and legislators commented about—the Brazilian Constitution of 1988 and the Bolivian national participation law promulgated in 1994.

The need for technical and managerial solutions has expanded in the past few decades, just as the breadth of new knowledge available to cities is expanding. Environmental and governance issues resulted in an elevation of standards, requiring cities to meet more rigorous requirements in operations and services. For instance, concerns about water expanded from the issue of supply and coverage, to that of quality, to increases in the number of pollutants being measured, and to complications regarding treatment and recycling. In governance, the standard practice of formulating a political program evolved into alternative competitive arrangements and in some cases publication of city budgets and procurement arrangements. Cities came under pressure to meet new accounting standards and to show how city business was being conducted free from the ever-present intrusions of corruption. Information technology makes real-time presence of data a reality for cities, and the pressure of democratic forces easier to transmit and be heard. The IT revolution from a city-management point of view also allows quicker access to, and more demand for, information about city operations and services.

The rise of horizontal cooperation

Except for mega-cities, most urban places have long been given short shrift by national governments. For the first several decades after World War I, national governments saw themselves as the guiding, designing and controlling elements in the public sector. The predominance of the nation-state both fed and was reinforced by the international distress of wartime conflicts and economic depression. In less than a decade after World War II, the first new pressures on cities exerted by demographic and environmental concerns began to reveal the fault-lines in the hegemony of nation-states as sole proprietors of wisdom and policy for cities.

With decentralization and democratization, together with globalization, many large cities are becoming more entrepreneurial in their quest for knowledge, more demanding for latest techniques, and in greater need of experienced hands to solve problems. Many obvious and a few not so obvious forces contributed to this transformation. One part of the story is that central governments have failed for decades to provide a policy framework in which cities can flourish. Cities were blamed for their countries' problems and largely left to their own devices. Decade after decade of failed or half-hearted policies did little to solve these

problems and even less to foster and support a capacity in cities to address growing urban challenges.

Today, and in the future, the city may be the only political unit on the planet
that is expanding in number and increasing in power, especially in comparison
to the nation-state, which is clearly losing ground, at least relative to the past.
Decentralization of governance in most countries around the world, though slow,
is contributing to this reverse of fortune. Globalization, the digital revolution,
democratization and decentralization are changing the pattern.

We need to look back once again to the era following World War II to see
how institutional capacity building was keeping pace with the demographic and
political change just discussed. The post-war institutional stock of actors was
influenced heavily by the arrival of the Council of European Municipalities (CEM),[9]
the Union Internationale des Maires (UIM) and Monde Bilingue[10] in the late 1940s
and early 1950s. The CEM was a move by the federalists of Europe to facilitate
political union—a continent of citizens guided by local self-governance; Monde
Bilingue was more preoccupied by the notion of universal brotherhood and
understanding. The Americans entered the fray with the Sister Cities[11] movement
in 1956, a twinning program based partly in a sly Cold War agenda mixed with
a more benign interest in citizen diplomacy, one of Eisenhower's antidotes to
the military-industrial complex.

Competition brewed between town-twinning organizations, and the number
of pairings grew rapidly in the 1950s and 1960s. Many city partnerships led to real
informational and interpersonal exchange: the twinned cities of Birmingham
and Frankfurt exchanged workers to encourage skills development and knowledge transfer; Dortmund, Leeds and Lille did similarly. Extra-European twinnings
emerged slowly, starting in the 1960s and 1970s. Soviet cities were paired with
others in the region while French municipalities matched up with cities in their
(often former) colonial territories. Meanwhile, intra-European twinnings accelerated; between 1963 and 1975, there were 50 a year between Germany and France
alone (Weyreter, 2003).

With the help of lobbying efforts by organizations like the United Towns
Organization (UTO), in 1971 the UN General Assembly passed a resolution on "city
twinnings as a means of international cooperation." The resolution endorsed the
idea of inter-municipal cooperation between the developed and developing
world. Efforts to link cities from the North and South gained momentum in the
ensuing decades and developed the concept of twinning from one based on
global understanding and cultural exchange to a relationship aimed more at promoting sustainable development and good governance.

Further development of the city-to-city relationship came from the idea of
"decentralized cooperation." Popularized at the EU's Lomé Convention in 1990,

decentralized cooperation can take the form of town twinning and use the relationship to foster better development strategies, often by involving develop-ment agencies in the practice. About 20 percent of all city-to-city partnerships in South Africa involve decentralized cooperation, funded by the development agencies of Sweden, the Netherlands, Belgium, Australia, Canada, the UK, Germany and Norway (de Villiers, 2007).

These trends reflected three changes. First, international development paradigms had shifted their focus increasingly toward urban development and multidisciplinary approaches, turning specifically to capacity building, institutional strengthening and good governance—all of which are supported by city-to-city relationships. Second, urban management issues had become more urgent and complex. Third, increased citizen participation had enhanced the possibilities of including a range of stakeholders in urban decision making (Bontenbal, 2009).

Since the 1990s the rise in city-to-city exchange has been further aided by a shift in development thinking away from a focus on *managing* cities to one on *governing* cities (Bontenbal, 2009). This places greater importance on the quality of local government. City-to-city exchange has also been catalyzed by a global recognition of local governments as development players. This chord was struck at the 1992 Rio Conference, after which many countries set out to decentralize development responsibilities to the municipal level.

Other factors associated with international development consensus enhanced the profile of horizontal relationships, namely: the 1996 UN-Habitat City Summit in Istanbul; the 2001 Istanbul +5 events focused on horizontal cooperation; the 2002 Summit on Sustainable Development in Johannesburg; and the 2005 founding of the Centre for C2C Cooperation in Seville. These efforts by the UN, its development subgroups, and its allies in the form of NGOs, constitute an international institutionalization and endorsement of municipalities' active participation in local urban development.

Twenty years after the Vancouver Conference, the major city associations and organizations—United Towns, Arab Cities and Towns, International Union of Local Authorities—began a process of merger. As a result of decentralization, a phenomenon, it must be noted, that coincided with the fall of the Berlin wall and the failure of the central-state model, scores of national associations of local governments were formed.

The 1996 meeting of the United Nations Centre for Human Settlements (UN-Habitat) in Istanbul will stand as another important waypoint in the development of the institutional capacity of cities and their affiliated organizations. Istanbul gave birth to United Cities and Local Governments (UCLG), a new amalgam of organizations and associations of both political and technical membership. The UCLG is symbolic of the transition by individual cities and individual organizations to a single voice, authorized to speak and be heard in the UN system, including the World Bank, to coordinate the concerns, political voice, and technical exchange between and among cities around the world. From the standpoint of city learning, the creation of the UCLG represents a milestone. It focused the voice of cities and city associations. More importantly, it represents a step toward efficiency because it consolidates city concerns into a single channel.

Emerging items on the agenda of urban learning—10 urban issues and the need to know for global learning

Although no formal agenda of action has been published by cities or affiliated organizations, an emerging set of key issues is facing cities in the coming decades. The following section might be seen as a list of wicked problems and a curriculum for city learning.

For political and practical reasons, first on the list is that most large cities are spreading out—decreasing in density—and solutions to metropolitan governance arise in every region of the world. Recall that Angel and his colleagues recently reported that average densities are falling in cities around the globe, and particularly in the developing regions (Angel et al., 2011). Angel's data are drawn from side-by-side comparisons of 1990 and 2000 satellite images of a representative sample of 120 cities. His team calculated that average density decrease is a direct function of spreading city perimeters.

Second, as settlements move beyond established administrative and jurisdictional boundaries, they stretch the customary definitions of city limits, spreading to adjacent metropolitan areas, contributing to fragmentation and deepening the question of governance in urbanized regions. A well-known example of this spreading urban region is the Boston–Washington corridor, a megalopolitan region with a population of 50 million and extending more than 600 km; far beyond the prospective planning competence of any of the more than five major metropolitan areas in the region.

The significance of spreading urban regions leads to a third issue: the increasing social distance implied in spreading metropolises. Though many low-income populations still settle in and around the urban core of large cities, increasingly, low-income settlements take up residence on low-cost land where property values are suppressed because of distance or due to clouded title, poor conditions of slope or vulnerability to flood. Metropolitan cities increase the importance of inter-jurisdictional coordination in planning, infrastructure investment, and services delivery to differing social classes residing in contiguous areas.

A fourth issue is that metropolitan centers have entered a more competitive environment. Liberalization of trade leaves cities much more exposed to outside competition because protectionist trade regimes no longer shield city industries from competitors. Further, competitive pressures are now global. The increasing velocity of international transactions—in trade, exchange of capital, and investment—means that metropolitan cities must move quickly to retain industries as well as to attract new ones.

Fifth is an issue of handling spillovers, both positive and negative. These are defining features of metropolitan areas. Smaller cities or units of government cannot generate the economies of scale that are typical of production in metropolitan cities. On the other side of the coin, major cities generate negative spillovers in pollution and congestion. The challenge of managing externalities is made sharper by the absence of coordinated national policies in developing countries to redress environmental imbalances.

Sixth is the issue of governance. Few organizational models seem to hold up under the pressures of changing economic and political circumstances. Virtually all the European countries are engaged in the question of metropolitan organization. Turkey has addressed the problem directly with reforms that link municipal, metropolitan and national tiers in planning and functions and the direct election of a metropolitan mayor. Many national governments have given capital cities special legal or financial status. Examples, including special districts, are Brasilia, Canberra and Abuja (Nigeria). These enjoy special spending or planning status, often linked directly to central government budgets. Cities in Europe, Canada, the US and Korea have experimented with a variety of governance configurations, with mixed success.

Many of the cities—London, Montreal and Toronto, for example—have reversed field, going from regional councils or area-wide governments to facilitate planning and investment in large-scale infrastructure back to small governance units, and back again to larger areas in a quest to capture a wider tax base. In the US, the policy battle has been over whether there is an economic pay-off for cities with regional authorities.

The seventh issue arises from the spreading social problems of poverty, insecurity and rising civic violence. The troubling trend toward the urbanization of poverty started with the great waves of migration after 1950 in Latin America and has returned into view in the past decade. Poverty has been growing faster than population, particularly during the economic stagnation of the 1980s. On the global level, a billion people live on less than a dollar a day. Additionally, the nature of poverty has begun to change. Increasingly, poor households are headed by women, and new problems related to drugs and violence make solutions even more complicated.

Eighth, with globalization of the economy cities face sharper, if not completely new, challenges to protect or grow their own economic interests. To put it simply, cities in the developing world cope either with overwhelming new immigration, often meaning rapidly growing slums, or declining economic fortunes, which translates into dereliction of large parts of the urban landscape. In both cases, the result is widespread unemployment, deteriorating housing and environmental conditions, and poverty. But a trend that holds across all regions is that many of the mid- to large-size cities are taking steps to tackle unemployment and job creation, and many more are interested in learning how they can address livelihood issues.

Corruption is the ninth issue, like others visible, but not prominent, in policy agendas of only two decades ago. Corruption threatens to undermine the very integrity of the governance systems, because "it generates economic costs by distorting incentives, political costs by undermining institutions, and social costs by redistributing wealth to the undeserving" (Klitgaard *et al.*, 2000: 4). Information and communication technology could add up to be a game-changer in many ways. Though many applications are being deployed—in procurement, system monitoring and reporting, direct service provision to citizens and businesses such as licensing and permits, land use planning, and many more. But a daunting field of obstacles still blocks the exploitation of IT's great promise to increase transparency and curb corruption (Schuppan, 2009).

Finally, large-scale disruption from natural and human-induced change has also grown in prominence and acuity over the past few decades. Climate change and other large-scale threats to national development—including pandemic health threats like HIV/AIDS, SARS and bird flu—emanate from or have direct impacts upon urban settlements. Cities in Africa have shouldered the burden of the decimating impact of AIDS in lost lives, lost labor pool, and lost resources in local health.

Certainly the most global of the newly emerging issues is climate change. While all cities concentrate activities that result in greenhouse gases, the larger and more immediate problem is one of adaptation (Working Group II Intergovernmental Panel on Climate Change *et al.*, 2008). This is because climate change increases the risk to public health and loss of life and property in places where basic infrastructure is already inadequate (Satterthwaite, 2009). It is no coincidence that many geographic areas of focus of climate adaptation are also areas of poverty and risky settlements.

Of less importance in the short to medium term, but ultimately crucial, is the mitigation of greenhouse gases. Recent discoveries have concluded that previous measurements greatly underestimate the contribution of biomass combustion (in non-urban areas) to the atmospheric brown clouds over South Asia (Szidat, 2009).

At the same time, there is clear evidence that cities are principal sources of greenhouse gases, and most probably the most important human-made source. However, cities in the developing world are not the most important emitters. Governance and management in cities everywhere, and a gradual move to more organized densities, is one of the frontlines in the battle to achieve sustainability.

The road ahead

The chapter has reviewed a straight historical timeline and examined some of the principal forces—some old, others recently emerged—that draw cities into knowledge exchange. Demographic growth was a transition that resulted not just in an urban planet, but also in a planet populated with at least a thousand cities, each potentially an important actor on the global arena. Migrations, in turn, have brought pressure on land and shelter, and these have spilled over into issues of environment, pollution, public health, and natural resource deple-tion. Meanwhile, new standards in development, new technologies in transport and communications, new approaches to the private sector, and a shift in central–local relationships have brought cities into a new realm of action as they awaken to a new imperative for knowledge exchange.

Today and in the future, cities are adapting to the tidal wave of challenges. They are forming mechanisms to facilitate a learning process. The next chapter will take measure of what we know about how cities learn.

Notes

1 The urban share of population in 1900 varied widely, from 80 percent in England to 40 percent in France, 25 percent in Italy, and 40 percent in Europe overall (Ewen and Hebbert, 2007).

2 The London-based Fabians made their international splash at the Second International Conference in London (1896). They advocated the necessity of having crucial services like gas, housing, and welfare delivered by the government, a message propagated by French and Belgian socialists in the early 20th century.

3 The study tours of the BCSMI focused on a wide variety of topics, including: the efficiency of Swiss municipalities' electric installations and the profitability of their utilities, Olso's specialized hospitals and its school system which offered free meals for students, Denmark's municipal health care model, Stockholm's telephone network, and urban management practices in Germany (Hietala, 1987).

4 The IULA's mission was to promote and unite democratic local governments worldwide and serve to promote professional standards, advocate for local governments, and be

a worldwide source of information, intelligence, and exchange to build local government capacity.

5 IULA attendance rates increased from 162 cities representing 28 countries in 1913 to 366 cities representing 39 countries in 1925. Municipal federations began to form and swell attendance. By 1932 membership in the IULA was estimated at 50,000 urban and local authorities (Dogliani, 2002: 585).

6 See the excellent Urban Development Timeline developed by Duane Kissick and PADCO, currently found at the AECOM website: http://www.urbantimeline.org/.

7 According to Local Government International Bureau, UK.

8 Hafteck, 2003.

9 CEM later lengthened its name by adding Regions to its purview: it became CEMR in 1984.

10 Monde Bilingue was reinvented in 1957 as the United Towns Organization (UTO), also known as the Fédération Mondiale des Cités Unies (FMCU). Monde Bilingue, for all intents and purposes, became FMCU-UTO.

11 The Sister Cities program, too, underwent an organizational evolution; it was institutionalized in 1967 as the non-profit Sister Cities International.

References

Amin, A. and J. J. Tomaney (1995). "The regional dilemma in a neo-liberal Europe," *European Urban and Regional Studies*, pp. 171–188.

Angel, S., D. Civico and A. Blei (2011). *Making room for a planet of cities*. Lincoln Institute of Land Policy, Cambridge, MA.

Beaverstock, J., R. Smith and P. Taylor (1999). "A roster of world cities," *Cities*, 16 (6), pp. 445–458.

Bontenbal, M. (2009). *Cities as partners. The challenge to strengthen urban governance through North–South city partnerships*, Eburon, Delft.

Campbell, T. (2003). *The quiet revolution: decentralization and the rise of political participation in Latin American cities*, University of Pittsburgh Press, Pittsburgh, PA.

Carson, R. (1962). *Silent spring*, Houghton Mifflin, Boston.

de Villiers, J. C. (2007). "Towards an understanding of the success factors in international twinning and sister-city relationships," *South African Journal of Business Management*, 38, 1–10.

Dobbs, R., S. Smit, J. Remes, J. Manyika, C. Roxburgh, and A. Restrepo (2011). *Urban world: mapping the economic power of cities*, McKinsey & Company, 49pp.

Dogliani, P. (2002). "European municipalism in the first half of the twentieth century: the socialist network," *Contemporary European History*, 11, pp. 573–596.

Ewen, S. and M. Hebbert (2007). "European cities in a networked world during the long 20th century," *Environment and Planning C: Government & Policy*, 25, pp. 327–340.

Gaspari, O. (2002). "Cities against states? Hopes, dreams and shortcomings of the European municipal movement, 1900–1960," *Contemporary European History,* 11, pp. 597–621.

Hafteck, P. (2003). "An introduction to decentralized cooperation–definitions, origins and conceptual mapping," *Public Administration and Development*, 23, pp. 333–345.

Hardy, D. (1991). *From garden cities to new towns: campaigning for town and country planning, 1899–1946*, Routledge, London.

Hietala, M. (1987). *Services and urbanization at the turn of the century: the diffusion of innovations*, Finnish Historical Society, Helsinki.

Klitgaard, R., R. MacLean-Abaroa and H. Parris (2000). *Corrupt cities: a practical guide to cure and prevention,* ICS Press and World Bank Institute, Oakland, CA and Washington, DC.

Kozinska-Witt, H. (2002). "The union of Polish cities in the Second Polish Republic, 1918–1939: discourses of local government in a divided land," *Contemporary European History*, 11, pp. 549–571.

Meadows, D., J. Randers, D. L. Meadows, and W. W. Behrens (1972). *The limits to growth: a report from the Club of Rome's project on the predicament of mankind*, Universe Books, New York.

Satterthwaite, D. (2009). "Addressing local and global environmental agendas in urban areas," Urban Strategy Review Background Paper, World Bank, Washington, DC.

Schuppan, T. (2009). "E-government in developing countries: experiences from sub-Saharan Africa," *Government Information Quarterly*, special issue: "From implementation to adoption: challenges to successful e-government diffussion," 26, pp. 118–127.

Szidat, S. (2009). "Sources of Asian haze," *Science*, 323, pp. 470–471.

Union of International Associations (2011). "Growth of international associations: non-governmental organizations (NGO) and intergovernmental organizations (IGO), 1909–1999" (paper), Union of International Associations, Brussels.

United Cities and Local Governments (ed.) (2008). *Decentralization and local democracy in the world*, First Global Report, United Cities and Local Governments and the World Bank, Barcelona, Spain and Washington, DC.

United Nations, Department of Economic and Social Affairs, Population Division (2010). World urbanization prospects. The 2009 revision. United Nations, New York.

Weyreter, M. (2003). "Germany and the town twinning movement," *Contemporary Review*, 282, pp. 37–43.

Working Group II Intergovernmental Panel on Climate Change, M. Parry, O. Canziani and J. Palutikof (2008). *Climate change 2007: Working Group II contribution to the Fourth Assessment Report of the Intergovernmental Panel on Climate Change*, Cambridge University Press, Cambridge, UK.

3 Cities as collective learners: what do we know?

The previous chapters have demonstrated a growing appetite for knowledge and technical exchange among cities around the globe. That discussion covered a few of the ways that cities go about gathering knowledge. We turn now to theoretical and practitioner literature to review what is known about organizational learning and to frame our understanding about cities as learners.

The central proposition in this book is that cities, though loose in terms of organization, mandate, bottom line and coherence, nevertheless learn. The last chapter showed us that very many cities, singly and in groups, are organizing ways to reach out to gather information about policy and practice from each other. They appear to acquire new knowledge just like any other organized entity. But given the diverse assemblage of powers, cross-cutting interests, and constantly evolving kaleidoscope of actors contained in them, how are cities able to retain and make use of knowledge? It is undeniable that cities innovate, reform, and make deliberate collective judgments with positive advances in economy, society and welfare. What do we know about collective learning and how might the present state of knowledge help us understand how cities go about the process—gathering, validating, storing and retrieving knowledge—and how is learning connected to innovation?

Notable recent works do not address the full range of these basic questions. Colin MacFarlane's *Learning the City* (2011), Safford's *Why the Garden Club Couldn't Save Youngstown* (2009), and Landry's *Creative City* (2000) are pertinent examples of works that address exchange of ideas and innovation or reform in cities. These contributions see cities in the light of collective action, and all of them in one way or another speak of transactions in ideas between cities, none drills down in to the detailed mechanics of learning.

Smart thinkers have written a covey of business books that trade on catchy phrases but shallow science, such as Peter Senge's *Fifth Discipline* (1990), Richard Ogle's *Smart World* (2007) and Malcolm Gladwell's *Tipping Point* (2002). But none of these penetrate beneath the silicon-thin surface of the digital age or pop network culture to see that human relationships still count in making sense of connectedness. Reliability and veracity of information are more important than global connections, high volume and blazing speed. We need to think beyond smart cities to understand the importance of meaning in information flow, be it over the internet or through personal networks of exchange.

Straying away from cities as protagonists in knowledge generation and transformation might be attributed in part to the digital revolution. The siren call of information flow that came with the digital revolution has been irresistible. The modern notions of the digitally connected are mostly a latter-day view of Meier's (1962) communications theory, with one major exception. Despite brilliant, groundbreaking work from thinkers like Jan van Dijk and Manuel Castells, some of the important elements of truth about urban development have not received much attention (Castells, 2009; van Dijk, 2005). Leading academic thinkers, cheered on by digital corporations, swerved toward the connectedness of networks and interaction with omnipresent media without giving full attention to deeper notions that make connectivity meaningful, particularly the ideas of human interaction that were at the heart of Meier's communications theory.

The magic of cities is that unlike corporations, where profit motives compel knowledge acquisition and management in predictable and replicable ways, cities seem to manage the same processes by civic assembly. By this I mean that cities have to find other ways to penetrate silos of information and achieve "buy-in" and alignment. And precisely because we have evidence of systematic change, we should explore the calculus of learning and pinpoint the locus of knowledge, and begin to shape policies to favor learning and innovation.

But we should also understand what is not covered in this present treatment of learning. The central idea in this book is collective learning, not individual values or specific skills. These are often the focus on twinning and international municipal cooperation and exchange. And though they are important, the key idea here—an idea that sets this work apart from much on municipal international cooperation (MIC) and twinning—is that cities or parts of them learn as a unit. They begin to reach agreement faster, they show a widespread common understanding of themselves. They achieve a collective city identity. All of this is based on common shared values, and this in turn on exposure to and working through the differences among key stakeholders in the city.

Cities as concentrators and transformers

It is almost inevitable that cities are often sources of innovation because they are the places where information is concentrated and exchanged. Urban thought pioneers like Richard Meier foresaw this as early as the early 1960s with his groundbreaking *Communications Theory of Urban Growth* (Meier, 1962). Meier saw cities much like nuclear reactors: they bring resources of all kinds into concentrations that are not found anywhere else. Individual agents—workers, CEOs, institutions, neighborhood activists and people in all walks of life—act to combine and recombine ideas. All this leads to the transformation of resources into something new. New emerging qualities appear. Of course, many negative outcomes arise as well: crime, corruption, pollution and a myriad of other ills. But the potential for innovation lies in this concentration of information, mixing of ideas, and transformation into something new.

Some of the key works in collective learning—Don Schön's *Beyond the Stable State* (1973), Chris Argyris and Schön's *Organizational Learning* (1978) and Nonaka's 1994 insights into innovation—developed important waypoints in the evolution of thinking about collective learning. Don Schön's work evolved in collaboration with Chris Argyris to address personal and organizational actions, particularly in connection with unintended outcomes of actions. Argyris and Schön made a critical distinction between common theories of action and more critical evaluation of underlying relationships. When experience confirms our assumptions about how the world works, we have single-loop learning; i.e., direct feedback. But when action A produces unintended consequences, then a deeper, more critical review of underlying values may be needed, a process Argyris and Schön refer to as "double-loop learning."

This simplified model of learning leads to more open, participatory feedback systems that help to stave off implicit biases and confront denial when outcomes look bad. Elaborated forms of the model led Schön, Argyris and followers like Peter Senge to develop strategies of cross-disciplinary, organizational learning based on systems thinking. And though these thinkers and the body of work they helped build led to many changes in the field of planning, they are nearly a half-century old: why refer to them at all?

The key reason is that at the heart of the matter for Argyris, Schön and others were issues of value sharing and trust among actors engaged in collective enterprises, whether in public settings or private organizations. These and related ideas are now reappearing in more recent literature in a half-dozen fields. Examples are in organizational learning, learning economies, regional competitiveness, capacity and institution building, together with, but to a lesser extent, the sociology and geography of networks. Each of these areas of work has some relevance to the question of cities as learning organizations. Still, only a minor share of any specific body of writing has been focused specifically on cities and almost nothing has been collated into a single volume treating the broad scope of learning and change. We turn now to a survey of some of this work to sharpen the question and review what is already known.

Coincidence and gaps: collective learning in urban development

Much of the academic and policy literature on regional competitiveness and clusters of industries alludes to the importance of underlying, "soft" infrastructure, described as an environment conducive to innovation that lies somewhat or mostly external to firms and companies. Aydalot's term *innovative milieu*, referring to an atmosphere of trust that is helpful for both collaboration and creativity in a locality (Aydalot, 1986), is a useful starting point in this stream of thought. Trust and collaboration are concepts that have been explored extensively in firms, regions and clusters by a large number of authors, of whom only a representative sample is cited here (Camagni, 1995; Kitson *et al.*, 2004; Kresl, 2007; Polenske, 2004; Porter, 2001).

Some analysts posit that learning, trust and creativity go together and are accepted parts of the soft infrastructure of city regions (Pinch *et al.*, 2003). But with few exceptions (Brandt *et al.*, 2009; Faulconbridge, 2007), most of the work just cited focuses on firms and clusters in city regions and not on cities or city-regions themselves. Moulaert and colleagues point to the initiatives taken by city-regions as "entrepreneurial urbanism" in the context of globalization (Moulaert *et al.*, 2005). It is only one short step further to see cooperative behaviors in learning. These linkages are the focus of Brandt and colleagues, who see inter-organizational relationships as a way to understand metropolitan regional growth (Brandt *et al.*, 2009). But what about the wider environment of the places where collaborating or innovative firms are located? What part of the innovative milieu arises from non-firm actors working together with private and civil sectors in the public goods areas of successful city-regions?[1]

Another largely separate but voluminous body of literature blossomed around organizational learning (and later learning organizations), with applications branching into behavior of both firms and public bureaucracies. Several reviews cover the main developments and watershed points in this vast domain (Dierkes *et al.*, 2001; Easterby-Smith and Lyles, 2002; Huber, 1991). Seminal in much of this, in fact the most frequently cited in Easterby-Smith and Lyles' comprehensive review, is the work of Ikujiro Nonaka.

Nonaka developed a key insight about industrial management. His concept relates to the conversion of tacit to explicit knowledge, a transformation involving a propitious environment for learning, something close to Aydalot's "innovative milieu," or in Nonaka's terminology a *ba* (Nonaka, 1994; Nonaka *et al.*, 2000). The "ba" refers to an atmosphere, an openness, in which managers and workers are free from the negative constraints of possible embarrassment, retribution or even fear. Figure 3.1 depicts Nonaka's idea of the ba.

The ba is a working environment created and maintained in a process of moving from open exchange (*socialization* in Figure 3.1), then moving clockwise through the other elements in Figure 3.1. In the expressing of tacit dimensions of knowledge, tacit knowledge is gradually externalized and adopted as accepted and shared knowledge by the larger peer group. It is something akin to play; individuals are given the freedom to think creatively. This insight harks back to the ideas of Dewey and Piaget about learning. The play is not invoked in most management studies, and the ba concept has been applied to city-regions in only one case found in the literature; that of Tampere, Finland (Kostiainen, 2002). We shall return to the idea of ba in the city in later chapters.

Other branches of organizational learning extend into capacity building and the concept of social capital. This body of work explores many areas, such as style and capacity of governance, the expression of voice, methods of conflict resolution, and the build-up of trust (Chaskin *et al.*, 2001; Ostrom *et al.*, 1994; Putnam, 2000; Uphoff, 2000). Others address conditions of creativity (Landry, 2000; Landry and Matarasso, 1998), facilitation of collective decisions and reduction of opportunistic behaviors (Grootaert and van Bastelaer, 2002), and the importance of information exchange. Examples include the cases of Tampere, Finland (Kostiainen, 2002; Kostiainen and Sotarauta, 2002); northern Denmark and southern Sweden (Malmberg and Maskell, 2006); and Curitiba, Brazil (Vassolar, 2007).

This last group of cases focuses on inter-network connections among the many regional organizations involved in research, urban planning and implementation.

Nonaka's "Ba"

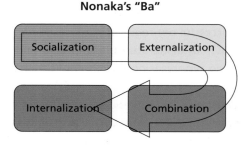

Figure 3.1 Nonaka's ba

But none of the authors cited in the preceding paragraph has drilled down systematically into either the sources of knowledge or the intra-city political or sociological dynamics of knowledge processing by individuals and groups involved in collective learning. In other words, they point to an assemblage of knowledge-intensive activities—universities, research institutions, firms dealing in high tech, and the like—but they do not specify the human relational elements that tie these knowledge places together. The elements of a city's own innovative milieu, its ba, lies outside and beyond the firms that operate there. Indeed the ba may be the very qualities that attract the firms in the first place.

The ties that bind

An equally large corpus of literature has been developed on social networks in organizations. The rapidly expanding field of social network analysis, understood as a branch of social capital, has covered many aspects of social and organizational life, again with a strong emphasis on business and innovation. Examples of thinkers from this area include Barabási, Newman and Watts (Barabási, 2002; Newman et al., 2006; Watts, 2003), to name the most recognizable. The distinguishing feature of these works is that they look at macroscopic properties of networks whose connected nodes reach into the many millions—on the internet, for instance, as well as in social and biological structures. Systems of cities fit this pattern and exhibit some of the macro-properties such as the power law found in natural systems. The authors develop axioms (e.g., preferential selection) to explain mathematical regularities found in large network structures.

More to the point, the network literature deals with power relationships, social movements, control of information flow and networks as learning tools for specific groups. Some of these ideas are relevant to the present discussion, for instance, intra-city partnerships and connections (Entwistle et al., 2007; Tresman et al., 2007), social movements (Mische, 2003; Parker, 2008; Passy, 2003) and governance of natural resources (Bodin and Crona, 2009). But while social network analysis (SNA) does provide a way to measure connections and trust, it has been applied only rarely to cities as units of analysis (Brandt et al., 2009; Cheng et al., 2004; Diani and McAdam, 2003; Fawaz, 2008). A key step still to be taken is to use the quantitative tools developed for social network analysis to probe the creation, maintenance and change of social and political values (Emirbayer and Goodwin, 1994), such as those suggested by the concepts of cohesiveness and trust, ingredients that are likely a part of "soft infrastructure" external to a firm.

In short, these separate but partially overlapping streams of work—on regional competitiveness, organizational learning, and social capital and networks—all contribute to a better understanding of the conditions and mechanisms of learning by multiple players in firms and organizations. Each body of thought recognizes that actors in open systems take part in collective learning, even when no explicit, formal arrangements govern the system. Further, trust and value sharing are seen as common denominators in a ba, an innovative milieu, the soft infrastructure or a creative city. These ideas provide an initial framework to explore learning environments in cities.

But numerous methodological questions arise when applying learning to cities as a unit of analysis. First, with rapidly changing leadership of cities, especially in the developing world, how can collective knowledge be identified, managed, and made available to future policy makers? And if "proactive" learning cities invest deliberately in learning, as claimed in the examples of Seattle, Bilbao and Curitiba (Campbell, 2009), have such cities achieved a civic ba, to employ Nonaka's term, or in other words, an innovative milieu in the civic realm? If so, how is this to be measured? Further, what connection is there between the collective learning being observed among leading cities and documented successes?

The conceptual model of networks in cities is straightforward and intuitive: cities exchange ideas, and individuals in cities process and validate new knowledge. There is no mathematical representation of city networks, either among cities or in terms of informal exchange within them. The litmus test of veracity and trust is met by individuals exchanging ideas and working together. Trust is often the governing factor in determining whether a network link has any meaning or significance for people learning in a city. In contrast to Barabási's insights on the making of individual connections and the production of regularities in large structures, the stories in Beyond Smart Cities provide everyday working examples at the level of individuals deciding whether or not to trust one another.

To the city

A growing body of literature speaks of cities as increasingly active players on an international stage, often in the context of transmitting policy ideas (Dolowitz and Marsh, 2000; Hewitt, 1999; Ward, 2007). Recall that only a few cases have employed learning concepts to examine cities directly. Some look at the role of crisis and leadership in subnational governments (Campbell and Fuhr, 2004) and the conditions of creativity (Landry, 2000; Landry and Matarasso, 1998); others highlight the importance of information, in Tampere, Finland (Kostiainen, 2002; Kostiainen and Sotarauta, 2002), for instance, or Curitiba (Vassolar, 2007).

These last two examples focus on inter-network connections among the many regional organizations involved in planning and implementation, but they have not drilled down into group or individual dynamics to illuminate the modes of learning, the use of knowledge, or the mechanisms of storage. Neither have they examined the impact or influence, if any, that the husbanding of knowledge has on the creation of soft infrastructure.

Richard Florida provides still another, one could say, back-door perspective on city learning by focusing on talent flows to cities (Florida, 2002). In other words, Florida's starting point for knowledge-based economies has more to do with talent seeking environment than environment seeking talent. His findings provide a fresh take on the entire development process. If talent drives knowledge economies, what drives talent to cities? His answer is agreeable environments— green, progressive and tolerant political and social values coupled with high technology. These are key factors that attract college-educated youngsters and those in the creative industries.

Florida introduces a new wrinkle in the common assumption, found most notably in the European literature on knowledge economies, that knowledge-based regions will have the talent they need. Florida's ideas about creative classes and their psychological and social preferences imply a reversal of the theory of change. Talent breeds its own innovative milieu. Accordingly, policies to foster knowledge economies may need to go much further than those typically found in OECD policy manuals about knowledge regions.

On the other hand, recent evidence from the financial crisis shows that even knowledge- and talent-intensive places like Portland are unable to keep all talent employed, and some of the talent in Portland is willing to sit it out on the street, as it were, rather than migrate to greener pastures for jobs. The quip line from "Portlandia" (a recent TV comedy series) captures it well: "Portland, the place where the young go to retire." So if talent is a factor in knowledge economies and learning, there must be more to the game. Cities like Portland still need to do the learning and networking to innovate and keep people employed.

Cities like Portland might gain insight from the "learning cities" movement in Europe and Australia. Learning Communities (via OECD and Pascal International) is a nascent movement that has grown out of an interest in lifelong education. Longworth's Learning Communities is a group of practitioners and academics, who apply concepts of lifelong learning and knowledge-based economies to cities and communities as an approach to economic development (Longworth, 2006). Strategic applications involve partnerships and networks. But again, the unit of analysis is high-technology and knowledge-intensive organizations and city-based knowledge industries but not, as in this volume, individual players within the city interacting with one another.

Summing up

Many domains of literature help us to understand the basic mechanisms of collective learning. But we are still in the dark about the interplay among individuals in social networks as they take part in collective learning and form an innovative milieu. Further, how do we fit these ideas of collective action to the zoology of city types we find operating in the real world? What framework can account for all the rich variety of learners, the individuals, the gadflies, the think tanks and private research and development centers, city twinning, and learning regions? How do the core of ideas of trust, interpersonal sharing of values, and the creation of an innovative milieu get installed in a city?

We shall see that the answers are found in the many ways that cities go about learning. Many cities have little or no idea about their learning; some knowledge agencies of cities are created mainly for non-learning purposes; and still others are designed with deliberate intent to capture new knowledge continuously. Above all, ready or not, cities are on the move. The chapters in Part II will document a surprisingly high volume of city-to-city visits and a wide variety of institutional arrangements.

Note

1   It can be said that Argyris and Schön focused on elements of the innovative milieu in city-based organizations in the sense that the transmission of ideas and sharing of values and deeper underlying structures of trust were part of double-loop learning (Argyris and Schön, 1978; Schön, 1973).

References

Argyris, C. and D. Schön (1978). *Organizational learning—a theory of action perspective*, Addison Wesley, Reading, MA.
Aydalot, P. (1986). *Milieux innovateurs en Europe*, GREMI, Paris.
Badshah, A. and J. Perlman (2002). "Mega-cities and the urban future: a model for replicating best practices," in G. Bridge and S. Watson, *The Blackwell City Reader*, Blackwell Publishing, Oxford, UK, pp. 549–559.
Barabási, A.-L. (2002). *Linked. The new science of networks*, Perseus Press, Cambridge, MA.
Bodin, Ö. and B. Crona (2009). "The role of social networks in natural resource governance: what relational patterns make a difference?," *Global Environmental Change*, 19, pp. 366–374.

Brandt, A., C. Hahn, S. Krätke and M. Kiese (2009). "Metropolitan regions in the knowledge economy: network analysis as a strategic information tool," *Tijdschrift voor Economische en Sociale Geografi*, 100, pp. 236–249.

Camagni, R. (1995). "The concept of innovative milieu and its relevance for public policies in European lagging tegions," *Journal of the Regional Science Association*, 74, pp. 317–340.

Campbell, T. (2009). "Learning cities. Knowledge, capacity and competitiveness," *Habitat International*, 33, pp. 195–201.

Campbell, T. and H. Fuhr (2004). *Leadership and innovation* (Development Series), World Bank Institute, Washington, DC.

Castells, M. (2009). *The rise of the network society*, Wiley-Blackwell, New York.

Chaskin, R., P. Brown, S. Venkatesh and A. Vidal (2001). *Building community capacity*, Aldine de Gruyter, New York.

Cheng, P., C. Choi, S. Chen, T. Eldomiaty and C. Millar (2004). "Knowledge repositories in knowledge cities: institutions, conventions and knowledge subnetworks," *Journal of Knowledge Management*, 8, pp. 96–106.

Diani, M. and D. McAdam (2003). *Social movements and networks: relational approaches to collective action*, Oxford University Press, Oxford, UK.

Dierkes, M., A. B. Antal, J. Child and I. Nonaka (2001). *Handbook of orgnizational learning and knowledge*, Oxford University Press, Oxford, UK.

Dolowitz, D. P. and D. Marsh (2000). "Learning from abroad: the role of policy transfer in contemporary policy-making," *Governance*, 13, pp. 5–23.

Easterby-Smith, M. and M. Lyles (2002). *The Blackwell handbook of organizational learning and knowledge management*, Blackwell Publishing, London.

Emirbayer, M. and J. Goodwin (1994). "Network analysis, culture and the problem of agency," *The American Journal of Sociology*, 99, pp. 1411–1454.

Entwistle, T., G. Bristow, F. Hines, S. Donaldson and S. Martin (2007). "The dysfunctions of markets, hierarchies and networks in the meta-governance of partnership," *Urban Studies*, 44, pp. 63–79.

Faulconbridge, J. (2007). "Exploring the role of professional associations in collective learning in London and New York's advertising and law professional service firm clusters," *Environment and Planning*, A39, pp. 964–985.

Fawaz, M. (2008). "An unusual clique of city-makers: social networks in the production of a neighborhood in Beirut (1950–75)," *International Journal of Urban and Regional Research*, 32, pp. 565–585.

Florida, R. (2002). *The rise of the creative class*, Basic Books, New York.

Gladwell, M. (2002). *The tipping point. How little things can make a big difference*, Little, Brown and Company, Boston.

Grootaert, C. and T. van Bastelaer (2002). *Understanding and measuring social capital. A synthesis of findings and recommendations from the social capital initiative* (Forum series on the Role of Institutions in Promoting Economic Growth), United States Agency for International Development, Washington, DC.

Hewitt, W. E. (1999). "Municipalities and the new internationalism. Cautionary notes from Canada," *Cities*, 16, pp. 435–444.

Huber, G. P. (1991). "Organizational learning: the contributing processes and the literatures," *Organization Science* (special issue: "Organizational learning: papers in honor of (and by) James G. March," 2, pp. 88–115.

Kitson, M., R. Martin and P. Tyler (2004). "Regional competitiveness—an elusive yet key concept," *Regional Studies*, 38, pp. 991–999.

Kostiainen, J. (2002). "Learning and the 'ba' in the development network of an urban region," *European Planning Studies*, 10, pp. 613–631.

Kostiainen, J. and M. Sotarauta (2002). *Tampere's path from industrial to knowledge economy. Finnish city reinvented.* MIT Industrial Performance Center, Cambridge, MA.

Kresl, P. (2007). *Planning cities for the future: the successes and failures of urban economic strategies in Europe,* Edward Elgar Publishing, Cheltenham and Camberley, UK.

Landry, C. (2000). *The creative city,* Earthscan, London.

Landry, C. and F. Matarasso (1998). *The learning city-region: approaching problems of the concept, its measurement and evaluation,* OECD, Paris.

Longworth, N. (2006). *Learning cities, learning regions, learning communities: lifelong learning and local government,* Routledge, Milton Park, UK.

MacFarlane, C. (2011). *Learning the city: translocal assemblage and urban politics,* WileyBlackwell, London.

Malmberg, A. and P. Maskell (2006). "Localized learning revisited," *Growth and Change,* 37, pp. 1–18.

Meier, R. L. (1962). *A communications theory of urban growth,* MIT Press, Cambridge, MA.

Mische, A. (2003). "Cross-talk in movements: reconceiving the culture-network link," in M. Diani and D. McAdam (eds), *Social movements and networks: relational approaches to collective action,* Oxford University Press, Oxford, UK.

Moulaert, F., A. Rodriguez and E. Swyngweddouw (2005). *The globalized city. Economic restructuring and social polarization in European cities,* Oxford University Press, Oxford, UK.

Newman, M., A. Barabási and D. Watts (2006). *The structure and dynamics of networks,* Princeton University Press, Princeton, NJ.

Nonaka, I. (1994). "A dynamic theory of organizational knowledge creation," *Organization Science,* 5, pp. 14–37.

Nonaka, I., R. Toyama and N. Konno (2000). "SECI, ba and leadership: a unified model of dynamic knowledge creation," *Long Range Planning,* 33, pp. 5–34.

Ogle, R. (2007). *Smart world. Breakthrough creativity and the new science of ideas,* Harvard Business School Press, Boston.

Ostrom, E., L. Schroeder and S. Wynne (1994). *Institutional incentives and sustainable development,* Westview Press, Boulder, CO.

Parker, R. (2008). "Networked governance or just networks? Local governance of the knowledge economy in Limerick (Ireland) and Karlskrona (Sweden)," *Political Studies,* 55, pp. 113–132.

Passy, F. (2003). "Social networks matter. But how?," in M. Diani and D. McAdam (eds), *Social movements and networks: relational approaches to collective action,* Oxford University Press, Oxford, UK, pp. 21–48.

Pinch, S., N. Henry, M. Jenkins and S. Tallman (2003). "From 'industrial districts' to 'knowledge clusters': a model of knowledge dissemination and competition in industrial agglomerations," *Journal of Economic Geography*, 3, pp. 373–398.

Polenske, K. (2004). "Competition, collaboration and cooperation: an uneasy triangle in networks of firms and regions," *Regional Studies*, 38, pp. 1029–1043.

Porter, M. (2001). "Regions and the new economics of competition," in A. Scott (ed.), *Global city-regions. Trends, theory, policy*, Oxford University Press, New York, pp. 139–157.

Putnam, R. D. (2000). *Bowling alone. The collapse and revival of American community*, Simon and Schuster, New York.

Safford, S. (2009). *Why the garden club couldn't save Youngstown*, Harvard University Press, Cambridge, MA.

Schön, D. A. (1973). *Beyond the stable state. Public and private learning in a changing society*, Penguin, Harmondsworth.

Senge, P. M. (1990). *The fifth discipline. The art and practice of the learning organization*, Doubleday Currency, New York.

Tresman, M., E. Pasher and F. Molinari (2007). "Conversing cities: the way forward," *Journal of Knowledge Management*, 11, pp. 55–64.

Uphoff, N. (2000). "Understanding social capital: learning from the analysis and experience of participation," in P. Dagupta and I. Serageldin (eds), *Social capital: a multifaceted perspective*, World Bank, Washington, DC, pp. 215–252.

van Dijk, J. (2005). *The network society: social aspects of new media*, Sage Publications, London.

Vassolar, I. (2007). *Urban Brazil. Visions, afflictions, and governance lessons*, Cambria Press, Youngstown, NY.

Ward, K. (2007). "Business improvement districts: policy origins, mobile policies and urban liveability," *Geography Compass*, 1, pp. 657–672.

Watts, D. (2003). *Six degrees: the science of a connected age*, W. W. Norton and Company, New York.

Part II
Framing a view

4 A gamut of learning types

Our run through the literature in the last chapter cut through many areas in organizational learning, networks and innovation. We saw that not so much has been written about deliberate city learning and innovation. We still know little about how cities, especially the innovators, might be working toward the construction of an innovative milieu. In this chapter, we shall see that some cities deliberately shape innovative milieus while others ignore them.

In a previous article, I suggested that active, innovative cities develop their own learning styles (Campbell, 2006). Cities like Bilbao and Curitiba have invested heavily over decades as part of a development strategy that has paid dividends in wholesale improvements. But we also know that cities take many approaches to learning. The World Bank and UN-Habitat, as well as the membership profiles of large, city-based organizations, tell us that a wide range of learning types can be found among the 4000 medium and larger cities in the world. We shall explore these ideas further in this and the following chapters.

A typology of city learners

UN-Habitat and others have developed frameworks (typologies) to form a map of the different ways that cities engage in city-to-city learning. In particular, the 2001 report by UN-Habitat is a useful guide (UN-Habitat and United Towns Organization, 2001). That framework is adopted here with several important modifications. First, the UN framework leaves out important categories of cities that are specialized as well as those that are not heavily engaged in learning, even though both specialists and slow movers are also acquiring and using knowledge. Second, the UN was not concerned with failure to learn, and so the framework does not include anything about why cities do not learn. We shall touch on that point at the end of this chapter.

The ways cities learn can be illustrated using five categories, distinguished by the degree to which the institutional effort in the city is organized and dedicated to seeking out and capturing information (see Table 4.1).

Many cities could be put in more than one category much of the time. A city department or mayor and accompanying constabulary will visit from time to time to kick the tires of a place, send a dedicated mission, participate in a conference, and join one or more networks. The point with these categories is not that they are tidy and mutually exclusive. Rather, we wish to cover the main mechanisms that cities use to get new ideas. The categories are distinguished partly by how much collective effort a city must exert in any given category in order to obtain new knowledge.

The rows of Table 4.1 depict a gradient of effort by the city, strong at the top levels and weaker lower down. Toward the bottom, cities are passive recipients rather than active learners. Linked to the level of effort is the order of learning. At the top of the table, cities learn things—ideas, practices, policies—that can be written down and transferred. A higher order of learning entails that exchange of values and tacit knowledge which leads to validation and innovation.

Table 4.1 Typology of city learning

Type	Principle	Example
1. Individual cities, one on many	Cities organize deliberate learning missions	Seattle, Denver
2. Individual cities, one on one	Cities engage in episodic visits or exchanges	EUROCITIES, VNG, Sister Cities
3. City clusters on clusters	Cities that share common program objectives or campaigns	UNESCO World Heritage Cities, Agenda 21 Cities (ICLEI)
4. Cities in active networks	Cities that are members in regional or global associations	UCLG and Metropolis, Healthy Cities, EUROCITIES, AsiaCities, CITYNET
5. Cities in passive networks	Cities that engage casually in conferences, events, and network bulletins	City Mayors, Local Government Information Network (LOGIN)

Source: Author

One of the key outcomes of putting effort into learning is that ground is formed, where participants from a city who take part in learning engage inadvertently or deliberately in the interpersonal transfer of values. This exchange and exposure lie at the heart of learning. We shall see that these gains tail off as we move down the list, even if the specific factual information or data accessed by a city might be valuable for it. By describing these attributes of information exchange we can understand something about how learning takes place. Later on, we can focus on how the city formalizes information and stores learning, if indeed it does so at all. In each of the five categories, case illustrations provide detail and context about the varieties of learning.

Type 1: one on many

Seattle is a prototype city; it is proactive, reformer and learner. Seattle created a process of learning that has ventured out to another city every year since 1992, making its study missions, in the words of the National League of Cities, "arguably the best city visit program in the U.S." Study missions are to be distinguished from trade and other missions, which depart regularly from the city every year. For instance, the Port of Seattle, which comprises its container port, airport and ferry facilities, also conducts and hosts visiting missions. The same can be said for each of the departments of water, parks, planning, and education, and a dozen other entities linked to the city. Although the study missions are the pre-eminent program, any time a group from the city engages in learning exchange, both "orders" of learning are achieved.

The study missions of Seattle are elaborate, highly organized, dedicated visits scheduled 18 to 24 months in advance and conducted on a yearly basis by the Trade Development Alliance, formerly a dependency of the Greater Seattle Chamber of Commerce and now independent. The study missions engage up to 100 business and civic leaders from the greater Seattle area each year. Mission membership turns over 60 to 80 percent each year, meaning that a rolling group of veterans is always involved. The overarching objective is to broaden and strengthen the understanding of city leaders about the position of Seattle vis-à-vis the visited city and its surrounding region.

According to Stafford (1999), six underlying goals of study missions are:

- to continue an ongoing process of relationship building among and between Seattle's civic leadership;
- to study and learn from the practices and programs of other cities and cultures that may provide solutions to Seattle's urban problems;

- to promote the region's business opportunities, including the ports, tourism, goods and services, educational opportunities, and venues for international meetings;
- to build relationships with the people and institutions in the cities visited;
- to organize special business and educational-opportunity meetings, such as the biomedical meeting in London between the leadership of Seattle's two industry associations, the meetings between female leaders in Singapore and Sydney, or the sharing of experiences with airport noise reduction;
- to help develop the most sophisticated civic leadership in the US on international issues.

Seattle began its study tour program in 1992 with a visit by a small delegation to the cities of Amsterdam, Rotterdam and Stuttgart. In 1993, Seattle was one of the first visiting delegations to Vietnam after the normalization of that country's relations with the US. In 1994 a delegation visited the Kansai region of Japan (Kobe and Osaka) and in 1995, Hong Kong. Succeeding missions visited London and Bristol in 1997; Singapore in 1998; and Sydney in 1999; Shanghai 2002; Barcelona 2003 and Munich 2004. All of these visits were organized by the Trade Development Alliance and included a similar profile of delegates.[1]

Participants on the missions include the top leadership figures of the city and county and its utilities, ports, universities, private firms and NGOs. Not all of the delegates are senior officials. The Boeing executive quoted in Chapter 1 pointed out that he persuaded Boeing to send three of their top younger people on the study tour because "it was the best value in training that money could buy." Each of the members, or their respective agencies, covers the travel and lodging and other costs. Often the receiving cities provide receptions and meals, and sometimes local transportation as well.

Most study tours involve detailed preparations with thick briefing books, seminars given in advance, and usually two preparatory visits by the chief organizer from Seattle. During the mission, the delegates meet over meals, discuss in plenary what they have seen, and hear presentations by their hosts. Agendas cover a wide variety of topics, including cultural, historical, economic and social issues. Speakers include US citizens working in the city, officials from the city and region, business leaders, and members of civil society. Each day involves a mixture of speakers, site visits and cultural affairs. Business promotion and networking do take place, but the participants on the study tours tend to spend most of their day together, in a group or subgroups, divided according to interest. For example, in Shanghai, a large delegation of health officials and university researchers (from the University of Washington's Fred Hutchinson Cancer Research Center) held parallel meetings with counterparts on issues of public health while elected officials and planners visited the city hall.

The heart of the learning experience takes place during these plenary sessions and afterwards when delegates sit during meals, in meeting halls, or on the bus in transit from one place to the next. They question and digest what they have seen and heard and exchange perceptions and opinions with each other. These transition moments allow them to absorb and gain perspective and insight on their own issues back home.

For instance, Seattle has long considered the merits and demerits of better public transit in the downtown area—light rail, in particular—and of the need for a third runway at Sea-Tac airport. Another issue is governance, or at least government coordination, in the greater Seattle area. Debates on these issues have been protracted over years and have emerged as subtext during city visits.

In this context, delegates visiting Shanghai were stunned to see a city nearly the size of Seattle in volume of buildings constructed in the Pudong region in less than 15 years. Surveying the ambitious progress made in Shanghai provoked a debate among the touring team at the closing meeting. The Seattle contingent spoke with growing unease about the swampy terrain of process-oriented planning in their own city. The Chinese in Shanghai were on the other end of this decision-making spectrum, where expedition and speed overrode all concerns for environmental care, permits, hearings, due process in courts, and so on.

But though Seattle may be pre-eminent, many other proactive cities are on an active and more or less regular search for knowledge. Major cities in the US and Europe—Bilbao is a good example—undertake similar study tours, organized with a specific program of events and themes to explore. Bilbao has reached out to other cities for consultation in order to guide its strategy for wholesale redevelopment along the Nervión River. Like Seattle, Bilbao's search for knowledge has run for several decades, but unlike Seattle, Bilbao's program has no fixed periodicity. Focused on strategic objectives of redevelopment in a formerly derelict part of town, Bilbao both ventured out for visits and invited peer cities to consult "in house" at conferences and seminars. Both visits and in-house events helped city leaders to set their sights as well as to gauge feasibility of the options they began to develop. As we shall see in Chapter 8, as the plan for massive infrastructure investments—in a new port, airport, rapid transit and other features like the Guggenheim Museum—city leadership constantly renewed its knowledge base as it implemented its redevelopment plan.

Other examples of proactive cities covered later include Amman, Charlotte, Portland, Turin and Barcelona. All are engaged in more or less continuous outreach efforts to solve specific problems or merely to keep up with developments in best practice around a range of issues. Mixed in with these efforts are study tours organized by chambers of commerce and NGOs. For instance, the Chamber of Commerce in Charlotte and Denver organized more or less annual events, visiting another city usually, but not always, in the US. Though no longer in the proactive category, Tijuana arranged a visit to Bilbao by the Arthur Anderson consulting firm. That experience marked a shift in vision and understanding for leaders in Tijuana, who were contemplating major invest-ments in the city. Many cities in Europe take advantage of the opportunities created by common goals and linkages created in the context of the European Union.

An important distinguishing feature of proactive learning cities is the high relative importance of second-order learning—managing knowledge, usually by placing responsibility for learning in the hands of an entity or agency—as opposed to merely acquiring new knowledge about policy and practice (first-order learning). Second-order learning refers to organizing and curating new knowledge. We shall return to orders of learning in later chapters.

Type 2: cities in one-on-one exchange—ad hoc and episodic

One-on-one exchanges take many forms. Perhaps the best known is twinning or city-to-city exchange in a binary fashion. These have been practiced for many decades, but started in earnest after World War II, as we saw in Chapter 2. Recent versions have taken a new twist, adding strategic and longer-term objectives that fulfill more programmatic needs of sponsoring entities, usually foreign assistance agencies. Many governments, including those of France, the Netherlands, Sweden, the UK and the US, make use of individual municipalities as technical agents of foreign assistance to local governments in recipient countries. Two such programs are illustrated below.

One of the oldest and most active is the VNG, the Association of Netherlands Municipalities, established in 1912. VNG International has operated or coordi-nated twinning assistance for local governments in the developing world since 1993. The most recent local government (LOGO) program, financed by the Dutch Ministry of Foreign Affairs, is aimed at specific countries in the global South (selected countries in Africa, the Americas, Asia and Eastern Europe). Based on its experience in the Netherlands, the VNG has many years experience with organizing direct inputs to local governments in developing countries by means of leveraging Dutch municipal officials or technicians with their counterparts abroad. Technical and managerial help on management, service delivery and improvement of technical skills is provided by direct peer-to-peer contact during short-term missions as well as exchange visits. The programs affect associations and individual municipalities in scores of countries (just under 60 in the 2007–2010 period).

A second example is City Links, a smaller program of twinning operated since 1997 by the International City and County Managers Association (ICMA) with USAID funding. Similar to the VNG, the ICMA is the professional and educational organization for appointed managers, administrators and assistants in cities, towns, counties and regional entities throughout the world. Since 1914, the ICMA has provided technical and management assistance, training, and information resources to its members and the local government community. The management decisions made by the ICMA's nearly 9000 members affect more than 100 million individuals in thousands of communities—from small towns with populations of a few hundred to metropolitan areas serving several million.

The ICMA's City Links program (inaugurated in 1997 as the Resource Cities Program) brings together the best management practitioners from the US with officials from client cities of USAID in developing and transitional countries to share resources and technical expertise with the aim of improving the lives of urban residents.

The City Links program facilitates the exchange of teams of local government officials—city managers, mayors and department heads—between US and overseas cities during a period lasting anywhere from 18 to 24 months. The exchanges enable officials to learn from their peers and adopt a pragmatic approach to urban management problems. The partners develop a work plan with clear objectives and expected outcomes to remedy whatever challenges the parties had agreed to address. Program funds cover international travel and accommodation costs, usually for trips by US staff to the host country and return trips by counterparts to the US city. Local officials contribute their time, making the program a cost-effective means to provide technical assistance to developing and transitional countries.

The program has launched nearly 80 partnerships under a global cooperative agreement. The partnerships address issues such as solid waste management, budgeting and financial planning, downtown revitalization, citizen participation, and water and wastewater treatment, among others. The collaborative effort helps partnerships make significant changes in urban management overseas.

In twinning programs, assistance is agreed in the course of the first of several preliminary site visits and, though it may be modified on the fly, is carried out in several successive visits by practitioner experts from the "resource" city to the other in the field, with return visits by field practitioners to the "resource" city. Knowledge is transferred in a direct manner, from practitioner to practitioner. The VNG and the ICMA cover distinct realms, but together include such things as strategic planning, conducting surveys, cadastre updates and reforms, budget management and forecasting, incubators for local economic development, procurement documents, auctioning public land, and so on.

For the most part, the city linkages achieve their objectives, usually two or three discrete management or service-delivery issues. USAID has concluded that when reforms are dramatic departures from conventional practice, as they were with the land auctions in former Soviet states, they can set up powerful models for change that other cities seek to achieve (USAID, 2001). Both the ICMA and the VNG have found that partnerships often result in unanticipated benefits to the overseas cities, for example, in management changes.

Several drawbacks limit learning. One problem with bilateral exchange is that a fixed horizon limits contact and support. Twinning programs by their nature are effective, but rather narrow in target, aiming to reach specific objectives in management, services or technical skills. Administrative turnover is sometimes a further limitation. US Sister Cities International learned this lesson long ago. That program has concluded that the most effective solution to sustainability—financial as well as institutional—is to build a relationship within the community, and not just among city officials.[2] Communities of interest become the glue of sustainability. When new leaders are voted into office, the relationship does not end. City-to-city relationships are important to a new mayor's constituency, without necessarily requiring a program commitment on the part of the mayor.

Additional problems arise from the tailor-made nature of assistance. Donor countries take the lead on sponsorship and the design of interventions, if not on execution, even though international agencies are well aware of the importance of ownership on the part of the recipient. Also, because of the tailored nature of direct help to local governments, the programs are limited in their reach. Assistance to national associations, on the other hand, has a built-in leveraging effect, since all members in the country are potential beneficiaries.

Type 3: city clusters on clusters

Learning through the mediation of international NGOs is fundamentally different in several ways from the previous cases. First, the focus shifts away from the city itself and moves instead to intermediate organizations. In effect, the agency of learning is shared, sometimes led, by an external actor, usually an international NGO. Second, network NGOs provide several forms of learning opportunities not provided by active cities. Networks provide conventions and standards (e.g., World Heritage Cities conventions or Agenda 21 and C-40 programs focusing on carbon footprint targets) as well as best practice and normative codes and legislation, which establish a framework of policy or practice.

The Organization of World Heritage Cities (OWHC) is an example of a growing international NGO that is instrumental in establishing a normative, even legal framework concerning the management of culturally significant places. The OWHC was established in 1993 to develop a sense of solidarity and a cooperative relationship between World Heritage cities. Made up of 218 cities having sites included on the UNESCO World Heritage List, the OWHC's mission is to promote the implementation of the World Heritage Convention by helping municipal administrators access the information they need to meet this challenge. To this end, the OWHC organizes symposia and seminars dealing with the challenges to be met in the realm of management and strategies pertaining to the development and preservation of historic sites.

The OWHC's headquarters, located in Quebec City, Canada, organizes the OWHC's initiatives, which are geared to the implementation of the World Heritage Convention. OWHC meetings lead to international conventions, some of which have the moral force of law, which help cities understand the rights and responsibilities of being designated as a World Heritage city. The OWHC also strives to heighten awareness of the importance of protecting historic cities among officials of the United Nations, UNESCO, the World Bank and the Council of Europe. In the coming years, the organization is to focus on the establishment of an electronic communications network linking member cities through the internet, and the creation of a data bank on historic cities.

A good example is the city of Hué, Vietnam (Yang, 2002). A former imperial capital of Vietnam, Hué was listed as a World Heritage city in 1993. Soon afterwards, UNESCO, with support from the Republic of Korea, helped to set up a GIS system to map the core area of Hué as a conservation management tool. However, urban migration, demographic changes and tourism demands began to take a toll on the city's cultural heritage. In response to unregulated urban development practices, UNESCO brokered a relationship between Hué and Lille Métropole in France to help cope with planning and management issues. With the hope of balancing protection with development needs, the collaborative effort began with five pilot project sites to develop an urban inventory and diagnosis of preservation priorities. The project engaged students from the Lille and Hué Schools of Architecture.

Further collaboration with Lille, as well as French and Brazilian banks, the city of Turin, and international development funds, facilitated the development of a revolving loan fund for housing loans and subsidies. Such collaborations helped generate a legal framework for urban conservation in Hué and have raised awareness of the value of inter-agency partnerships within local government. It has also spurred the city to engage citizens more actively in urban planning initiatives, and given the Hué Heritage House (an important Vietnamese cultural center) an important role guiding the future of coordination of urban preservation and development.

The ICLEI, now Agenda 21, is another important network, with more than 700 cities engaged in climate action. Originally the International Council on Local Environmental Initiatives, the organization was formed in 1990 when its key founder, Jeffery Brugmann, discovered that it was possible to affect behaviors of cities—that is, to change operational policies—in a way that would have positive impact on greenhouse gases. His experience with a single municipality in Southern California mushroomed into a solid organization that made Local Agenda 21 a cornerstone of its actions.

The ICLEI's mandate has evolved to address the sustainable cities agenda. ICLEI members carry out campaigns to improve environmental conditions.

> A fundamental component of our performance-based campaign model is the milestone process. Each campaign incorporates a five-milestone structure that participating local governments work through: (1) establish a baseline; (2) set a target; (3) develop a local action plan; (4) implement the local action plan; and (5) measure results.
>
> (ICLEI, 2003: 8)

The ICLEI has developed a network of activists operating at the municipal level in scores of cities around the globe to lobby city councils, provide public education, and promote community support for environmental improvements. The ICLEI has built up a database of more than 70 successful sustainable city case studies.

Box 4.1 *Potchefstroom, South Africa*

Potchefstroom is a rapidly urbanizing municipality in the Northern Cape province of South Africa. In 2001, the medium-sized city of 125,000 joined the ICLEI's Cities for Climate Protection (CCP) program, which provides local governments with a framework to identify GHG emissions while improving local communities' living conditions. Soon after, in 2002, Potchefstroom volunteered to implement the ICLEI's Local Agenda 21 to develop a comprehensive sustainable development action plan. The subsequent integrated development plan (IDP) included regulating local practices and standards to reduce energy consumption, improve indoor air quality, and reduce emissions and waste. The CCP provided the city with an approach and case studies that helped Potchefstroom design and implement targeted sustainability programs, including the design and construction of energy-efficient buildings, a tree-planting project, a program to upgrade streetlight efficiency, the recovery of methane from a local sewage-filtration system, and retro-fitting of the city airport's infrastructure. According to local reporting, the successful implementation of a sustainable development plan led to a 39.8 percent reduction in the city's carbon footprint in 2003.

Source: Du Plessis *et al.*, 2004

A second kind of service is the wide access to many different practitioners. Occasional contact at large-scale conferences of membership and thematic organizations creates a loose bond in networks. For instance the UCLG or Metropolis semiannual meetings and Bertelsmann Cities of Change periodic meetings provide an opportunity for "weak ties," which in Granovetter's logic is a source of fresh, out-of-the-box thinking (Granovetter, 1973) and reference contacts for consultation and advice.

Type 4: cities in active networks

Many other organizations offer platforms for learning by cities, even though the primary objective is not learning per se. One study shows that since the 1980s NGOs dedicated to city sustainability have flowered from a handful to more than 50 (Keiner and Kim, 2007). Examples include both national and international associations. The Council of European Municipalities and Regions (CEMR) and United Cities and Local Governments (UCLG) are two of the most visible in the past decade. The CEMR represents some 100,000 local government units in Europe. Most nations have local government associations of some kind.

UCLG, an NGO, is a confederation of national elected officials and local government associations. It was organized to give political voice to local governments at the regional and international levels and was launched in 1996 at the UN Conference on Human Settlements held in Istanbul. The UCLG and Metropolis were forged from the previous worldwide federations of the Union of Local Authorities (of elected city representatives), Cités Unies/United Towns, and their counterparts in the Arabic-speaking world and in sub-Saharan Africa. Today they lobby for the interests of more than 10,000 local governments and officials and regularly stage studies, seminars and learning events for their membership.

Many regional organizations—EUROCITIES, Merco-ciudades (an association of cities in the Mercosur trading bloc) and CITYNET are good examples—also maintain active networks of exchange in which apex secretariats sift demands and problems from among the membership and frame learning events for cities in their respective domains. Ishinabe provides a good review of Asian networks (Ishinabe, 2010).

In this class of cases, networks, organized as secretariats with technical staff of various sizes, are the centers of action. As opposed to passive networks (see the next section, below) each of the regional organizations has the means, budget, technical information, and staff to foster learning events that attract cities as members and clients. The main dynamic of learning takes place in face-to-face meetings, in plenaries, parallel groups and myriad bilateral exchanges.

The importance of these groups is that the agenda is broadly agreed and framed to serve the common interests of cities in relation to higher powers. Typical topics of study include political issues such as federalism, finance and fiscal relations, as well as technical areas of service delivery. The upshot for most members is to build a common understanding about the role of cities and an agenda for action at regional and global levels.

Type 5: cities in passive networks

In contrast to the active push of network clusters, discussed immediately above, resources like the City Mayor website, UN-Habitat Best Practices, and Open Society's "LOGIN" websites on urban and technical issues operate in a more passive mode. Organizations in this type of learning develop information that is of interest to members and make it available—for those who wish to access it—via electronic or print media, often reinforced by meetings.

UN-Habitat Best Practice is not the only award-conferring sponsor of best practice cities, but it is certainly the best known globally. The structure resembles (and may have been patterned after) the Kennedy School of Government Innovations program for cities and counties. The Best Practices database features winners of best practice selected by an international jury. Winners are posted on the database with brief write ups. These are widely recognized, if not actively promoted, by international agencies. The database does offer stimulating ideas in many experiences, but there is little or no effort to certify or adopt award-winning practices as a standard of excellence and little evidence that these are replicated or even followed up in any systematic way.

The Local Government Information Network (LOGIN) is a development partnership to increase the flow of useful information and experience to those people who develop, enact, implement and monitor policy. LOGIN can be characterized as city network cooperation. LOGIN's main objectives are to promote the professional development of local government officials and to build their capacity to make better policy decisions through large-scale, extensive provision of

Box 4.2 *Best practices awards*

Every two years, up to 10 outstanding initiatives receive the Dubai International Award for Best Practices to Improve the Living Environment, a biennial environmental award established in 1995 by the Municipality of Dubai, United Arab Emirates. Those initiatives meeting the criteria for a Best Practice are included in the Best Practices database. The lessons learned from selected best practices are analyzed and made available to other countries, cities or communities. A searchable database contains over 2150 proven solutions from more than 140 countries to the common social, economic and environmental problems of an urbanizing world. It demonstrates the practical ways in which public, private and civil society sectors are working together to improve governance, eradicate poverty, provide access to shelter, land and basic services, protect the environment and support economic development.

information. Another purpose of the program is to strengthen the capabilities of organizations that support the reform of public administration in the framework of decentralization. LOGIN also aims at facilitating the exchange of best practices and other policy-related information at inter- and intra-regional level in the area of local governance.

Funding resources originate from local partner contributions and development project and program funds, as well as from resources from foundations and trust funds. LOGIN's major financial support comes from Steering Committee member organizations: the Open Society Institute, the UNDP, the Council of Europe, USAID and the World Bank. Other donors include the Danish and Czech governments. Local partner organizations also contribute to the program with their own financial resources.

The Committee provides policy guidance and oversight for project implementation. The LOGIN Program Manager prepares the agenda and background materials for the meetings, which take place eight or nine times a year, using a video conference facility. The Steering Committee makes its decisions by unanimous vote (thus every member has the power of veto).

Both UN Best Practices and LOGIN enjoy recognition and a growing demand from their respective constituents. Their survival and expansion attests to some measure of success in filling an information niche in this "passive" segment of the knowledge market.

Observations from cases

This typology illustrates the widely varying arrangements in which cities tap knowledge and effect learning. The "universe" considered here is not exhaustive, but it is reasonably representative of typical arrangements reported by practitioners, field observers and academics. The important point about this collection of learning modalities is not simply the examples that are described. They are representative, but are only single cases, and scores operate in each category.

The types of city learning differ in important dimensions: in purpose; sponsorship; mechanics of learning, including first- and second-order learning; and whether or not institutional capacity is affected.

Why learn?

Cities will learn by accident, but they can learn in deeply transforming ways if they see a purpose in doing so. Finding the reason to learn, and assembling a platform that reflects the common interests of key stakeholders, constitute indispensable parts of the process. Bilbao is a good place to start on the question of motive. That city's leadership elite foresaw a pending crisis and successfully mobilized broad-based support to take action and avert an economic meltdown.

Seattle's motivation was similarly triggered by the recession in 1993 and layoffs by Boeing. But the purpose of learning among Seattle elites was one of understanding competition. In Bilbao, the purpose moved into wholesale retooling of the city. The one-on-one relationships in City Links, Sister Cities International, and other binary exchanges are typified by smaller-scale objectives, such as the practical issues of framing a plan, getting educated on best practice in land use, adaptation to climate change, or managerial issues.

The point is not how big the problem, but how big the motivation. When purpose is not clear, or motivation not widely shared, learning does not get started. The first step is often identifying a problem. Much of the literature on learning regions and firms starts with the issue of economic survival, and this can be seen in some cases discussed here as well. On the other hand, many cases of failure—in the City Links, for instance—were traced to difficulty in reaching an agreement, or even the absence of an agreement, about whether a problem had existed in the first place (USAID, 2001).

Agency, mandate, leadership and support

Four key features stand out in the city agencies that are responsible for learning: leadership, mandate and focus of actions, plan and time horizon, and degree of community engagement.

In the case of types 1 through 4—direct agents, binary pairing, one on many, and clusters—the leading force has been a collection of stakeholders, a small cadre of individuals who share a vision or commitment to a long-term goal. But it is implied that broad-based community support lies behind most of these cases. In the case of Curitiba, where a small number of individuals were identified with that city's success, the leadership changed hands over the years but the fundamental direction was sustained by broad-based community support, reaffirmed periodically at the ballot box. We shall learn more about these dynamics in Chapter 7.

On the other hand, the formality of arrangements was mixed in types 1 and 2. Seattle's group was organized by an institution (the Chamber of Commerce of Greater Seattle and later, the Trade Development Alliance), but members in the group participated on an informal basis. The Seattle case demonstrates the construction of a governing elite, teaching itself the ways of the world by going and looking. In effect, the city has deputized the TDA to be its scout, and has engaged in shared values of exploration and bonding to build a leadership group and loose governance structure. In contrast, Bilbao's Metropoli-30 was highly organized, with staff, budget, responsibilities, and a mandate that was geared to form the big picture. In Curitiba, a strong internal focus and specific organizational arrangements were drawn up to protect the agency from political manipulation.

The reliance on external agents by the other learning types, 2 through 4, brings inherent risks. Partly because of external agency with accountabilities related to public budgets, these efforts focused on a comparatively narrow set of objectives. Types 2 through 4 are also subject to extraneous forces that make it difficult to sustain learning over time. Further, because external organizations like UCLG are viable only with economies of scale, they tend to be less focused on the needs of specific places. Progressively, the active and, in an even more pronounced way, the passive networks rely on the initiative of cities themselves to access information and knowledge about best practice.

This is not to say that passive sources of knowledge cannot play an important role in inspiring new ideas, even for the active type 1 and 2 cases. Granovetter's idea of weak ties bridging to novel information is one route to discovery. Numerous examples of this kind were documented in a World Bank research project on innovation in decentralized settings. Sources of inspiration for innovative leaders were frequently an idea or practice found outside the immediate setting, and often in international settings discovered by accident. For example, the city of Tijuana drew on ballot referendum as seen in neighboring California as a way to demonstrate public support for indebtedness (Campbell, 2001).

Leadership by individuals or small groups needs to drive the effort forward, and even cities with strong leaders cannot move far without support from the larger community. Single leaders do not succeed by themselves. The best efforts, as shown in the learning city-regions and managed networks, are those that consist of a group that sees its own self-interest aligned with the larger interests of the city. At the same time, as illustrated by Seattle and Bilbao, without concrete achievements it is unlikely that broad-based community support can be sustained.

Of equal importance is the extent to which the cities have nurtured broad community support into the learning effort. The type 1 and 2 cities in this review are clearly engaged in dedicated institutional capacity building that extends far beyond agency boundaries. The most active cities were also the most concerned with community participation, but civic involvement did not extend to citywide consultations. The focus was on blending key leadership groups and cutting across bureaucratic walls. Indeed in the Seattle case, one of the objectives of study tours is to create a permeable layer across boundaries of all kinds, including jurisdictional, agency and public–private realms. The most purposeful of these cases—represented in different ways by Bilbao, Seattle and Curitiba, among many others—are cities that are able to create learning experiences and draw on stored memory in order to bring that knowledge to bear on present and newly emerging problems.

Mechanics of learning

A key feature highlighted in this typology is the degree to which the city or agency takes the initiative to learn deliberately. The most intensive learners are those proactive cities categorized in types 1 and 2. They share several distinguishing features.

Perhaps the most important is the extent to which a city commits to learning as a continuing practice. Cities can opt for a style that sets up a system that generates its own knowledge internally, or seeks knowledge from outside its domain. Cases range from benchmarking and competitiveness in types 1 and 2, to the search for best practices and specific techniques in types 3, 4 and 5. Cities operate with different formulations of the sources of knowledge.

Types 1 and 2 have demonstrated styles of finding knowledge at its origin and either bringing it home or sending a legation for study at its source. Bilbao brought experience from many quarters to its stakeholders at home. Seattle is singular in the cases reviewed here in demonstrating a commitment to see best practice in its native habitat. Other cities not reviewed here—Johannesburg and Barcelona, for example—also recruited world-class sources of information for presentation to the home team.

The regularity of learning events, their duration, and follow-up activities are another signal feature of the most active learners. Regular, long-term, sequential and follow-up activities have all proved important for the active cities. These same traits will emerge again in the following chapters as indicators of serial learning cities.

It should be noted that the source of knowledge in virtually all of the cases is overwhelmingly from other cities. Though many avenues are available to transmit information and experience—policy seminars, conferences, small group meetings—virtually all of the official development assistance organizations rely on city-to-city exposure as a key ingredient. In all of these cases, knowledge agents play an important role, for instance, international organizations such as in the UN family, as well as specialized organizations working on environmental, governance or other issues.

Type 1 and 2 cities also featured high-level persons in both public and private sectors as regular participants in the learning process. Exposure to new ideas in their native context enriches the Arthur Koestler "aha" experience, especially if this takes place in the company of a core leadership group, as in the case of Seattle. City Rounds in the World Bank Institute endorse the importance of observing best practice in the native setting of the practitioner.[3] Learning practitioners know that context is everything in the understanding of how things fit together and where the weak points are likely to be. In the words of Bill Stafford, Seattle Trade Development Alliance:

> Cities learn from each other because they understand and trust each other more than commercial firms that have something to sell or even international institutions which are laying conditions on lending.[4]

First- and second-order learning

Recall that first-order learning consists of discovery and findings about things and processes. It entails questions like: Does it work? How much does it cost? What is the payback? Can it be implemented back home? Virtually all of the types discussed in this chapter satisfy first-order learning to some degree. But it is what I call the second-order products of learning that determine the outcomes for cities. What counts over the long term are the very processes entailed in the exploration—to use those words often cited in Seattle, "building relationships" internally, and "getting to know who we are." These second-order effects turn out to be the most important. All learning cities construct a way to conduct interchange among themselves, the visiting team, task forces or work groups. The highest pay off results more from a focused, dedicated effort that is sustained over time. Further, the larger the group, the better is the outcome. Sending a scout can work; sending a posse is better. A large, cross-cutting delegation enables the formation of trusting relationships.

Institution building—managing knowledge

The special-purpose agencies show that cities dedicated to learning invest in policy and in a learning effort that is sustained over a long period of time. Seattle is running into its second decade of sustained policy support to learn, Bilbao is entering its third, and Curitiba its fifth. Some form of institutionalization is achieved. In London, it was the Economic Intelligence Unit; in Barcelona it is the metropolitan planning organization. Financial support is supplied in different ways. Seattle employs a pay-as-you-go scheme; Bilbao drew cleverly on EU funds, incurred debt, and solicited private donations; London dipped into its own city budget; and Barcelona's metropolitan planning unit is shared by the city, the surrounding municipalities and the province.

Summing up and looking ahead

The gamut of learning types helps us see the range of effort, the form of agency, the purpose of learning, and the means of support. Of course, many other subcategories of learning types can be imagined. In particular, virtual learning has been excluded as a type here. It is rapidly growing because virtual or distance learning has several attractive features, low cost being one of the most important. Virtual learning is particularly apt for technical skills and for applications where a team has already been formed. But distance learning is limited in other ways. Because it is often geared to technical skills, higher-level managers are frequently reluctant to join. The ideas of learning that we are pursuing in these chapters focus partly on the very formation of organizational tissue. This requires assembling minds from across many departments and disciplines and walks of life.

In fact, most cities in the survey described in the following chapter are on the hunt for first-order outcomes. Beyond those sizeable numbers of cities that conduct visits are many more that take part in less active ways, monitoring and exchanging information organized along thematic or geographic lines. The many urban membership associations, together with sector-specific agendas, like sustainability, health and clean air, all sponsor and actively promote circulation of information through meetings, conferences, seminars and reports.

The gamut of learners presented in this chapter highlights the proactive types that invest in learning by organizing a systematic effort. The examples in this category are well known, but how many others are like them? We find some answers in the next chapter.

Notes

1 The Trade Development Alliance has also helped trade development missions, separate from its study tour mandate. The TDA organized 26 outbound missions in its 10 years of operation and assisted in the development of 14 others.
2 Personal communication, Tim Honey, former executive director, Sister Cities International.
3 City Rounds involved city-to-city visits and presentations by experts and practitioners from peer cities. See www.worldbank.org/wbi/urban.
4 Personal communication, Bill Stafford, Trade Development Alliance.

References

Campbell, T. (2001). "Innovation and risk-taking: urban governance in Latin America," in A. Scott (ed.), *Global city-regions—trends, theory, policy*, Oxford University Press, New York, pp. 214–235.

Campbell, T. (2006). "Smart cities—the case of Bilbao," *Urban Land*, 65, pp. 56–59.

Du Plessis, A., E. Le Roux, W. B. P. Bluemer and J. Lommen (2004). "Greener governance in southern SADC: success report on medium sized local authorities," North West University, Potchefstroom, South Africa.

Granovetter, M. (1973). "The strength of weak ties," *The American Journal of Sociology*, 78, pp. 1360–1380.

ICLEI (International Council of Local Environmental Initiatives) (2003). *2003 triennial report. Local governments implementing sustainable development*, International Council of Local Environmental Initiatives, Toronto, p. 28.

Ishinabe, N. (2010). "Analysis of international city-to-city cooperation and intercity networks for Japanese national and local governments," Institute for Global Environmental Strategies (IGES) Discussion Paper, Hayama, Japan.

Keiner, M. and A. Kim (2007). "Transnational city networks for sustainability," *European Planning Studies*, 15, pp. 1360–1395.

Stafford, W. (1999). "Globally competitive regions: What Seattle is learning from the rest of the world" (pamphlet), Trade Development Alliance of Greater Seattle.

Trade Development Alliance (2001). "Crossroads10!," in Trade Development Alliance of Greater Seattle (ed.) *Crossroads*, Trade Development Alliance of Greater Seattle, Seattle.

UN-Habitat and United Towns Organization (2001). "City-to-city cooperation: issues arising from experience," UN-Habitat, Nairobi.

USAID (2001). "Evaluation of resource cities program design," Washington, DC.

Yang, M. (2002). "Protecting the urban morphology of Asian cities," in *World heritage 2002: shared legacy, common responsibility*, UNESCO World Heritage Centre, Urbino, Italy, pp. 30–31.

5 Light on a shadow economy: city learning in 53 cities[1]

The previous chapter focused on proactive cities. They devote effort to learning in a deliberate and systematic way. But how common are they? Are these just a handful of outliers? A more basic question is: How widespread is city-to-city exchange and to what extent are less proactive cities also in the mix?

If there is any doubt about the level of activity as regards cities as learners, this chapter should shift the debate. It's not whether, but how much. The quantitative evidence in the following pages demonstrates a previously unreported flurry of business being undertaken by cities as they exchange ideas with each other. Cities of all sizes and from all geographical regions are engaged in shopping at a bazaar of knowledge. The data in this chapter show the pace of knowledge gathering among cities. They form a picture of eager traders, on the prowl to learn new ideas, accumulate experience, understand the pitfalls of policy, examine technical solutions, and find shortcuts to solve the problems they face at home. Curiously, this exchange is being undertaken largely outside the policy vision of nations and international financial and technical assistance organizations. The chapter also throws further light on proactive learners: How do they consolidate their learning? What topics are of greatest interest to them? How much effort they put into learning?

Pulling back the curtain

Curious about the growing evidence of city-to-city exchange, in 2004, together with Sylvia Blanco at the University of Washington, I organized a systematic survey of visits from other cities to Seattle. Our aim was to tabulate the number and types of incoming city delegations on technical visits, as opposed to cultural, ceremonial or friendship exchanges.

The number and range of visits were startling. We found that in the year 2002 Seattle hosted more than 150 delegations, mostly from outside the US. Visiting delegations averaged seven persons per group and stayed around four days. We are sure that this was an undercount, because our database did not reflect a full 12 months and missed a number of city departments.

The delegations consisted largely of technical and policy teams, mostly from Asia, and covered topics in governance and policy, private–public cooperation, legal and regulatory systems, health care, primary and secondary education, environmental quality, and community-based planning. One group of visiting Chinese city officials illustrates a typical harvest. The official responsible for litter removal mentioned that he had several thousand workers in his department and was baffled to see why his Seattle counterpart had less than a few dozen. The answer he got brought an "aha" expression to his face. The several dozen Seattle workers concentrate on public education, especially in schools. Mechanized equipment does the rest.

I found that anecdotal evidence from other cities corroborated a high flow rate of visitors. Similar volumes of visits were reported by Baltimore, Barcelona, London, Stockholm, Toronto and Vancouver. Each of these cities has reported significant numbers of visits from their urban counterparts elsewhere in the world. Many host cities handle these exchanges though international affairs divisions. The city of Stockholm maintains a fee structure designed to cover administrative and overhead costs connected to the provision of services to visiting delegations.

The numbers from the Seattle study formed the basis for a wider, more comprehensive survey of city-to-city exchange. As part of the background research for this book, a web-based survey was conducted during the period 2007–2009 to throw new light on the extent and outcomes of city learning.[2] The data reveal thousands of technical visits annually. Cities ranging in size from less than 100,000 to 10 million have formed a market of exchange operating in the shadows.

Survey of city learners—a word on methods

We saw in Chapter 4 that leading cities invest substantial human and financial resources in learning. How wide is this practice and what modalities of learning are involved? Is it all twinning and single-city missions, as in Seattle? Or are university studies, private consulting firms and in-house expertise also playing a role? The survey aimed to answer these questions and to probe in a preliminary fashion whether city size, wealth or some other characteristics, particularly innovation and reform, might be associated with pace and mode of learning.

The survey was distributed to about 300 cities in two waves by means of intermediaries, mostly membership associations of cities such as UCLG, Metropolis, CITYNET in Yokohama, and the Administrative Staff College of India (ASCI), among others. I also made contact with many city executives with whom I had worked in the past. Each organization was asked to identify knowledgeable respondents from selected cities drawn from among their respective membership bases in order to capture a representative distribution by size.

The 48 cities that responded fit a smooth bell-curve by size, but are concentrated in Asia, Europe and Latin America (only one response was received from Africa and one from North Africa). The survey did not pretend to collect an official response from the city, but rather to gauge level and type of learning in cities by knowledgeable officials or semi-official professionals working in or for the city. Respondents included mayors, other elected officials, advisors, consultants or city officers. The list of cities and categories of size and region, among others (as explained below), are in Appendix 2.

Several steps were taken to limit biases and errors intrinsic to this indirect, single-respondent approach. First is the problem of representing a complex organization—a city that can involve scores, if not hundreds, of departments and units—by a single respondent. Survey takers were asked to base their responses on their personal experience with the city, but where relevant they were asked to speak for the city as a whole to the best of their knowledge (for instance, to report or estimate the number of learning events for the entire city and whether learning was recorded and documented in some way by the city). For the most part, respondents were high-level officials or advisors, but we cannot be completely sure that the quality of information they provided is even across all survey takers.

A second problem is the self-declarative nature of the survey. It relies on individuals, and the idiosyncrasies of judgment, to classify important information. For example, respondents were asked to gauge the amount of time they spent learning, how many trips their city had made in the previous three years, and whether their city could be classified as a reformer or not (detail on this question is covered later). In each of these instances, the questions were explained and guidance was given in written form. Triangulation and spot checking on known city reforms are the main means of cross-checking answers for accuracy and consistency.

Another issue is small sample size. Though it has some value in terms of statistical significance for testing hypotheses, the findings are also rich with suggestive clues and provide useful benchmarks and directions for further work. An additional issue may be that individuals were specially selected by intermediaries (explained below), with a consequent bias.

To limit these possible drawbacks, detailed instructions and selection criteria were provided to the intermediary organizations, explaining the purpose and offering guidelines for survey takers.

The central questions in the inquiry are aimed at understanding the importance of learning as a deliberate activity of cities and to explore what is specific to proactive cities. After many years of working with cities in the World Bank, and with city-based organizations like Sister Cities International, the ICMA, the VNG in the Netherlands and others, I was quite sure that cities were engaged in a significant level of learning activity. But I was not quite so sure about the mix and intensity of exchange. An important debate was shaping up about North–South relations, and a growing unease about whether yet another form of dependency was emerging at the city level. Also, were proactive cities translating the knowledge they picked up into innovation or reform? Do reformers assign more time and attention to the learning process than non-reformers?

Findings—how much exchange?

One of the foremost concerns was to quantify the number of learning exchanges being undertaken by cities. To measure this, survey takers were asked how they learned, what kinds of learning they liked, and how much of it was city to city. The survey takers were asked to indicate how many trips were made by their respective cities over the previous three years, taking into account tours and visits at the national or international level to other cities. These were to include visits to companies, universities or development assistance organizations for policy or technical purposes.

The initial responses were puzzling. The data showed that almost all of the respondents indicated that their city engaged in more than 10 city-to-city learning events per year. The range of responses offered to respondents was based on numerous case observations (in Toronto, Stockholm and Baltimore) and case study findings in Seattle, Bilbao and Curitiba. The range turned out to be far too limited (see Table 5.1).

Recall that the survey was administered in two waves. In the initial phase, responding cities were all bunched at the upper end of the scale, i.e., more than 10 per year. The range was expanded in the second wave (26 additional cities in 2009) so that respondents could register up to 30 visits per year. The data showed that more than 40 percent of the second wave of survey takers fell also into the even higher end of the scale on numbers of visits.

Despite this rather untidy process, the results are startling. If these survey data are even reasonably representative of the total volume of city-to-city exchanges

Table 5.1 Number of study tours and exchanges

Scale used on first-wave number of trips in past three years	First-wave total N=27 (%)	Scale used on second-wave number of trips in past year (%)	Second-wave total N=26 (%)
None	0	None	0
1–10	0	1–5	4
More than 10	59	6–10	25
Don't know	7	11–15	8
No answer	33	16–20	4
		21–30	17
		More than 30	42
		Don't know	0

Source: Author

being undertaken around the globe, the total numbers for cities of substantial size, say, a quarter million or more, of which more than 1000 are currently on the planet, then the traffic in visits could be in the neighborhood of tens of thousands per year: a high—and heretofore unrecognized—volume of exchange.

But how is it possible that a city conducts dozens or scores of visits a year? The answer is that large cities, those with more than 500,000 in population, have thousands of employees in scores of departments. For instance, a typical million-size city has departments on the order of 10 to 20 that cover finance, land registry, parks, markets, public transit, business licensing, water, sewerage, power, social welfare, housing, local economic development, personnel, administration, and others. Larger cities work with semi-dependent entities that handle utilities, transportation, telecommunications and other services. Each of these has its own internal structure of management and administration.

In addition, the private sector typically organizes visits, often in conjunction with the conduct of trade and commerce in the city. These in turn are often linked to conferences of some kind. And, by the way, the sponsor or organizer of the outgoing missions very much shapes the content and prospects for long-term learning, as we shall see in the case studies presented in Part III. Several small delegations from chambers of commerce, plus the multitude of city departments, plus higher-level delegations, quickly bring up the total. Delegations in the visits can be small, from a couple of department heads to 20 or 30 or more. Turin, Barcelona and Seattle annually organize delegations of up to 100 persons. The documentation of visits to Seattle referred to in an earlier chapter suggested that the 150 visits to that city consisted of an average of seven persons staying four nights. If these numbers were typical, the expenditures of study tours could easily be in the range of US$100 million per year.[3]

Findings—content, processing, proactive reformers

The survey was designed to see whether the typology used in the previous chapter would hold up in a wider survey. To address this question of proactive reformers, respondents were asked to "self-declare" whether their city was a reformer or non-reformer. In this chapter and elsewhere, I use the term "reform" synony-mously with the term "innovation." In cities, making change in policy or practice is often, if not always, an innovative application of a proven idea or practice. My scale of measurement is very crude. Those cities indicating that "many" inno-vations or reforms were undertaken in the previous three years are classified as "reformers." Those recording "some," "few" or "none" were, for purposes of analysis, categorized as non-reformers. Half the responding cities fell into each category of "reformer" and "non-reformer."

Spot checks of many of the cities show that, with some notable exceptions, the reformers line up quite well with anecdotal evidence of cities that have demonstrated innovation and reform. One of the exceptions is Stockholm. Its survey respondent declared that Stockholm made only one or two reforms in the past three years. While this might be true in the strict sense of the term, Stockholm accomplished major reforms in congestion charging and other changes over the past decade. Turin is another example: its respondent declared it a non-reformer, even though Turin achieved major changes in strategic planning and the Olympic Games in the dozen years *prior* to 2005. Survey takers appear to have been observing the instructions rigorously.

One question of immediate interest is how reformers match up with those proactive learners introduced in the previous chapter. Having observed that Seattle and other cities mulled over and deliberated their experiences after study tours, I tightened the definition of proactive cities using a composite indicator. First, proactive cities are those taking more than 10 visits per year. Second, they have accomplished many or some reforms in the previous three years. Third, they take steps to institutionalize their learning, for instance, by establishing an office, or routinely following up their learning events with home-based seminars or conferences. We shall see that many also document learning by writing up reports, or otherwise follow up with monitoring new ideas or tracking newly implemented projects (see Table 5.2 for a list of 17 proactive cities).

Table 5.2 Seventeen proactive cities, innovation, and institutional practices

City	Pop. (million)	Reformer	Has office	Holds own sessions	Agency documents	Follows	Tracks
Amman	2.8	1	1	2	1	0	0
Bangkok	6.3	1	1	2	0	0	1
Barcelona	1.6	1	1	1	1	1	0
Charlotte	0.71	1	2	1	1	1	0
Da Nang	0.75	1	1	2	1	1	1
Madrid	3.3	1	1	1	1	1	1
Manila City	2.5	1	1	1	1	1	1
Paris region	11.6	1	1	1	1	1	0
San Salvador	1.5	1	1	1	1	1	0
Toronto	5.5	1	1	1	1	1	0
Berlin	4.2	2	1	1	1	1	1
Buenos Aires, DF	2.5	2	2	2	1	1	1
Istanbul	8	2	1	2	0	1	0
Kathmandu	0.67	2	1	2	0	0	1
Mashhad	2.4	2	1	1	1	1	1
Naga City	0.1	2	1	2	0	0	1
Seoul Metro	23.9	2	1	1	1	0	1

Key:
Reformer: 1 = many reforms in the past three years; 2 = some.
Office: 1 = has designated department (office) and officer to manage learning; 2 = has no office.
Holds own sessions: 1 = holds many learning sessions at home; 2 holds some, few or none.
Agency documents learning: 1 = sending agency documents, learning visits; 0 = does not comment.
Follow-up on learning: 1 = yes; 0 = no.
Tracks lessons and monitors innovations: 1 = yes; 0 = no.

Our definition of proactive learning cities is narrowed down qualitatively and quantitatively. These are cities for the most part with populations of over a million. Some cities, like Turin and Stockholm, are not on the list because they did not define themselves as proactive. More than half are from the developing world. In any case, proactive cities make an effort, deliberately and continuously, to capture knowledge. They seek ideas from many sources, and most of them visit other cities for this purpose. They rank city-to-city exchange as having the highest pay-off for learning (this point is taken up in greater detail, below). Also, proactive cities process their ideas by following up on the ideas that have been discovered, for instance, by organizing seminars and conferences or meetings to deepen the understanding of new knowledge. These activities (which I refer to as "agency") are usually associated with one another.[4] Moreover, documenting learning and tracking outcomes are also good predictors of reformer cities.[5]

We know, however, that merely writing down lessons and tracking their outcomes already presumes substantial institutional capacity. We have pulled back one layer of the onion of soft infrastructure only to be confronted with another set of questions about how this capacity gets established. Getting a start on learning can be as simple as assigning this function to a relevant part of the city, or alternatively to a university or NGO. Part III is composed of case studies that explore these stories in greater detail. Without getting ahead of myself, let us say for the moment that the cases will show many ways of getting the job done. Moreover, the stories illustrate the vital importance of a complementary form of storage—what I call soft storage in personal networks—as part of the mechanism of learning and innovation.[6]

Proactive cities and innovation

Though Table 5.2 shows that proactive cities are reformers, it is also true that nearly as many cities with records of reform are not proactive, in that they visit less frequently or do not take steps to establish an office or conduct follow-up efforts. In part, this ambiguous finding is also a result of the blunt definitions for "reform" and "innovation" that I have used in the survey. The idea was to separate the very active reformers from the pack. I'm afraid I succeeded only partially. The data and cases show that these relationships of gathering knowledge, storing it, and translating it into innovation or reform are more nuanced. Measurement of innovation and reform requires more careful specification. Still, we find many intriguing and some quite strong and statistically significant relationships from the survey, and these help us to focus on details in case studies and policy. With this in mind, let's push forward to find out more about the patterns of learning.

Patterns in geography

Survey respondents named on average more than four sources of knowledge; the range was 0–10. Mapped schematically in a way that more or less shows the cities' relative geographic positions, Figure 5.1 produces a complicated picture. Visiting cities are represented in red; hosts in blue. Reformers are shown as diamonds. The graphic shows that cities are crossing the globe as they visit both reformers

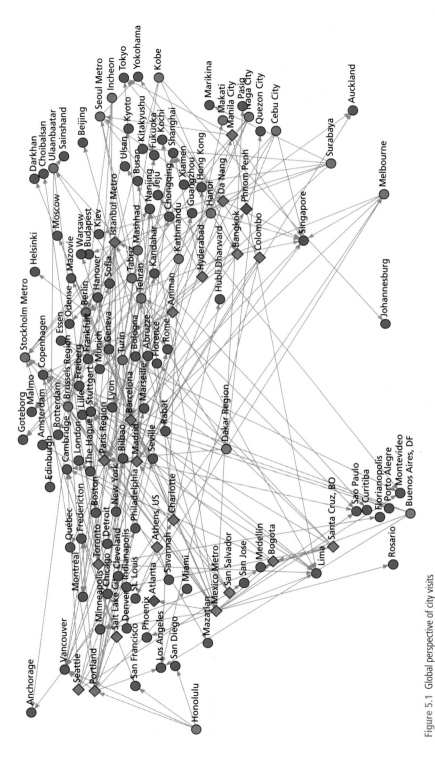

Figure 5.1 Global perspective of city visits

Key: red = visiting city; blue = host; diamond = reformer

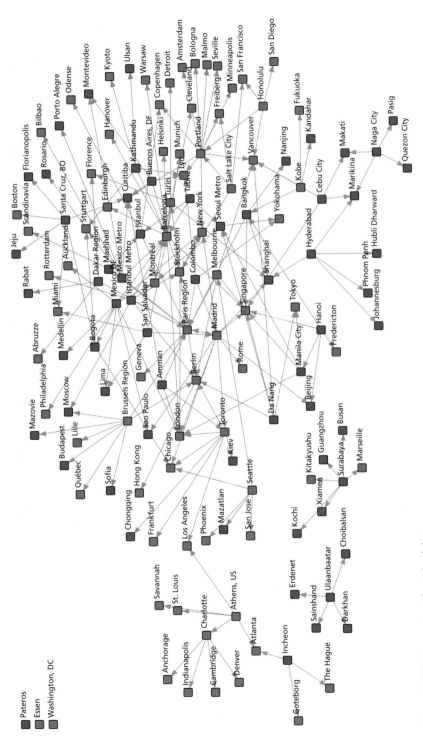

Figure 5.2 Global perspective with peripheral clusters

Key: blue = global South; red = global North

and non-reformers. Some of the more popular hosts—for instance, Singapore in the lower center-right—have not been classified in terms of reform.

A different way of picturing the exchanges brings out other details. Figure 5.2 makes it clear that some cities stick close to home; for instance, Surabaya stayed within its region, and Ulaanbataar (bottom left) visited only cities in Mongolia.

Larger host cities tend to be regional favorites—like Seoul and Singapore in East Asia; Vancouver in North America; and London, Paris, Berlin and Barcelona in Europe. A third pattern is that intermediate cities do cut across regions in their visits; for instance, Santa Cruz (upper right) and Tabriz (center right).

Greater detail about North–South exchange is shown in Figure 5.3. Northern cities are depicted at the top of the graph and Southern on the bottom. Visiting cities show distinct preferences about where they choose to go. Even the reformers and non-reformers favor Northern neighbors over those in the South. These revealed preferences are somewhat out of sync with those of development assistance agencies, especially given the recent interest among agencies in supporting South–South exchange.

Table 5.3 synthesizes the information in Figure 5.3. Travel takes place in all directions, but on balance cities in both North and South favor the North. A sharp distinction can be seen between reformer cities and the observed direction of travel. While those cities claiming to have made reforms are evenly split between the North and South, non-reformers are much more likely to be in the South (Table 5.4). This raises important questions—not just about South–South exchange, but about exchange in all directions. Are the lessons being transmitted the "right" lessons? Is good practice being exchanged or should we be worrying that cities are regressing to a mean, or worse, racing to the bottom?

Figures 5.4 and 5.5 provide more detail on the inter-regional exchange of visits, giving more clarity about how much of the exchange stays within the Asian and European regions, respectively. The figures also show the most popular sites for visits, suggesting that regional "hubs" may be important as learning centers.

Table 5.3 Direction of visitor flows

		Hosts	
		North	South
Visitors	North	74	14
	South	62	49

Pearson coefficient 18.9. Sig = <0.0001

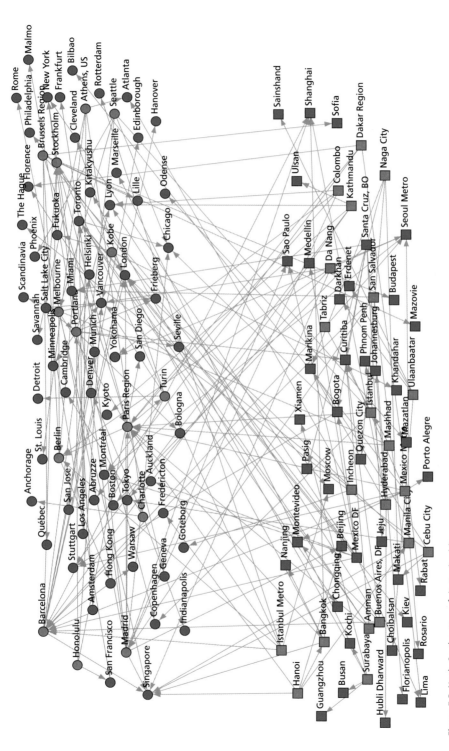

Figure 5.3 North–South pattern of city-to-city visits

Key: round = North; square = South

Table 5.4 Reformers by North or South

		Geographical area	
		North	South
Status	Reformer	13	12
	Non-reformer	5	18
	Pearson coefficient 4.68. Sig = <0.0305		

Size of visitors and hosts

The choice of target cities by size reveals a preference for mid-size cities or smaller (Table 5.5). The smallest cities in the group tended to visit peers of a similar size, and as the visitor size grows into the higher range, the choice of host city grows also, up to cities in the 1 million–5 million category. In other words, bigger cities get fewer visits, proportionately, even from similar-size "peers." Altogether, it seems that visits showed a marked preference for cities in the 1 million–5 million range. We have no direct information from the survey takers about why this apparent pattern emerges. Perhaps these medium-size cities, examples of which

Table 5.5 City visitors and hosts by population size

Population range			Hosts			
Visitors	Small (%)	Medium (%)	Large (%)	Very large (%)	Mega-cities (%)	Totals by visitors
Small	44	6	33	11	6	18
Medium	5	0	67	24	5	21
Large	14	6	40	29	11	63
Very large	5	5	42	25	22	40
Mega-cities	0	13	52	17	17	23
Total visits to hosts	20	10	74	39	22	165

Key: small = 50,000–500,000; medium = 500,000–1 million; large = 1 million–5 million; very large = 5 million–10 million; mega-cities = 10 million and higher. Percentages are rounded up to whole numbers.

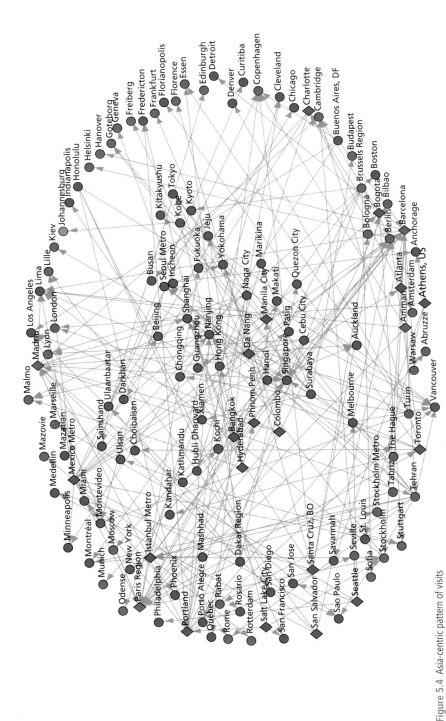

Figure 5.4 Asia-centric pattern of visits

Key: blue = Americas; green = Asia; red = Europe; diamond = reformers

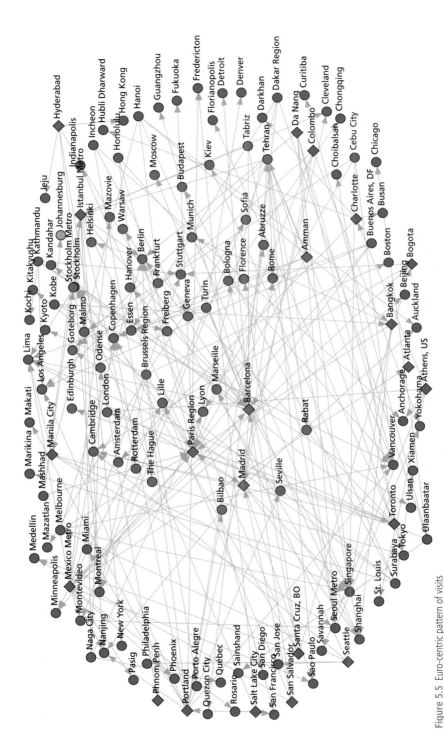

Figure 5.5 Euro-centric pattern of visits

Key: blue = Americas; green = Asia; red = Europe; diamond = reformers

include most Scandinavian and Northern European cities (Stockholm, Denmark, The Hague) as well as Vancouver, represent destinations where it is possible, as one participant put it, "to get your arms around" the whole thing, i.e., to understand the detail within the larger setting.

Effort devoted to learning

In an attempt to gauge the importance respondents assign to learning activities, I asked them to indicate how much time they *personally* devoted to learning, that is, to gathering and processing new knowledge in visits, seminars, conferences, and the like. The responses can be no more than roughly indicative, but they do show some correlation with whether the city was proactive, and whether it was a reformer or non-reformer. For the group as a whole, the modal range of time spent by respondents on learning is between two and three weeks per year (see Table 5.6).

Non-reformers were even more heavily represented (54 percent) in the two to three week range. In contrast, nearly 60 percent of respondents from reform cities were in the above-four-week range, roughly twice the proportion of non-reformers and equivalent roughly to 8 to 12 percent of the work year.[7]

As a benchmark, the amount of time devoted to learning in organizations of OECD countries and US corporations runs in a similar range to the respondents from reformer cities in the survey. For example, investments in learning at the national level, admittedly a gross aggregate, is in the 3–6 percent range for OECD countries (Hwang and Gerami, 2006). A better comparator is a corporate benchmark. According to O'Leonard, somewhere between 5 percent and 7 percent of staff time (17 to 25 hours per staff member) was devoted to training in US

Table 5.6 Time spent in city learning

	Weeks						
Respondents	None	<1	2–3	4–6	>6	Don't know	Total
	(%)						
Reformers (22)	4	4	34	29	23	6	100
Proactive (17)	0	6	18	35	35	6	100
Others (31)	6	13	52	6	23		100

Note: figures rounded to the nearest whole digit.

corporations in that period (2007 and 2008) (O'Leonard, 2008). The well-known 15 percent rule of Minnesota Mining and Manufacturing (a Fortune 500 company) states that every employee can use up to 15 percent of his or her time on ideas not related to daily work and responsibilities (Kanter *et al.*, 1997). With these as rough guides, it seems that at the very least we can say that representatives of reformer cities (those who answered the survey) are meeting or exceeding comparable benchmarks for learning.

Content of learning

To understand what city delegations seek to learn, respondents were also asked to give open-ended and closed responses to what kinds of topics most matched their objectives. The 42 cities responding to this question reported 172 learning exchanges involving 103 cities. The topics linked to these visits covered the gamut, ranging across topics as varied as bus rapid transit, disaster coordination in connection with earthquakes, snow-sweeping policies, preservation of open spaces, practices covering walking and cycling, tourism and cultural policies and downtown renewal and preservation of heritage areas.

Respondents were also asked to indicate interest in a "closed" (limited) list of 10 substantive and seven skill or management areas (by "voting" for the top three). The choices of topics for both substantive and managerial areas were

Table 5.7 Substantive areas of learning

Topic	Reformers (72)	Proactive reformers (45)	Others (103)
		(%)	
Urban renewal	12	10	12
Urban planning	15	13	16
Water and waste	7	3	6
Solid waste	10	7	8
Land use and planning	7	3	6
Transport	24	20	19
Climate	10	17	11
HIV	1	0	1
Local economic development	20	13	12
Housing	7	7	7
Other	0	7	4

derived from pre-survey interviews with experienced urbanists and managers of city associations. In the substantive areas (Table 5.7) urban transport was the walk-away winner, whatever the classification of the city—reformer, proactive or other (referring to all those not otherwise classified, for example, as reformers only, or proactive reformers). Local economic development followed as a close second for reformer groups, and climate change for proactive cities. Recall that the main difference between "reformers" and "proactive" is that, while both are reformers, the proactive group visits more and tends to do more codification and processing of knowledge. Utilities, such as water and electricity, solid waste and topics like HIV trailed behind for all groups.

On management issues (Table 5.8), each of the three groups of cities expressed interest in metropolitan governance, ranking it first or second. After that the groups diverge: proactive cities seek policy analysis; reformers vote for methods and tools; and the rest of the cities go after financial management, ranking it above all else. These findings raise interesting questions as to whether proactive and reforming cities have already achieved some level of comfort in the areas where the non-reformers ("Others" in Table 5.8) are voting, such as project evaluation. Further detail on these topics would allow national and international development assistance organizations to tailor their technical-assistance offerings better.

A glance at the program content for technical assistance and training offerings of the World Bank and Asian Development Bank reveals that programmatic

Table 5.8 Management areas of learning

Topic	Reformers N = 67	Proactive reformers N = 53	Others N = 31
		(%)	
Policy analysis	21	19	14
Methods/tools	16	15	12
Project evaluation	11	11	17
Problem solving	10	8	10
Metro governance	19	23	17
Negotiation	9	6	8
Financial management	13	17	18
Other*	1	2	3

* Security, disaster management

content is weighted toward topics like financial management, gender, HIV, corruption, climate change and analytical tools. Relatively little or no attention is given to formal means of policy analysis. Although a lot of attention is paid to metro governance, there is little offered by way of normative content.

Modalities of learning

Respondents were asked about the degree of impact of different modalities of learning, for instance, seminars, private sector sources, university courses, activities of associations and city-to-city exchanges (see list in Table 5.9). City-to-city exchanges were ranked by all respondents as having the most impact, followed by professional associations, organizations and in-house seminars. Except for surveys and on-the-job training, the "other" categories in written comments turned out largely to replicate the categories already mentioned (city to city, professional groups and associations) and do not change the outcome.

The high marks given by all groups for city-to-city exchanges fit with the pattern of high numbers of city visits that we saw at the beginning of this chapter. Cities meet high costs of travel to get the goods despite the risks of political heat back home. These results beg the question—one that needs to be pondered by the helping institutions and national policy—about the factors that produce impact and alternative ways to get the same bang for buck. On the other end of the spectrum, universities, professional reports and consultant firms came out at the bottom in terms of impact. Is there room for new or improved players in this drama?

Table 5.9 Impact of learning events (average impact rating in range of none (1) to very high (5))

Modality	Reformers (22)	Proactive (17)	Others (31)
In-house seminars	3.31	3.6	3.45
Consultant firms	3.47	3.59	3.00
University courses	3.08	4.15	3.27
Prof. publications/reports	3.15	3.47	3.40
C2C exchanges	4.38	4.38	4.29
Assns/city orgs	3.63	3.94	3.90
Prof. organizations	3.27	3.94	3.53

Summing up and looking ahead

The survey data suggest that a large volume of exchange has been taking place in cities of significant size, that cities prefer to learn from each other, and that they are aware of sources of further information they would like to explore. Above all, our proactive reformers appear to engage in more or less the same proportion of city-to-city learning as reformers, but the proactive group is distinct in its dedication of time and effort in gathering knowledge and processing it, through both documents and discussion. Though imprecise, our measure shows that the respondents in the survey, at least, dedicate an amount of time comparable to or even exceeding corporate benchmarks of investment in knowledge.

All cities appear to be looking for knowledge on transport and metropolitan management, the two most widely cited issues, but many more are on the list of concerns. Further work will help to understand how cities choose their "targets" for learning about these topics and to establish a stronger connection between learning—i.e., the number and kinds of events—with the size, wealth and other policy variables in cities that might affect the motivation for and processing of city learning.

Learning as building blocks to an innovative milieu?

Survey data have shown that self-declared reformer cities take steps to institutionalize the learning process. They codify knowledge, conduct follow-up, monitor new ideas, organize internal learning events, and store knowledge in document form. The main point is that key features in proactive cities are beginning to take shape. They could well be interpreted as building blocks in the innovative milieu, that soft infrastructure discussed so widely in the literature in connection with creative and knowledge economies.

These findings line up with research on twinning. De Villiers found in a survey of 171 city-twinning projects that strategies, experience and level of resources made no difference in outcomes of adopting change. Rather, a written plan, community awareness, managerial commitment and personalities were the difference makers. Active marketing also correlated with community commitment and public understanding of the city-to-city engagements (de Villiers, 2007). Similarly, van Lindert and Bontenbal document individual and collective cases showing a variety of outcomes and commonly found issues, such as ownership, control over content, financing, and depth of participation (Bontenbal, 2009; Bontenbal and van Lindert, 2009).

Exchange in the shadows

The term "shadow" has been used in the chapter title to reflect the largely hidden exchange of knowledge taking place around the world. For the most part, this activity is outside the policy awareness of cities and states. More importantly, cities typically have to fight a battle against accusations from local political opposition and national figures, who see only junkets in these exchanges. Even the international development-assistance agencies are not convinced that city-to-city visits are worth the high cost they entail. And the academic community, though exploring such ideas as city networks, the transfer and use of knowledge in knowledge economies, and the uptake of policy and practice from one city to another (in policy migration), has not produced an approach to gauge the pay-off of city visits. It would be useful to have metrics of this kind. At least then a basis for policy could be grounded in empirical estimates of cost and benefit. As it stands, cities operate in the shadows, often not trumpeting their efforts until and unless a pay-off can be demonstrated.

Cities meet the high costs of knowledge for good reasons. City leaders search outward for ideas because they have short terms of office and they know that learning from others is cheaper and less risky than pursuing untested ideas and ending up in false starts. Conversely, many mayors I have spoken with confess a suspicion about the agendas in the back of the minds of World Bank experts who visit them in connection with policy reforms linked to lending or other forms of financial assistance. Mayors understand that an agenda of policy reforms can often be a direct threat to one's hold on political power. Mayors are even more suspicious of the hidden and not-so-hidden motives of private businesses who offer products or services touted to be cutting edge or state of the art.

Talking across the table directly to another mayor who has no policy agenda or product to sell puts the conversation immediately on a different, more equal footing. Cities share a world-view and understand the amalgam of political conditions that typically face local governments. Mayors and their policy and tech-nical people are in the business of making political calculations about risk reward. Getting high-quality information that addresses these risks at the same time as new and best practice is being transmitted offers a double pay-off.

These perspectives are corroborated by many anecdotal sources of infor-mation, and they hold important clues to improving the process and the yield of city-to-city visits.

What's next?

We turn now to explore specific cases in depth. Our aim is to gain further insight into the DNA of learning by diving more deeply into three styles of proactive learners. We shall see that important mechanisms of the learning process are the same as those in innovation, and that these mechanisms lie at the heart of the urban ba.

Notes

1   I am grateful for the assistance of David Leipziger in the management and analysis of survey data.
2   The survey was implemented in two waves: the first in the fall of 2008, which returned 27 responses; and a follow-up with slight modifications in the fall of 2009, with 29 additional responses. Three responses were discarded for various reasons (redundancy, incomplete information). Each version was posted on SurveyMonkey on the web, with Spanish and Portuguese versions available. Except where indicated, the data reported here reflect combined responses to identical questions.
3   This number assumes seven-person teams staying four nights; around $800 per capita plus $1500 in airfares.
4   Cities that document their findings and organize their own sessions at home are significantly related ($chi^2 = 6.84$, df = 4, p = 0.002; kendall tau b = -0.488, approx Tb = −5.07, p < 0.001).
5   Significant at 0.038 and 0.027 levels, respectively.
6   By "soft" storage, I mean to refer to informal networks of the urban community (Campbell, 2009). Soft storage is tantamount to tacit knowledge, as described by Nonaka and colleagues (Nonaka *et al.*, 2000).
7   Though customs vary from country to country, the number of working weeks in a calendar year is assumed to be 46, allowing for holidays and vacation time.

References

Bontenbal, M. (2009). *Cities as partners. The challenge to strengthen urban governance through North–South city partnerships*, Eburon, Delft.
Bontenbal, M. and P. van Lindert (2009). "Transnational city-to-city cooperation: issues arising from theory and practice," *Habitat International*, 33, pp. 131–133.
Campbell, T. (2009). *Torino as a learning city*, The German Marshall Fund of the United States, Washington, DC.
de Villiers, J. C. (2007). "Towards an understanding of the success factors in international

twinning and sister-city relationships," *South African Journal of Business Management,* 38, pp. 1–10.

Hwang, J. and M. Gerami (2006). "Analysis of investment in knowledge inside OECD countries," *International Journal of Social Sciences*, 1, pp. 99–104.

Kanter, R., J. Kao and F. Wiersema (1997). *Innovation: breakthrough thinking at 3M, DuPont, GE, Pfizer, and Rubbermaid*, HarperBusiness, London.

Nonaka, I., R. Toyama and N. Konno (2000). "SECI, ba and leadership: a unified model of dynamic knowledge creation," *Long Range Planning*, 33, pp. 5–34.

O'Leonard, K. (2008). *The corporate learning factbook. benchmarks, facts, and analysis in US corporate learning and development*, Bersin and Associates, San Francisco.

Part III

Crucibles of learning:
proactive learner-reformers

6 Informal learners–Turin, Portland and Charlotte[1]

The gamut of learning styles explored in the previous chapters suggests that cities go about their business of learning in very different ways. Even the most assiduous among them, those proactive learners, have built up city learning capacity using different styles. And though style is undoubtedly a result of social, cultural and historical circumstances that shape the ways cities do business, different learning styles nevertheless have important features in common.

Three typical styles of proactive reformers are represented in this and the following two chapters. For the most part, the stories demonstrate that cities acquire and process new ideas in a more or less systematic way, despite their widely differing organizational arrangements. They construct the basic machinery needed to gather new ideas, to evaluate them for use locally, and then apply them with appropriate and sometimes novel adjustments. These last steps lie at the heart of innovation.

The three styles presented are called simply: (1) informal; (2) technical; and (3) corporate. In preparing this book, I have personally observed the organizational arrangements cities have set up to manage learning. This present chapter will explore the cases of Turin, Italy and Portland, Oregon as informal learners.[2] Others that can be placed in this category include Barcelona, Cape Town and Charlotte, and examples will be brought into the discussion where appropriate. Successive chapters will explore technical and corporate cases.

The case of Turin

Turin has achieved a wholesale turnaround without adopting an official position on learning, knowledge acquisition, knowledge intensiveness or even a lead agency. The term "informal" is meant to denote that no formal organization is erected and no written game rules govern the practice of learning as was done with Metropoli-30 in Bilbao or the promotion apparatus in Tampere, Finland. Further, the purposes, mission and outcomes evolved over time and were not pre-scribed in any formal way—i.e., put in writing and adopted or explicitly acknowl-edged by the city or stakeholders in civic, commercial and academic circles.

The story of Turin will show that the city has put in place informal arrange-ments that resemble the "soft" infrastructure that Aydalot called *innovative milieu*, an atmosphere of trust, collaboration and creativity in a locality or region (Aydalot, 1986; Camagni, 1991, 1995). At the heart of the matter for Turin are network mechanisms of public, private and civic leaders who were assembled for planning purposes and who then continued to operate in a consultative way, building on trust that was created in the early stages of the planning process.

This network machinery became a critical tool to gauge ideas, inform policy, and facilitate management, particularly during the strategic planning for the city and later for the 2006 Winter Olympic Games. These planning exercises took place during the mayoral administrations of Valentino Castellani (1993–2000) and Sergio Chiamparino (2001–2010). Let's look first at the context of learning and then turn to the modalities of how things were learned.

The setting—reform and decentralization

Like many cities successful in learning and reform, Turin's story begins with a political and financial crisis in the late 1980s and early 1990s. Turin's history is intimately tied to Fiat motors. Founded in 1908, the very name—Fabbrica Italiana Automobili Torino—reflects the tight relationship between the company and the city. For more than half a century, Fiat was the main economic stalwart on which the city was strongly dependent. In the 1970s and 1980s, the company was plunged into a crisis of poor management and falling demand, which cost tens of thousands of jobs. This catastrophe was exacerbated by a political crisis, a failure of morality in politics in Turin that turned it into a bastion of corruption so pervasive that the city came to be known as "*tangentopolis*" (roughly "pay-off city"). National political reforms at the beginning of the 1990s led to the direct election of Mayor Valentino Castellani.

The new mayor, formerly a professor of engineering at Turin's prestigious Politecnico, campaigned both to diversify the economic base of the city and to reform its political process. Upon winning, as described in greater detail later, he immediately launched a process of fact finding together with an open and active deliberation involving hundreds of citizens and thousands more taking part in a more passive way, attending presentations made for a wider public about how the economy, the city's infrastructure base and other neglected needs could be addressed.

An overview of lessons learned in Turin: the substance of what and the style of how

To keep our discussion manageable, we shall focus on new ideas and knowledge related to planning in Turin, particularly certain aspects of strategic planning in the late 1990s and early 2000s. The content of Turin's learning can be characterized both as substantive—lessons about "what" to do—as well as stylistic—lessons about "how" to do it. Let's take the concrete substantive lessons first.

For starters, the city discovered the meaning of strategic planning, as opposed to master planning, which had been the sole requirement of long-time practice in Italian cities before 1993. Much effort was exerted by the city, driven largely by Castellani himself, to explore the terrain of a strategic approach to the future. Not even Castellani was fully aware of the differences between strategic versus structure or land use planning when he took office. His first exposure to strategic views came in Barcelona a decade earlier. On one of several visits there, Castellani met with city leaders and planners who had begun to think about an approach which links long-term change in economic, political, and social factors with not just the shape and equipment of the city but the very identity as well.

As we shall see in more detail later, Castellani and his team arranged to disseminate the lessons and the promise of strategic planning not only to key stakeholders in Turin, but through all of Italy. When he took office, the idea of planning was deeply rooted in the fortunes of Fiat and the physical parameters of planning inherited from the previous 50 years. Turin had followed national law, and more importantly, the exigencies of Fiat, for key directions in planning, for instance, in the provision of infrastructure like streets and utilities to serve the residential areas populated by the Fiat labor force. Castellani sensed, and later convinced planning elites, that, like many other European cities, Turin needed longer-range planning to go hand in hand with the changing form and economic fortunes of Europe.

In contrast to structure plans, which seek to lay out rational grids and meet growing needs in infrastructure and facilities, strategic visions have an eye outward, on how the city is to make its living, how it fits into a larger assemblage of city-regions in Europe. Strategic planning considers competition from other cities and looks toward comparative advantages in image and identity, as well as more typical issues of completed grid works for inner-city circulation.

European practices in planning, regional development, economic change and other reforms were already taking shape to complement the physical and knowledge-intensive planning in Turin. Castellani and his planning lieutenants observed that a key insight was the realization that "things can be done" and that cities (and mayors) "are not alone." By this, Castellani was referring to a slowly emerging alteration in the proportions of power with decentralization in Italy and elsewhere in Europe. These shifts in power led to new opportunities for cities to initiate actions. Besides the transformation in Barcelona after the death of Franco, Castellani witnessed Lyon engaging in new challenges, like economic development and social progress. Several interviewees spoke of the psychological value of seeing that "others have done it," referring often to Glasgow, but also to Barcelona, particularly in connection with the Olympic Games.

One of the first examples of learning was about connectivity. City leaders discovered that the longer-term view of strategic planning needed to be geared to the city's economic fortunes by means of inter-city linkages—especially high-speed rail—as well as to intra-city connectivity, road, rail and forms of land use. Direct exposure of the city's leadership to progressive cities in Europe like Barcelona, Glasgow and Lyon, as well as to committee work on regionalism in the European Union, made it clear that the city needed to be unencumbered from the rail lines that had served Fiat well earlier in the century, but had become an insurmountable barrier that divided the city sharply as Turin grew. The rationale for gearing the city's physical infrastructure to its changing economic structure soon came to suit Fiat as well during its recovery.

Europe was growing more tightly connected as prospects for high-speed rail grew closer to reality, leading to tighter inter-regional connections toward the east and south to Milan and Genoa on the one hand, and on the other, toward the west into Spain and France, particularly Lyon and Barcelona. This implied a greater understanding of regional markets and trade and strategic alliances in knowledge-intensive industries. Also, Turin was getting acquainted with global standards in connection with the 2006 Winter Olympic Games, for which high international levels of quality—in hotel and food services, for instance—needed to be met and monitored.

In addition to a new approach to planning, the city learned about knowledge intensiveness. With the beginning of Sergio Chiamparino's administration, a second strategic plan was organized to build on the preceding one by enhancing the city's knowledge-related institutions, like universities, libraries and museums. This software side of Turin was to complement the strategic deployment of "hard" infrastructure planned and started under Castellani's administration. Both hard and soft investments were being implemented as Turin was preparing to stage the 2006 Winter Olympic Games.

The shift to a focus on building a knowledge economy under Chiamparino's administration raised many questions of institutional standards and practice. In the first place, the concept of knowledge economies was beginning to take hold throughout Europe in the 1990s. One consequence was that new standards needed to be observed in the competitive allocation of resources in university departments, research programs and private sector proposals for public sector procurement, practices that took on special relevance in connection with the competitive process for accessing EU research and cohesiveness funds.

Stylistically, the accomplishment of the Games taught Turin that it could meet world-class deadlines, a lesson that could only have come with a commitment to undertake a world-class event. One of the most enduring stylistic lessons was the public–private way of doing business. Many interviewees spoke of the mutual distrust that once characterized relations between the public and private realms in Turin. Spirited and often ideological discord divided public–private relations in the early 1990s. A bitter legacy of the decades-long struggles between labor unions and management at Fiat had shaped the very identities of these institutions and engendered deep mistrust and ill-feeling.

The strategic planning processes and the Olympic Games created a high-pressure cauldron for more collaborative working arrangements. These circumstances seemed to dissolve some of the mistrust of the past. By the time Chiamparino was completing his first term, attitudes appeared to have changed fundamentally. Many interviewees spoke of this transformation. For example, one participant contrasted the acrimony and mistrust of the past with the present-day situation. In the words of one member of the chamber of commerce, "Today, not even a small proposal would be presented without an open and deliberate round of consultations between the private sector and the public sector—including commune, province, and region." Several observers stated that the new working style is a matter of "mutual respect." This stylistic change was a milestone in the city's learning process and set the stage for a new phase of learning.

To sum up, Turin's exposure to external knowledge came from: (1) other cities; (2) methods and practices in the EU; (3) global practice through industries in a growing knowledge economy; (4) global practice assimilated through the successful bid for and hosting of the Winter Olympics in 2006; (5) the international business practice of Fiat. The internal mechanism is the network of connections between and among players taking part in one or more of the previous five realms.

Turin's learning apparatus

Up to now, the reader might be tempted to conclude that strong mayoral leadership was the main factor in Turin's learning. In fact, leadership was important, but not the most important factor. Two successive mayors locked onto an approach to the city's future, but both administrations needed many dedicated participants from key segments in the city to bring a new future into reality. Dozens of public, private and civic actors peopled the machinery of learning in Turin.

Before turning to explore the actors that took part in planning, we should take note of Turin's formalized institutions that nominally would be responsible for strategy and planning. Four are worth noting here. First is the city's Department of External Affairs, a typical municipal arrangement to handle external relationships, including inbound and outbound missions, and to plan and keep track of official visits, including those of the mayor and members of industry. A second is a special agency, Torino Internazionale, set up specifically to implement the strategic plans. It is perhaps uniquely suited to developing and managing a learning process. Third is the Politecnico (the Polytechnic University), whose Rector, Francesco Profumo, quietly conducted a long-term campaign to expand the capacity and physical plant of the university, to integrate it with the city in order to enable the university to compete on a global basis. It was his vision, and no doubt his influence, that geared the second strategic plan to knowledge intensiveness. A fourth group is several agencies (one succeeding the other) whose main mandate is the economic and social development of the Piedmont region. Closely allied but with a broader and more purely industrial and commercial outlook is the Chamber of Commerce.

Organizations of these types—city-based, plan-based, a university, regional authorities and commercial interests—are found in many cities. Often they are very effective in accomplishing their goals. But none of the four in Turin is specifically tasked to gather new knowledge, keep Turin up to speed on urban developments and best practice, to conduct research, and develop ideas a city may need to remain competitive. Instead, these tasks were carried out by ad hoc, informal groups drawn from all of these and many other organizations, businesses and NGOs, working hand in hand, step by step, as needs required.

Exposure to outside influences

The preceding section on lessons shows how important were Turin's connections to sources of new ideas in Europe. In particular, Turin made specific and well-targeted connections to key cities undergoing strategic planning and used these connections to help guide its own work. As mentioned earlier, guest presentations were made by visiting delegations from European cities during each of two strategic plans. During the first, when the idea of a strategic plan was novel in Turin, five cities (Barcelona, Bilbao, Glasgow, Lyon and Stockholm) were invited to present their experience. The audience included Turin's political leadership and technical professionals, as well as the broader public.

Sine then, delegations from Turin have averaged more than 30 visits per year to other cities, mostly in Europe but also to Seoul, Korea, where metropolitan planning arrangements is a key area of interest. Urban renewal has continued to be a theme of interest. Climate change has grown in importance, as have metropolitan governance, project evaluation and negotiation skills.

For many years, Barcelona was an important source of knowledge. During both the first and second of Turin's strategic plans, it benefited from Barcelona's experience in developing an overall scope of strategic planning, as well as in the mechanics and process of putting a plan together. Mayor Castellani's time in Barcelona in the 1980s, and later in the 1990s, led to the appointment of a former mayor of Barcelona, Pasqual Maragall, to be head of Turin's Scientific Committee, a group of advisors for the first strategic plan. Additionally, one of Maragall's deputies made repeated visits to Turin and, according to one former deputy mayor of Turin, "tutored the city" in the methodology of strategic planning. Turin was the first Italian city to adopt and publish a strategic plan and subsequently became a founding member of the Italian Network of Strategic Cities.[3]

Other figures in Turin gathered ideas and contacts in Europe. Mercedes Bresso served on the EU Committee of the Regions and was in a position to observe a wide variety of practices and opportunities being afforded cities and regions by the EU. Castellani also sat on the the Committee of the Regions. This and the contact with other cities enabled Turin's leaders to see how other cities set objectives, and in Castellani's words, "how cities developed methods" to solve their problems.

In succeeding years, when a second, knowledge-intensive strategic plan and preparations for the Olympic Games were under way, similar references were made to European counterparts where knowledge economies were being built and, as in the case of Barcelona, where Olympic Games had been hosted.

Turin also drew on ties with EUROCITIES and on relationships with such associations as the French NGO Quartiers en Crise (Neighborhoods in Crisis). With the help of local firms, this last contact was essential to framing an approach to social issues dealing with poverty on the periphery of Turin during the first strategic plan.

Internal networks

Though a large volume of ideas was gathered from outside Turin, much was also generated internally. More important, all the learning, the acquiring, processing and validating of new information, was undertaken by a group of civic leaders, working not as a formally instituted agency but rather more like an informal posse. Much has been said in previous chapters about soft infrastructure in cities, and Turin is a good illustration of how that milieu develops. Recall how Seattle's study-mission members aim to "get to know" each other. They are participating in breaking down the redoubts of uncertainty and mistrust that obstruct cooperative behaviors. Turin is a case where special relationships and trust were developed from scratch. We can learn a lot from Turin about how this process works.

A key step in the formation of Turin's milieu was Mayor Castellani's conviction that a new start was needed following the moral and political meltdown of Turin in the decades preceding his election. An officer at one of Turin's main foundations put it terms of having "to shuffle the deck" to bring in new people and open up the system. From the very beginning, Turin's planning elites were opened to the intermingling of fresh blood with the old guard. The process wasn't accidental; it was a deliberate strategy.

Even before taking office, Mayor Elect Castellani viewed the population of Turin as somewhat "in a shell" and recognized that the multiple crises of preceding decades required the laying of fresh foundations in Turin's public choice-making mechanisms. The Mayor deliberately created a development forum to open up the process. Specific groups were engaged in hearing outside speakers, a dozen commissions of 15 to 20 persons each were formed to think through specific ideas on an informal basis. Each group set its own agenda and constituted its membership, pulling people in as and when needed.

One high-level official in Castellani's administrations cited the "Friday tea with the Mayor" as an illustration of the openness of the process. Groups of people (altogether perhaps 150 people, according to one of Castellani's deputies at the time), including members from the opposition parties, were invited and mixed in small Friday sessions to discuss in complete freedom a "soft agenda" with "open minds." The official observes that "the strategic plan was an instrument to create networks . . . to put networks together."

The Rector of the Politecnico is a good example of an agent of external and internal knowledge who moved with impact through the informal networks in Turin during and after the strategic planning. Before assuming the position of rector, Profumo had traveled widely, spending up to a year in each of Japan, the US and Eastern Europe, each time interspersed with a return stay in Turin.

A common thread linked the stops in his academic migration. He was observing the relationship—physical, academic and financial—between universities and the mother cities he visited.

His vision of strong civic–academic integration was put to the test in 2002, when a Vice President of General Motors visited Mayor Chiamparino to explore major investments that would create a research center in the city linked to GM's partnership with Fiat. One of the key issues was public administration: could GM count on the city to meet its side of the bargain for facilities and other arrangements? More particularly, could the city commit a champion to drive the process? On the spot, with GM officials still in his office, the Mayor phoned Profumo and gave him a three-minute summary. The parties met at eight the next morning, framed a memorandum of understanding, and within three months of signing had 220 GM researchers installed at the Politecnico. That beginning led to a much expanded physical campus that today forms a significant part of Turin's revitalization.

The deal moved quickly because the groundwork had been started a half-dozen years earlier with Profumo's self-organized study tour and his active and trusted participation in the strategic planning process. His image of city–university arrangements, and above all his personal style—trusted, competent, in charge of his domain—had laid the groundwork for the deal.

My interviews in Turin uncovered a system of trusted ties between and among key players who were engaged in the planning process (see Appendix 3 for more detail about the interview process). In interviews, I asked each informant to name persons he or she regarded as: (1) trustworthy; and (2) active in the community like himself or herself. These last questions were crucial to understanding linkages of trust. In Table 6.1, "sources" refers to the interviewees; "references" refer to those persons named by interviewees as persons of trust. Table 6.2 tabulates the frequencies with which a given person was named.

Table 6.1 Sources, by sector

Sector	Sources interviewed	References made, by sector
Public	6	31
Private	6	40
Civic	1	4
University	2	19
Foundation	2	6
Unknown	0	4
Total	17	104

Table 6.2 Frequencies of persons named

No. times named	No. persons
1	97
2	12
3	5
4	5
5	1
6	2
7	2
8	2

A total of 104 unique individuals were named as trusted ties; seven persons were named more than once, and six were named more than three times. Several persons were named eight times. These individuals form the nodes in the resulting network of ties shown in Figure 6.1. Grouped and presented as a single picture, these data give us what I call a *cloud of trust*, a constellation of network ties between persons where trust is indicated by the direction of arrows from the source.

In Figure 6.1, interviewees are represented as circles, trusted ties as squares. The overall structure of the network shows rather tight clusters, and that several interviewees function as bridges, connecting separate clusters (left center and lower left). This picture is somewhat akin to the pattern found in a study by Belligni and his team at the University of Turin (Belligni *et al.*, 2008). At the same time, the figure shows a central cluster of nodes, persons named by multiple interviewees (as reflected in Table 6.2).

What about the relationships among the interviewees themselves, a group we might think of as elites? Do they have many common ties, revealing a cohesive structure? Standard measures (density 0.23, compactness 0.92) mean that nearly a quarter of all possible connections is present in the network, but that the "distance" between any two persons in the network is just a bit more (1.17) than only one link away. High cohesiveness of this kind is normally interpreted as meaning that actors are able to respond quickly and effectively to stimuli. Again, a few persons are key nodes in the network. Overall, this tightness may be one of the factors thought to be important in the magic sauce that plays a role in Turin's innovation, responsiveness and competitiveness.

Another key finding uncovered in the interviews but reflected only weakly in the data is that new members were imported into networks during the planning process. According to participants involved, this new mixing was both unexpected

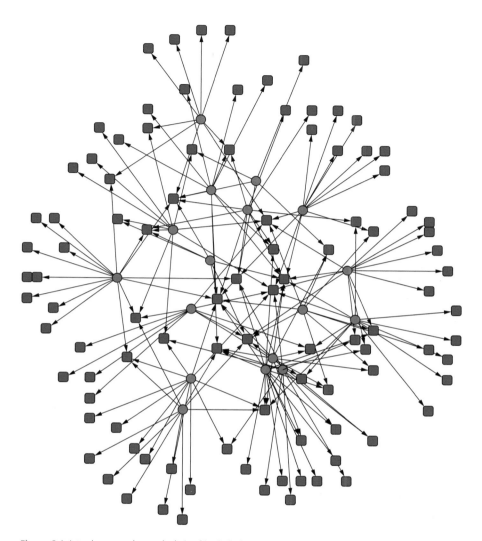

Figure 6.1 Interviewees and trusted relationships in Turin

Key: red circles = interviewees; blue squares = trusted others

and unprecedented. Two distinct episodes of opening took place; one in the first strategic plan in the mid-1990s, and a second during the second strategic plan in the early 2000s. Particularly in the first strategic plan, persons whose skills and creativity had not been previously tapped were brought into deliberations without regard to political affiliation, family background or industrial sector.

Several interviewees explained that they had not anticipated nor could they have expected to be a part of the deliberative efforts in city planning. For instance, interviewees told of having been invited to take part in meetings and discussions

Table 6.3 Age distribution

Age	Source	Name
0*	0	6
70	2	7
60	3	32
50	6	24
40	4	28
30	2	6
20	0	1
Total	17	104

* Unknown or deceased

around strategic planning without having a family, industrial, or social "patron." They described having received calls "out of the blue" by persons whose names they recognized by position or title, but with whom they had no previous relationship.

Age differences are a partial reflection of this mixing, as suggested in Table 6.3. Many of the newly invited individuals were separated in age by a decade or more from most of their "peers" at the meetings they were invited to attend. The network data related to age appear to corroborate these anecdotal stories. The "Name" column in Table 6.3 shows a mild bimodal distribution with soft peaks of age in the 60s and 40s.

The work of Belligni and his colleagues is confined to the period 2001–2006 and focuses on somewhat static "milieus"—i.e., sub-networks in Belligni's nomenclature—each of which has distinct characteristics in terms of religious, political or business affiliations, as well as in terms of composition and interconnectedness. The present analysis suggests a dynamic quality in the functioning of the networks in Turin, as newcomers crossed over socio-economic lines.

Some interviewees reflecting on the process found it entirely innovative, and in several cases persons making these "crossovers" progressed to new and important institutional positions. These findings add a new dimension to recent works on governance networks in Turin by Belligni. The significance of this finding is that mobilizing new generations of activists might offer lessons to other cities seeking to build new cadres of leadership.

on their flanks. Another ugly incident made headlines when a biker, confronted by a bus driver and an angry bus passenger, came to blows. These are a few of the many incidents that illustrated the growing problem of two cultures in the throes of blending. Maus started his blog and began to be the beacon on these issues for bikers.

Biker advocates like Mia Birk were on the European study tours along with public officials, transport planners, politicians and businesspeople. They all saw the simple genius of the bike corrals and green boxes, and when these ideas were put on the blog, new knowledge was spread quickly. One degree away from Maus was the biker in the traffic police division, and with support from the Mayor and his biker-advocate, the first installations were in place in a matter of weeks.[4] The idea had spread quickly, reached a point of validation when viewed in situ, and spread link by link into the right clusters of interest, from bikers, to traffic police, the Mayor, and back.

This small example captures many of the main steps in learning. The identification of an idea, in this case along the lines of Copenhagen and Amsterdam, is recognized as closely related to the objectives in a community of interest— the bikers. Then comes circulation of the idea for processing and deliberation within practitioner circles as well as more widely in the community. Deeper and more elaborate processing cutting across outside interest groups then leads to more complete integration—in this case of biking into the regional transit scheme, into the green pathways and walking routes, into City Hall and eventually Metro's plans. Associations of bikers have formed and have been influential in a larger movement that seeks not only to integrate biking into the city's transit system but also into the local economy—for example, in biking destinations for tourists, local organized "rides" (touring), local businesses that manufacture equipment and apparel. Even pop culture has flowered from the biking community (see Box 6.2).

Box 6.2 *Pop culture of biking*

One of the delights of cities is the creative pop cultures that emerge with the propinquity of interests. In the case of Portland, bikers have shown flair and playfulness in celebrating their culture. "Zoo bombers" are an organized gathering of bikers who glide their favorite two-wheeler down a hillside from the zoo into the city center in a high-speed parade. Subgroups have formed to celebrate tiny bikes, tall bikes and sprocketless bikes; to play bike polo, ride after hours ("Knight riders"), ride in costume, take part in scavenger hunts and video contests; and, for fundraising and high art, to take part in bridge breakfasts or bike in an operatic review in the park (the zoo bombers and bridge breakfasters of course get permits and reserve public spaces).

In contrast to the examples discussed in the Turin case, the anecdotes about improving biking safety in Portland illustrate the connections of already well-formed groups turning over new ideas, evaluating their benefits and drawbacks, and either helping out, getting out of the way or voicing opposition. The strategic planning anecdotes in Turin, on the other hand, are about a strategic planning group being formed on the march. The emphasis in Turin was on new relationships as they were being created; the lesson from Portland is about the linkages between groups. In both cases, effective knowledge exchange depends on trusted relationships.

Internal trust networks

Planning and charting the city is carried out by a wide, but much smaller group of actors. These may respond to political pressures and reflect the priorities and interests of their constituents, but at early moments in the game, before political interests and outcomes are entirely clear, city leaders are learning and exploring, and it is this phase of the game—that of interactions among trusting members—that is most crucial for developing future pathways of growth.

I conducted in Portland the same kind of exploratory analysis of participant groups as in Turin. As noted earlier, the difference between the two cases is one of maturity in formation. The Portland system is a collection of mature interest groups. The graphics for Portland show eight distinct subgroups, representing bikers, parks and urban wilderness, home builders, local commerce, business development and manufacturing, economic development, and political and policy interests, including Metro. These groups have formed and consolidated an identity and exerted an influence over planning in Portland for the past two decades. The Turin group on the other hand is new. Its members all had one thing in common: direct participation in Turin's strategic plans.

Accordingly, the graphics below depicting Portland networked groups are not strictly comparable to those of Turin. Figure 6.2 shows the interconnections among, for instance, the leader of the urban parks and wilderness group with others in business, city officials, Metro and economic development, all of which

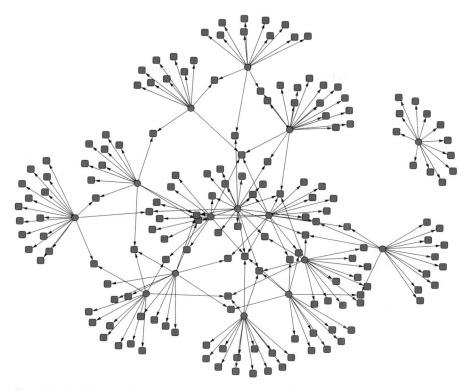

Figure 6.2 Cloud of trust in Portland

Key: red circles = interviewees; blue squares = trusted others

played a role in the creation of an interconnected wilderness parkway in Portland and the surrounding communities. Comparisons of networks are discussed in more detail in Chapter 10.

Benchmarking against other informal models

Turin has invented a process that created a series of overlapping networks among what we might call the planning elites to figure out a way forward for the city after the political and economic low in the 1990s. A somewhat similar invention is still under way today in Charlotte, North Carolina. The difference is that Charlotte already had a major clique that effectively forged a new image of the city. Hugh McColl (Bank of America), Ed Crutchfield (First Union), Rolfe Neal (*Charlotte Observer*) and Bill Lee (Duke Energy) formed a core of key players. Each sat at the commanding heights of his respective domain—banking, newspaper and media, electric utility. That group steered the city toward a wholesale transformation, which is mostly complete today, at least in terms of the downtown physical form.

But with the passing of the power elites and the banking crisis of 2009–2011, Charlotte is now in a pickle. Key members of the clique are deceased, retired or inactive. The future of the city's main industry is in question. Meanwhile, a still-undefined leadership in Charlotte has a handful of knotty problems to solve, including leadership itself, a racial divide, inequities in schools, neighborhood disparities, and growing immigration by Latino and other ethnic communities. This is not to imply that the city is in disarray. On the contrary, social capital is coming out of the woodwork to solve the city's problems.

This is precisely the interesting feature about informal learning in Charlotte. Without the stiff backbone of the old guard, how does the new generation form a new, stable elite to guide the city? Turin's problems were quite different. A new leader appeared on the scene and immediately perceived the need to mobilize civil society by forming linkages. In Portland, the learning process accreted over time; new ideas were imported and digested within and among the many well-defined interest groups.

Accordingly, the lessons Charlotte most needs to learn—those second-order processes of engagement and trust—are not found in the most common forms of external learning undertaken by the city. The Chamber of Commerce plays the dominant role in organizing study missions, and the topics and targets for the most part have not focused on rebuilding the leadership at the center. It was perhaps for this reason that one of the most recent visits was to Charlotte itself. The Chamber structured a round of internal visits and sparked something of an awakening. Certainly the "self-visit" got rave reviews from the many participants.

Internal learning is the order of the day, and Charlotte's many civic players, led by the Foundation for the Carolinas, have picked up this mantle of service. In Charlotte, leadership groups formed with the purpose of examining the very idea of future leadership attract members from all the traditional institutions—religious, civic, public and private. Moreover, foundation sponsors intentionally work with partners to pair actors, individuals and organizations in a way that forges inter-institutional ties. Identities and ideas are deliberately mixed so as to achieve a blend. Interviews in Charlotte made it plain that these informal mechanisms were critical to the processing of information and to break through to new understandings.

The institutional tissue formed by these participatory efforts equates to informal networks and nascent social capital. The interlacing creates ties across public, private and civic sectors. These inter-digitations of civic roles perhaps constitute the hallmark of modern governance and are vital for learning exchange.

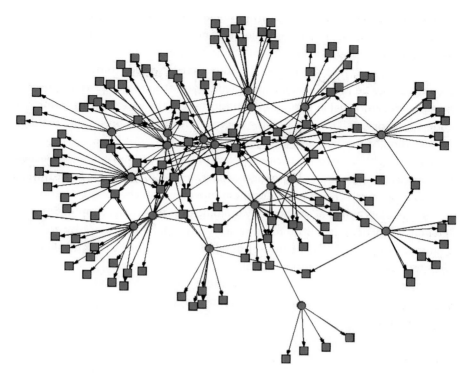

Figure 6.3 Cloud of trust in Charlotte

A glance at the cloud of trust in Charlotte gives a reflection of this crossover design. As in Turin, the graphic in Figure 6.3 reflects a density of ties among key actors. In this case, the graphic highlights crossovers between and among public, private and civic members.

Conclusions

Turin, Portland and Charlotte fit the proactive-reformer mold, yet each had a distinct task that was undertaken in an informal way. By any standard Turin launched a unique and highly productive process of creating a new planning tissue of networked groups that have lasted for more than two decades, but is now dissipating. Portland is in full march, near the top of its game, processing new ideas and sending them through the networked system of interest groups. Charlotte is exerting energies to build a new layer of leaders. In each of these cases, the process of learning and the discovery of new ideas help to forge a cohesiveness, and in turn rely upon connectedness among key players.

Each of the cities started from different initial conditions. Portland with a big bang of reform has been at the learning task much longer than the others. Turin was launched into learning because of political and economic calamity. The Turin story also suggests that the informal system that emerged from a cauldron of deep crisis may be idiosyncratic and difficult not just to replicate in other cities but to guide a renewal in Turin itself. Charlotte is at the very stage of forming a leadership cadre. Can this city find the energy to form a new urban elite without the prodding of a critical emergency?

Turin and Charlotte found their own ways to forge new links in their respective networks of activists. Turin's city leaders deliberately recruited actors from outside the established elites and engaged them in a common challenge. Charlotte's informal leaders aimed at deliberately building bridges across communities. The dynamic in Portland is a little more of a free-for-all held in place by an environmental ethos. Each of the cities will need to sustain efforts to link and liberate the latent potential in its social capital.

The key actors in these city stories consist of an amalgam of elected officials, corporations and commercial establishments, developers and home builders, neighborhood associations, NGOs and large civic institutions like universities and hospitals. In each of these cities, any one member of these groups is only a few degrees away from another. New knowledge acquired in one of them—about bike corrals in Copenhagen, Olympic events in Barcelona, or the internal dynamics within the home city itself—sooner or later flows into adjacent groups through network contacts. But the speed and success of uptake depend in the first instance on whether the idea is flowing across a bond of trust.

These informal cities, like many others with different styles, find themselves facing constantly changing challenges, whether metro regional governance, regional development, high-speed rail, keeping global talent or fiber optic infrastructure. Meeting challenges requires some kind of system for learning and innovation. The following chapter on technical learners, with Curitiba as the protagonist, illustrates an entirely different system reflecting an utterly different set of circumstances, yet learning, networking and innovation are also part of the story.

Notes

1   The author wishes to acknowledge the generous support of the Gordon and Betty Moore Foundation, which played a part in making possible the development of this chapter.
2   The fieldwork, conducted in Barcelona and Turin in June and July of 2009, was supported by a grant from the Comparative Domestic Policy Program of the German Marshall Fund of the United States.

3   Today, 55 Italian cities are members of the network.
4   A fuller account of the biker story in Portland and beyond can be found in Birk *et al.*, (2010).

References

Aydalot, P. (1986). *Milieux innovateurs en Europe*, GREMI, Paris.

Belligni, S., S. Ravazzi and R. Salerno (2008). *L'élite che governa Torino. Il potere nella rete*, Political Science Department, University of Turin, Turin.

Birk, M., J. Kurmaskie and J. Moore (2010). *Joyride: pedaling toward a healthier planet*, Cadence Press, Portland, OR.

Camagni, R. (1991). *Innovation networks*, Spatial Perspectives, London.

Camagni, R. (1995). "The concept of innovative milieu and its relevance for public policies in European lagging regions," *Journal of the Regional Science Association*, 74, pp. 317–340.

Cortright, J. and C. Colleta (2005). "The young and the restless: how Portland competes for talent," in J. Cortright and C. Colleta (eds), *The young and the restless*, Impresa Consulting, Portland, OR.

Florida, R. (2002). *The rise of the creative class*, Basic Books, New York.

In contrast to the informal approach described in the last chapter is a more technical mode of learning, as seen in places like Curitiba. The chief distinguishing
characteristic is the presence of some form of semi- or wholly independent think
tank, attached directly to City Hall or closely allied to it, consisting of professional
analysts who have a responsibility to research and develop ideas for the city.
Amman, Budapest, Curitiba, Ho Chi Minh City, Juárez, Lyon and Philadelphia are
a few of the many cities that have such a body. And though these cities vary in
the extent to which they press the advantage of a dedicated city think agency,
they share the distinction of having made an institutional and budgetary commitment to generating, processing and storing knowledge. High levels of budgetary
commitment make it difficult for most places to clear the institutional threshold
to establish this model. And though it is effective for learning it has distinct drawbacks, as we shall see by focusing on the case of Curitiba, Brazil.

The choice of Curitiba is based on the city's long history of innovations in
multiple areas, making it a well-known case of good management. Bus rapid transit, land use controls, green space and environmental sustainability are only a few
of the many innovations that Curitiba's think tank has implemented over the past
four decades. Though it is often overshadowed by the famous native-son architect
and political leader Jaime Lerner, the think tank IPPUC (its Portuguese acronym
pronounced i-poo-kee, which stands for Instituto de Pesquisa y Planejamento
Urbano de Curitiba—Curitiba Institute for Urban Planning and Research) has
operated since the dawn of the city's trend-setting changes in the 1960s.

In this sense, the agency is a device that functions in similar ways to Turin's
informal networks. Both models gather and sift through ideas for possible application to the city, and both show how dedicated attention can build a shared
vision over time and create a self-aware organization. But some aspects of the

freewheeling style and openness of Turin are not so easily achieved in technical agencies like IPPUC. This chapter explores the roots of insights and learning, showing how they mature into innovative changes in the city. Along the way, we shall make reference to other cities with think tanks to illustrate the many advantages of technical agencies, as well as their weaknesses, in generating new knowledge, learning and innovating.

Founding moments in Curitiba—responding to growth pressures

Capital of the state of Paraná and neighbor to São Paulo in central South Brazil, Curitiba has 1.6 million inhabitants in the city proper and 2.3 million in the metropolitan area. From the 1950s to the 1970s, Curitiba was Brazil's fastest-growing city. Beginning in the 1940s with the collapse of coffee prices, mechanization in agriculture, and de-industrialization in the neighboring industrial powerhouse of São Paulo, strong migratory flows pushed into Curitiba, its growth rates reaching over 7 percent per year during some decades between the 1950s and 1980s.

Curitiba's position as the state's capital and center of services, together with its central geographical location—linking agricultural production areas in the west to the main port on the Atlantic coast—helped to fuel the city's growth, from 140,000 inhabitants in 1940 to 180,000 in 1950, and 360,000 by the 1960s. The demographic transformation was brusque and unrelenting. In 1961 nearly 70 percent of the state's population lived in rural areas, and by 1991 nearly 75 percent of the population lived in urban districts (Lowry, 2002).

Rapid growth brought problems and environmental challenges typical of many cities in Latin America during its period of high rural-to-urban migration. The city suffered from excessive spillovers in airborne and waterborne industrial contaminants and congestion on the one hand, and, on the other, shortage of facilities, infrastructure and services. One consequence of the demographic pressures was that incoming populations began to settle in floodplains surrounding the city, resulting in recurring losses of property and life when annual floods reached into the low-lying areas of the spreading urban fringe.

The political context during this period was an important factor in shaping options for the cities of Brazil. Just as Curitiba was about to give birth to a master plan and to conceive IPPUC, Brazil was entering a military dictatorship (1964–1979). Under military rule, cities were expected to follow the dictates of central government irrespective of local sentiment. Cities were financially dependent on the state and federal governments, making them vulnerable to changing

macroeconomic and political conditions. Local governments had very little autonomy to launch initiatives or independently to establish their own priorities.
Second, at the outset of the era, the mass media were under censorship, and
public participation in political affairs was at times severely restricted. Public
involvement was nevertheless brought into the early planning stages in Curitiba
and would gradually increase.

Third, the military government gradually replaced import substitution policies
with inflows of foreign capital accompanied by a rise in major infrastructure
projects, many of them leading to an increase in urban investment. Most Brazilian
cities took advantage of that investment to build motorways and viaducts, thus
establishing the predominance of the private car. Curitiba, however, developed
an alternative course of action and created IPPUC to help implement it.

Planning process: the Agache Plan

The independent course chosen by Curitiba was in part made possible two decades
earlier in the 1940s with the Agache Plan, the first formal attempt to respond to
urban growth in Curitiba. The Agache Plan, named after French urban planner
Alfred Agache in 1943, proposed a well-defined central area surrounded by residential zones, with a traffic system composed of concentric (ring) roads linked to
the central area by radial avenues. Agache's spoke-and-wheel design reflected a
classic planning concept. He could not have known that the concept would be
overwhelmed by the powerful impact of booming ownership of private automobiles. However, the plan did foresee and made provision for transit rights of way
along the spokes, and, fortunately for the city, some of these along with radial
rights of way were preserved over the decades. Though the city subsequently
grew beyond the physical limits envisaged by the Agache Plan, the outlines for
access to the periphery were in place.

Box 7.1 *Origins of urban planning in Curitiba*

Toward the end of the 1940s and into the mid-1950s there began a
noteworthy transformation in Curitiba with the implementation of the
Preliminary Urban Plan. At this time, architect and city planner Alfredo
Agache, co-founder of the French Society of Urban Studies, wanted to intro-
duce a new standard of urban space design. Agache was commissioned to

create an urban plan for Curitiba and designed a development scheme that gave priority to public services such as sanitation, easing traffic congestion, and creating centers that enabled the growth of both social life and commerce. After two years of preparation, economic setbacks curtailed the full implementation of the plan. However, initial parts of his plan included large avenues, an obligatory setback of five meters from the curb as a buffer zone for new buildings, an industrial district, the civic center and the municipal market. While the Agache Plan was not completely realized, from its inception it is evident that the people of Curitiba benefited from the visionary framework it established.

In the 1960s when the pressures of growth were being felt acutely in the city, Mayor Ivo Arzua Pereira commissioned a new urban plan for Curitiba adapted to modern needs. In his words: "One of the sharpest needs felt by the population was a revision of the Agache Plan, not because it had defects, but because (with the growth of the city and state interference) it . . . had become obsolete."[2]

In addition to the basic radial pattern, a key legacy of the Agache Plan was the perception that planning could help solve problems arising from rapid urban growth. This perception was acted upon in 1964 when the city government organized a competition for the preparation of the "Preliminary Urban Plan," which later became the Curitiba Master Plan.

Curitiba Master Plan

Curitiba's Preliminary Urban Plan was developed in 1964 by SERETE (Society of Studies and Projects) and Jorge Wilheim of Associated Architects, with the collaboration of local technicians. Among these technicians were Jaime Lerner and Lubomir Ficinski, key figures whose vision of planning and expert guidance were to be felt in Curitiba for many decades. Within a year, a series of public deliberations and seminars was organized in partnership with the mayor's office and civil society on the topic of "Curitiba Tomorrow." These events brought the plan into public debate: its objectives of open and transparent planning engaged the local population.

The general approach of the new plan was to improve the quality of life in the city, and in particular to create an integrated transport system coordinated with land use. These ideas aimed to reduce congestion and preserve the traditional center of the city, to contain the growth of the city within its physical and

territorial limits, and to create supportive economic conditions for urban development. The master plan laid the groundwork for a range of transport innovations,
among them that commerce, services, and residential areas should expand in a
linear manner from the city center along "structural axes." The plan laid out
guidelines to:

- change the radial urban growth trend to a more linear form by integrating
  the road network, transport, and land use;
- decongest the central business district while preserving its historic center;
- manage, rather than prevent, population growth;
- provide economic support to urban development; and
- support greater mobility by improving infrastructure.

Profile and governance of IPPUC

City officials and planning elites in Curitiba—the mayors, leading political officials,
and planners—realized that a strong technical capacity would be needed to carry
the plan forward. Then Mayor Ivo Arzua, believing that a mere advisory office
would not be sufficient to lead the reforms foreseen in the plan, made sure that
a new agency had specific duties related to implementation. He sought and
obtained the support of the association of architects, commercial associations and
other interested groups to create a special body for this purpose.[3]

IPPUC was created in 1965 with its main mission the implementation of the
Master Plan. The Institute was founded as a municipal autarchy, giving it a certain
administrative and functional independence.[4] It was governed by a board of
directors and had a deliberative council, chaired by the mayor, along with a
president. The board was composed mainly of the directors of departments in the
City Hall and city council representatives, with the Institute's president, who was
appointed by the mayor. Despite these formal arrangements, IPPUC does not fit
the same corporatist mold as, say, Bilbao's Metropoli-30, which is covered in the
next chapter. Metropoli-30 has a much broader, agenda-setting and visionary role
than does IPPUC.

At the heart of IPPUC were three technical departments (*superintendencias*);
one for planning, another for project execution, and a third for urban research.
In addition, support structures, including administration and finance, handled the
internal mechanisms of the institution's operation. A Center of Data Processing
(CPD) was in charge of processing the data needed for municipal planning and
administration.

As an autarchy, the Institute was created with its own payroll, separate from
that of the municipal government. Although IPPUC expenses were approved by

the board, independence in personnel and legal matters made it possible for the Institute to escape the deadening impact often seen in the quasi-public or fully public sector planning agencies of many Latin American cities.

Roots of learning in IPPUC

Having key political leaders and technical professionals on the board and council made it easier to gain approval for IPPUC's policies and work program. The deliberative council was empowered to propose laws on matters that were important but not considered in the Master Plan, such as land density regulations and fiscal mechanisms. In addition, the council supervised the work of IPPUC in the implementation of the plan.

IPPUC's independence also made it easier to attract and contract professionals, including foreign experts. According to Santoro, experts from Brazil and abroad enriched the original proposals foreseen in the plan.[5] Within a few years of its founding, more than 60 technicians were working in IPPUC. Among them were architects, engineers, lawyers, sociologists and educators. They were drawn from pools of immigrants and fresh recruits—Polish, Chilean, Argentine, Bolivian and French—all of them well traveled and for the most part hired on a competitive basis. The Institute's duties, according to Law 2660 of December 1, 1965, were:

1   to elaborate and direct to the executive branch a bill establishing Curitiba's Urban Plan;
2   to promote studies and research of an integrated plan for the development of the municipality of Curitiba;
3   to judge bills and administrative measures that could impact the municipality's development in all of its aspects;
4   to create conditions for implementation and continuity, which would allow a constant adaptation of sectoral and global plans to the dynamics of municipal development;
5   to make the local plan compatible with regional or state plan guidelines.

IPPUC's first bylaws, approved by Decree 1910/65, added other duties, such as:

6   preparation of studies aiming to improve adaptation of municipal works to the Municipal Master Guiding Plan along with tax or administrative restrictions and incentives needed for the implementation of the Master Plan;
7   exploration of the feasibility of sectoral programs;
8   the promotion of agreements with technical entities and universities for the training of professionals;

9   offering internships to university students; and

10   the execution of other activities linked to urban development.

These remits involved research and developmental functions ranging from basic data gathering, to concept schemes, to site plans and engineering, and even to forecasting. In other words, the Institute was charged with generating and developing data and information about the city and translating it into proposals and plans based on objective evidence.

As a part of the mission, IPPUC technicians scouted out ideas and practice from around the nation. For example, in 1967, a year after Curitiba's city council approved the city's Master Plan, which had been prepared by IPPUC, an agreement was ratified between the State of Paraná's government and 10 municipalities that were part of Curitiba's metropolitan region. This resulted in the creation of the Metropolitan Council, of which IPPUC was a part, and which considered development issues over the entire urbanized region of greater Curitiba. IPPUC's participation in this agreement allowed it to prepare technical studies and program works related to integrated regional planning, in addition to coordinating works, projects, services and activities of interest to the whole region. With this swift organizational step, IPPUC was put in position to develop proposals and projects for a wide metropolitan area without the usual problems of partisan political bickering.

By the end of 1967, Curitiba had created an agency not only engaged in the mechanics of urban growth, but also able to take initiative on issues and practices that could affect the sustainability of development over a wide area. Directly linked to the mayor's office and with a status above municipal departments (secretários do município), IPPUC was capable of following and studying as well as providing for the implementation through project contracting of all of the major elements in the city's growth process. Moreover, though not conceived as an institution dedicated to sustainability, IPPUC had in its founding terms of reference all the elements the institution needed to achieve sustainable development (Oliveira, 2001).

Mechanisms of success in sustainability—channeling advice to the city

Though it moved through various phases—at first active, then quiet in the face of public reaction, then active again—IPPUC created a long record of contributions to various aspects of urban development in the city. Santoro and Leitmann (2004) and Oliveira (2001) see the early years in several distinct phases. An initial period that Oliveira calls "institutionalization" (1962–1966, see above) was followed by an incubation period (1965–1970), at which time conflicts arose over the vision and strategy of projects conceived by IPPUC on the one hand and, on the other, those developed by the municipal administration. During this period, in Oliveira's words, IPPUC was "in the icebox," its actions and activity on hold (Oliveira, 2001: 99). During this period, IPPUC developed projects under its director Jaime Lerner. Beginning in 1970 with the appointment of Lerner as mayor, IPPUC launched its first important phase of implementation.

The rough chronological order follows the evolution of thinking and trial and error concerning land use, transport and social and environmental issues in Curitiba. Each section illustrates a modality of action—on learning and innovative solutions—to problems that are common in fast-growing cities.

Establishing rudiments of urban form—1967–1972

The use of land and a special program for vehicles and pedestrian circulation became the focus of attention under Mayors Ivo Arzua and Jaime Lerner, with engineers José Portella and later Cássio Tanigushi directing the Institute. IPPUC began to plan radical changes for the city. The key features of restructuring would be linear access routes radiating out from the city, along with the creation of new residential and commercial establishments formed with the help of land use controls, zoning measures and building regulations.

One of the seminal and most difficult proposals advanced by IPPUC was a large sidewalk mall in the middle of downtown, later to become Flower Street. The idea was to keep the block free from automobiles and reserved for pedestrians. Though common in many cities today, the idea of a pedestrian mall in the city center was unheard of in Brazil at that time. Initially, the idea was hatched in IPPUC based on examples of European pedestrian streets, which were beginning to emerge in downtown core areas. Several of the IPPUC staff, and Lerner himself, having traveled, worked or lived in Europe, were aware of these developments. Lerner's acute sense of design was quick to see the logic in the alternative use of commercial street space. The trick would be to implant the idea in a form that would be acceptable to commercial interests.

Lerner's team in IPPUC pored over the Master Plan and selected a single block in downtown Curitiba for a pilot project. The proposal aroused stiff opposition from commercial businesses in the city center. Shop owners felt that their success depended upon access by and parking spaces for private automobiles. In contrast, the IPPUC team and Lerner in particular felt that the first step in gaining control over the automobile was the creation of automobile-free areas downtown.

Many meetings were required with the Chamber of Commerce and other departments before IPPUC, using technical arguments, eventually persuaded these groups that the proposed closing of downtown streets made sense. One element in the argument was that Flower Street was not an isolated project, but rather was part of a larger scheme to manage traffic flows in and out of the city. The IPPUC plan would divert traffic to parallel streets. But resistance was still quite strong. Lerner then adopted a quick-strike strategy, closing the selected block for a street fair on a Sunday during which schoolchildren could participate in an art project that was spread across the street surface. The combination of the fair and a larger than normal pedestrian flow of parents, regular shoppers and schoolkids carried the day, and the pedestrian mall idea took hold.

Succeeding phases of the transit plan began to widen the focus to larger questions of traffic flow, congestion, access and pedestrian ways. This sequence of steps produced a signal feature that is seen in many other places: an innovation that is initially relatively small opens the door to far wider change.

The rather small step—in Curitiba's case the closing of a single block—demonstrated the possibility of vibrant commercial life without automobiles in a dense, downtown area. That initial change, embellished by enhanced use of the street with flower vendors and civic activities like street painting by schoolchildren, demonstrated a new, convivial use of space. Resistance by commerciantes began to evaporate as once-a-week closures gave way to a permanent arrangement. Gradually, the larger public began to see the advantages of this re-arrangement in the way the city worked.

IPPUC technical planners built on this initial innovation by adopting additional European and home-cooked ideas into the scheme, such as extending the pedestrian mall, establishing parallel one-way routes in alternate blocks, and designating "fast routes" to run from neighborhoods to downtown, greatly facilitating access to the city center. Though the ideas were not complicated technically, IPPUC and the administration had to spend three years developing these initial changes and achieving consensus before the transit plan would become reality.

Later, new routes were created for the traffic flows crossing Curitiba's traditional downtown. Buses were given dedicated lanes. Small lane curbs were built to help ward off intruding automobile traffic. Running parallel to main transit lines were single lanes that functioned as access ways for neighborhood traffic. Density changes were introduced to encourage commercial and real estate development along the access corridors in order to take advantage of and mutually support public transit.

With these main components of the traffic management plan, the rudimentary elements of Latin America's first rapid bus transit system were put in place. The dominance of the automobile was being broken in Curitiba. More important, a platform was established that enabled much more elaborate and larger-scale systems to be built up in the following years.

Education of the public was no small part of the solution. IPPUC helped to develop materials, film, television pieces and pamphlets to accompany the plans and educate the public. A publicity campaign helped the citizens to see the new and emerging patterns of accessing the city and managing the use of urban land.

The Curitiba story illustrates vividly the effective use of a technical team when managed by a talented and visionary planner like Jaime Lerner. His genius is captured in the seminal experience of Flower Street. Lerner and his team did not merely transplant the idea of pedestrian malls from European cities. The genius was in seeing the potential and adapting the concept into a much larger scheme of city traffic, but most of all, showing how this innovation could be introduced into an otherwise reluctant environment. A decade later, the technical team, this time with Lerner as mayor, would produce a much wider and equally innovative transit scheme for the entire city.

Structuring the transport system—1972–1983

The next phase of development for IPPUC and the city of Curitiba is marked by three factors. The first is the appointment, by the governor, of two technicians as mayors—Jaime Lerner and Saul Ruiz—both of whom were familiar with and relied upon the planning, urban development, and expertise of IPPUC. Both retained the same director, Lubomir Ficinski. This continuity of thought and personnel signaled a growing acceptance and rising technical strength of the Institute as a thought leader for the city.

The remaining factors helping to define this phase originated outside Curitiba. In 1973, the oil crisis brought a doubling of gasoline prices. The price shocks helped to strengthen the conviction of Curitiba's leadership in supporting extensive public transportation. Not long afterward, in 1975, Curitiba felt the effects of the second exogenous influence: the city became one of the beneficiaries of proceeds from a World Bank loan to improve public transit in the cities of Brazil. IPPUC would play a key role in meeting these challenges.

Integration of land use and public transport

IPPUC technicians began to develop a broader road scheme for the entire city that took advantage of the basic premise of integrated road and land use. An express route for the exclusive use of buses ran north and south, forming the central axis between the "fast lanes" already developed. With 30-meter widths, the lanes provided ample volume for through traffic. At the same time, pedestrian and slower traffic was accommodated on parallel strips.

In addition, a new land use plan was approved. Taking a lead from European rights of way planning, IPPUC proposed building regulations that permitted construction of up to 22 times the areal size of the land between the "fast routes." The Master Plan required that buildings facing streets of public transportation have a fixed percentage of their areas dedicated to commercial establishments. On streets that crossed fast lanes, construction was allowed up to 12 times the area of the land and had to have five-meter setbacks. In this way a pyramid of land use density was being formed.

With trial and error, IPPUC and other technicians determined that it was desirable to increase the density of built-up areas even further. Other initiatives expanded parking and created a beltway around the city to relieve pressure and interruptions from traffic cutting through the downtown area merely to get to the other side of town (Ranhagen and Trobeck, 1998).

These solutions were a blend of homegrown ingenuity and borrowing of ideas from many places. IPPUC drew on practices that were beginning to emerge in many cities in Brazil and around the world. But IPPUC's visible and proactive role in applying lessons began to attract the attention of the state and federal governments, and this exposure enhanced the role and legitimacy given to IPPUC. A short time later, Curitiba received US$54 million as a part of proceeds from yet another World Bank loan. Interaction with transport planners and engineers from the World Bank and consultants brought in from many parts of the world served to increase IPPUC technicians' access to world-class knowledge in transport planning.

IPPUC was made the supervising agency for national transport projects managed by the federal transport authorities (Empresa Brasileira de Transporte Urbano, EBTU). With growing capacity and confidence, access to loan funds allowed IPPUC and the city to accelerate projects that had already been started—for instance, in road paving, public lighting and transport terminals. As a consequence, Curitiba sprang forward relative to its own timetable and relative to other cities taking part in the EBTU World Bank urban transport project. In effect, IPPUC's presence made the difference in speed and effectiveness of change.

With each expansion and improvement, it became possible to build onto the existing platform of innovations, for instance in signaling systems, buses and tariffs. With the help of technicians from Europe, IPPUC's technical department created a traffic control center and drew upon experience in the Netherlands, Germany and the US of an electronically coordinated signaling system that relied on TV cameras and electronic scanners installed in the roadway at strategic places in the main intersections in town. These fed data to a computerized control system that regulated traffic lights, enabling "green waves" and speedier traffic flow for special periods during the day. Though it is common in many cities of today, IPPUC was among the first of Brazilian cities to make use of high-tech gear in traffic management.

One of the most important innovations was in transit revenues. Partly due to the pressure of the oil crisis, IPPUC began work on a unified tariff scheme for public transport. In 1979, a system of single tariffs—part of the Integrated Transportation Network (RIT)—was established across the city. This innovation made it possible for operators of small bus lines, including feeder and transfer lines on the periphery where little money could be made, to stay in service. A cross-subsidy built into the integrated transportation network compensated operators on smaller and less popular routes, while larger ones running bus routes in the more lucrative downtown areas could still turn a profit (Rabinovitch and Leitmann, 1996).

The idea of revenue sharing underscores a feature of planning in Curitiba that runs right through the city's experience from the very beginning of IPPUC. The many innovations in Curitiba contributed and benefited from an intangible factor that characterized planning in the 1970s and 1980s. An atmosphere had been created in Curitiba in which planning was an accepted practice. The visible and interventionist role of IPPUC was tolerated partly because the system had demonstrated concrete achievements. Building up step by step, planning, and particularly transit planning, could point to tangible benefits and these in turn reinforced a sense of acceptance in the wider political environment. These circumstances were tested in a subsequent period of development.

Box 7.2 *Coordinating and managing public works*

In March 1977 the municipality signed an agreement that drew upon IPPUC's comparative advantage in data gathering and management to improve coordination of public works and services. IPPUC's Data Processing Center together with other units developed a management system for public works on roads. Later they began to compile an urban infrastructure information system. The management and information systems were intended to increase the efficiency of the supervision process, improve production of reports, and streamline evaluation of contractors and cadastre information by tracking subterranean networks of water pipes, drainage and sewerage lines, underground wires, gas lines, and other infrastructure.

IPPUC created and maintained an up-to-date database of urban spaces. With the introduction of computers, IPPUC could authorize works almost immediately and inform contractors and state agencies about the subterranean networks existing in the section, thus avoiding accidental destruction and breakdowns. The database grew to include bus routes in service, open markets, schools, parking lots, gas stations and hospitals.

Applying innovation to environmental and social issues

The discussion about IPPUC's role in learning and innovation has been quite selective so far, because it has focused on a specific segment of history and a narrow range of applications in transit and land use. Brazil's transition from military to civilian leadership beginning in the 1980s brought new and powerful currents of economic change. First, a protracted period of hyperinflation drove the cost of living up by thousands of percentage points per year. Brazil's macroeconomic performance, and particularly its efforts to control inflation, became an all-consuming effort throughout the 1980s. Second, in the latter half of the 1980s Brazil entered a period of political and administrative decentralization, in which a new constitution and reforms of the state were to bring about popular election of mayors and new powers and prerogatives in planning, spending and management for all of Brazil's local governments.

The first elections in Curitiba were won by somewhat populist figures whose political objectives aimed in part to soften the impact of hyperinflation on the poor. The city elected two consecutive populist governments between 1983 and 1988. The period was also marked by strong partisan political influences. Because IPPUC was largely identified with the party out of favor, the organization began to shape an adaptive strategy. It shifted its focus from physical infrastructure toward a more socially relevant agenda. At the same time, IPPUC was downgraded from a semi-autonomous agency directly linked to the mayor to a typical municipal bureau (secretariat), on a par with public works and engineering. Many foreign technicians left the Institute. Shifts in the political environment at the national level influenced the allocation of international financial assistance, which was diverted to other cities, drying up external financial flows once enjoyed by IPPUC.

Yet IPPUC was left with a heritage of valuable assets in the form of large databases on social and physical infrastructure, including a geographical information system that covered schools, health clinics and daycare centers in each of seven distinct regions that had been identified by socio-economic and research units beginning in the late 1970s. In 1985, IPPUC participated in the census of Curitiba together with the Brazilian Institute of Statistics (IBGE). A new data management unit was created (SCITAN), and it mapped highly detailed information for every city block. Today, IPPUC's data form the basis for cadastre registers (land ownership and value) for the municipality and provide an important input to IBGE for the national census on residential housing carried out every 10 years.

This database came in handy for social planning. With the turn toward social concerns, the structuring of neighborhood associations began to be encouraged and consolidated, and IPPUC could offer comparative data to deal directly with these associations. About 500 neighborhood associations were organized by the populist local governments, and IPPUC played a role in exploring or creating site-specific solutions for problems in many of these neighborhoods. For instance, about 50 daycare centers and 25 health clinics were created to extend better service in selected areas of town. IPPUC's technical units in social analysis began to work more closely with municipal bureaus of health, youth and education.

IPPUC took part in creating many social innovations during this period (see Box 7.3, below). The "trash that is not trash" program is one of the most inventive. Squatter settlements in Curitiba, as in most cities of Latin America, form in high densities in areas such as hillsides and flood plains. In these areas, customary mechanized methods of solid waste removal do not work well. The "trash that is not trash" program was aimed at solving this problem. The first step was to shift popular understanding about household wastes. The central idea was to create incentives for residents in *favela* areas to recycle their own wastes in exchange for bus tokens, and later food staples.

Residents separated and recycled waste, carrying it to dumpsters placed conveniently around the edge of densely settled areas. A private contractor emptied the dumpster bins once a week, and took the bags to a processing center owned by the city. The facility employed homeless people and recovering alcoholics to sort the trash into their respective waste streams by type. The trash-purchase scheme and the "trash that is not trash" program were linked. The proceeds from the sale of the recycled materials went to finance the purchase of surplus food from farmers. The food was then given in exchange for collected trash (Tlayle and Biller, 1994: 92).

Box 7.3 *Social innovations*

These and other schemes arose in part due to a shift in focus onto fine-grain social problems, in keeping with the electoral changes registered at the polls during the difficult economic times of the late 1980s. IPPUC analysts

were involved directly and indirectly in the creation of numerous innovations to solve typical urban problems. Besides trash recycling, other
programs helped to solve the problems of congestion and the choking of
downtown streets by street vendors.

- The problem of street vendors clogging thoroughfares is common
  throughout the developing world. In Curitiba, the number of vendors
  reached a peak in the mid-1980s. IPPUC participated in the organization
  of these small-scale merchants (often known as the "informal sector")
  into an association, in which 600 people were registered. A visual communication program was launched to support a project to design and
  build 600 metal carts on wheels. These were attractively painted, covered
  with small awnings and placed in regulated parking lots in 200 corners
  in the downtown area. The carts were leased at low rates to the vendors,
  who through their own association exerted a preventive force to keep
  new "informal" vendors from establishing themselves in the downtown
  area.

- One of the most notable innovations was the "tube station." Shaped
  like a long cylinder, the station is an above-grade loading platform
  where passengers embark and disembark at the level of the bus carriage,
  much like a passenger platform at a metro station. Bus fares are paid
  inside the tube before boarding. These two innovations—level of entry
  and pre-paid fares—greatly accelerated the speed of passenger transit
  time between bus stops. In a second innovation, small express buses
  (*ligeirinhos*) were added on fast routes with fewer stops. The combination of these changes helped to solve the problem of traffic jams.

- In 1985, a compulsory transportation voucher, to be deducted from
  worker payrolls, was established by federal law. Curitiba was well prepared to implement this policy. Transportation vouchers in the form of
  coins had already been created. These were sold in advance and kept
  their value for public transit in spite of constant increases in the cost of
  living during hyperinflationary years.

- All of the schools teaching physically or mentally handicapped students
  were registered with the city. Buses amended regular routes to cover
  those schools, with public servants working as attendants in these buses
  between home and school.

Flood control and parks

Curitiba lies at the confluence of several key tributaries that flow to the Paraná River at the border between Brazil, Paraguay and Argentina. One feeder system, dominated by the Iguaçu River, cuts through Curitiba. When the city was small, the rise of the Iguaçu during the rainy season was uneventful because a wide floodplain absorbed the high waters. Starting in the 1950s, the city's horizontal expansion spread onto this floodplain, resulting in chronic losses of property and life.

Engineering solutions to this problem were unsuccessful because channeling the rivers simply transferred the floods to other areas. City authorities realized that it was necessary to recover the floodplain. A concerted effort to expropriate areas along the courses of the rivers and build small dams led to the creation of large parks and lakes that today are Curitiba's main recreational sites. Concurrently, new land use regulations regarding the division of land into plots for housing development prohibit the construction of streets and buildings in strips subject to flooding.

In creating parklands and recreational areas, IPPUC was instrumental in devising and analyzing land swaps and management schemes. For instance, the Passaúna Park was created to protect a river and its system of springs that supply one-third of Curitiba's water. The area was declared an "environmental protection area" under legislation that grants tax incentives for the preservation of forest cover. Further, the law allows only up to 30 percent of the area to be used for construction. The choice of sites and the building parameters are subject to local approval. Similarly, new housing developments in non-drainage areas must dedicate 35 percent of the land area to the public domain for environmental purposes.

The overall result is a city with one of the highest ratios of green areas per capita (50 square meters per inhabitant) among Western cities, providing its citizens ample recreational and cultural sites, more than 140 km of bicycle paths, neighborhood parks, and in-city forest reserves (Tlayle and Biller, 1994). With the expansion of park and flood control areas, Curitiba increased green space per capita by a factor of 10, giving the city a claim to being "an ecological city." Oliveira (2001) challenges this claim, suggesting that environmental sustainability of parkland, solid waste and transport were more of a packaged afterthought than an explicit objective driving these programs. Whether premeditated or not, the progress and innovative solutions to typical urban problems produced results that are studied and replicated in many cities in Latin America.

Some of the ideas for these innovations were dreamt up locally, others were borrowed from outside. Land swaps to accommodate control over floodplains were inspired by Japan's land-swap system. The Normandy Basin Authority in

France shared its educational kits to measure water quality for use by students in secondary educational institutions. Some novelties originated inside IPPUC, such as educating children and parents about riverways and flood risk using creative devices like colorful artwork depicting inquisitive fish painted on elevator walls and in school stairwells. The fish inquired of the viewer: "Where is the nearest water?" The images implanted a daily reminder about the city's relationship to natural waterways and its vulnerability to floods.

Other think tank cities

IPPUC in Curitiba may not be the first or even the best think tank for a city.[6] But IPPUC represents a sustained and productive record of innovations over five decades. Moreover, the IPPUC case illustrates many key lessons that other cities—Juárez and Amman are discussed below—have learned in adopting a technical learning model like a think tank.

IMIP in Juárez

Though Juárez has been overwhelmed in recent years by the devastating violence of arms and drug trade between Mexico and the US, the city set a standard for planning with the its Instituto Municipal de Investigación y Planeación (IMIP—Municipal Institute for Planning and Research). In 1994, Francisco Villareal, one of the mayoral candidates for Juárez, visited Curitiba to learn more about its successes. He was impressed with the way IPPUC was shielded from partisan political influences in the management of day-to-day technical decisions. The short terms of office in the Mexican municipal system precluded the institutionalization of technical capacity. A typical scenario featured a new mayor every three years and a wholesale turnover of technical staff along with those holding posts of confidence. Sometimes even files and archives about municipal business were removed from offices with the outgoing administration.

After he was elected, Villareal founded IMIP. By having IMIP created in state legislation, he aimed to build a strong wall of separation from political influence and to lay the groundwork for institutional stability. In addition, the enabling legislation stipulated that private and civic individuals were placed on the board, that the board was empowered to hire the director, and that the terms of office were staggered with those of municipal elections.

With a guaranteed percentage of the municipal budget, and the rights to hire and fire employees on a private sector basis, IMIP enjoyed success. Its independence allowed it to build up a strong professional team. In turn, high-quality technical work earned the respect of business and civic and local officials. These factors helped to clear away conflicts of interest in land use planning and to manage urban growth. The management system had an open style. Each of the half dozen key topical areas—for example, land, legal, social, geographical information system (GIS)—was managed by a technical coordinator. The team members were encouraged to challenge each other and were permitted to speak independently with the public and the press.

The founding director, Luis Felipe Siqueiros, feels that the rich backgrounds of his technical staff were especially important for IMIP's research, which the director feels is one of the institute's main functions. The team put together high-quality maps and data based on a geographical information system that covered the social and physical parameters of the city. IMIP built a library of documents, maps and planning materials, including interactive data from the GIS. The library became one of the most important in northern Mexico.

That richness was strengthened by regular sabbatical visits from Brazilians. According to one World Bank officer, Curitiba began to refer to IMIP as its "franchise" in Mexico.[7] Exposure to outside ideas helped to form the technical and operating style of IMIP. Periodic exchanges on the part of the director to Canada, the US and Europe built upon years of academic study in France. Both the director, who earned his doctorate in urban planning in Paris, and the mayor, who spent years in Paris, were strongly influenced by European urbanism.

Institutes similar to IMIP began to spring up in other cities in Mexico. León established its own planning institute at about the same time as IMIP was being formed. By 2005, 11 institutes belonged to the Mexican Association of Municipal Planning Institutes and nearly 30 more were in the process of formation.

Ai in Amman

A similar pattern of exerting rational control over urban planning is found in Amman, Jordan with the founding of the Amman Institute (Ai) in 2005. The Ai was created on the fly, so to speak, to cope with burgeoning speculative construction of high-rise buildings in downtown Amman. The pooling of petrodollars in oil-exporting countries, together with tensions in several countries of the Middle East, stand in contrast to the relative stability of Jordan, making Amman an attractive place for investment. Proposals for dozens of high-rise towers financed by funds from Iraq, Saudi Arabia and other Middle Eastern nations began to flood into the city for approval in the early 2000s. The first of these produced large, speculative buildings that were out of character with their surroundings;

sitting on the ridge outcroppings of Amman's many arroyos, they were conspicuous in size, prominence and form.

Alarmed at the prospect of runaway growth, King Abdullah II turned to his mayor, Omar Maani, a successful entrepreneur whom the King had recently appointed. Through the Prime Minister, the King instructed Maani to prepare new regulations and land use plans for the downtown area. Maani in turn mobilized the expertise of BearingPoint consultancy, which was already on contract to the city to conduct real estate analysis. Seeing the broad scope of work and far-reaching implications of the new plan, one of BearingPoint's principals, Gerry Post, proposed that the team being assembled for the analysis and planning effort be transformed into a city-owned, for-profit entity, which came to be called the Amman Institute. Ai has undertaken a half-dozen innovative initiatives to tax building, reform the business process and reshape the organizational structure of the city, improve transit and solid waste, and mobilize popular participation in city affairs.

The pressure of growth and need for fresh planning expertise were part of the impetus for city think tanks in many cities, including Ho Chi Minh City, Budapest and Philadelphia. Think tanks or technical teams owned by or formed within their respective cities grew up organically. For instance, the Institute for Development Studies (IDS) in Ho Chi Minh City and the Economy League in Philadelphia evolved over time. The IDS is the latest incarnation of a city agency with a tradition of research, analysis and advice, particularly in connection with land development in Ho Chi Minh dating back to before the Vietnam War. The agency gathers and maintains data on land, property markets and building, conducts studies and forecasts trends.

The Economy League of Philadelphia arose from a tradition of industrial efficiency in the early 20th century. The Economy League cut its teeth by gathering the equivalent of time and motion data for the city. The mission gradually morphed over the decades to become a watchdog, a conductor of studies, an analyst of data, and more recently a convener with an appetite to play a stronger mobilization role in building a constituency for economic development in the greater Philadelphia area, covering nine counties and parts of four states (New Jersey, New York, Pennsylvania and Delaware).

Comparing think tanks

IPPUC, IMIP and Ai may be neither the first nor even the best think tanks, but they do represent sustained and productive records. With the help of Table 7.1 we can examine some of the key features that each of these cases has in common

Table 7.1 Comparing think tanks

Factors	Curitiba IPPUC	Juárez IMIP	Amman Ai	Economy League of Greater Philadelphia
How are they born	Floods, congestion, strong leader and planning tradition	Idea transfer from Curitiba model, need for independent analysis	Emerging wave of speculative high-rise construction downtown leads to Royal imperative	Business community wanted efficiency studies of public sector (1909)
Relationship to the city	Private, city owns main share, sits on board	Autonomous public, city on board	Private, city main shareholder, earns revenues	Work on projects in relation to the city
Finance	City budget, consulting revenues, fees for service	Fixed percentage of city budget, consulting fees	City budget, consulting revenues, tax increment shares	Business and individual contributions, foundation support, project counselling fees
Learning modality	Internal staffing, extensive exchange	Internal staffing, some exchange	Internal staffing, international exchange	Internal staffing, growing domestic exchange

with the others. These include the circumstances of their origin, organizational and financial relationships with the mother city, and the dimension of learning and "atmospherics" related to innovation.

Origins and structure

IPPUC originated with the conviction that a strong institution would be needed to implement Curitiba's Master Plan, and behind this conviction lay the urgency

of protecting the city from disorganized growth that was leading to vulnerability of losses in flooding and increasing congestion. These tasks required some
degree of functional autonomy as well as certainty about income, both of which
were built into its original design. These in turn provided a degree of insulation
from political interference in connection with choice of issues and scope of inter-
vention. Fortunately for Curitiba, many of the outcomes related to these issues
were favorable, and management control by the governing council, with broad-
based linkages to stakeholders, helped to maintain its autonomy to some degree.

Getting a hold of key issues like land is a common theme that runs right across
the examples in Table 7.1. Perhaps the most telling example of this, and one that
is fitting in the learning context, is the formation of IMIP in Juárez, Mexico.

Making a living

Financial sustainability is perhaps the most pressing issue facing city think tanks.
Unless they are created by a higher-level jurisdiction, and therefore likely to be
protected, think tanks are vulnerable to rising and falling political fortunes. All
were put on a partially commercial footing and all were able to hire on a market
basis, a factor that is important both in keeping high standards in professional
skill areas and also in ensuring the caliber of people needed to create new value
in knowledge generation. The think tanks vary in the extent to which they meet
a market test by selling data or analysis, but rarely are more than half the recurrent
costs met in this way. For example, Ai earns 40 percent of its income from outside
of Jordan, and IPPUC has long sold transport and data services to cities and states
in Brazil.

Learning modality and atmospherics

The many innovations in Curitiba contributed to and benefited from an intangible
factor that characterized planning in the 1970s and 1980s. For starters, an atmosphere had been created in Curitiba in which planning was an accepted practice,
and IPPUC had a visible and interventionist role, with concrete achievements. With
a string of solid accomplishments, followed by creative invention, IPPUC earned
acceptance as a think group. In the beginning, one of IPPUC's strongest comparative advantages was its high-quality professional staff and an internal working
environment that was characterized by encouragement of what today is called
"out of the box" thinking. Jaime Lerner, the one-time director and several-time
mayor of Curitiba, told me that in the early days of the organization the atmosphere

the plan. In 1990, the city launched Bilbao Metropoli-30, a public–private, non-profit association charged with planning, research and promotion of projects. A group of 19 founding members was drawn from across a broad spectrum of entities in the region, including cities, banks, businesses, universities, publishers, utilities, the port, railroad, and others. The mission of Metropoli-30 was to carry out the revitalization of metropolitan Bilbao.

After long deliberation—a process that involved hundreds of community and regional meetings, together with international learning seminars staged in the city, technical studies and strategy meetings—the association arrived at ambitious and far-reaching conclusions: the future economy of Bilbao would center on the creative arts, information and culture, and learning institutions. This was a radical departure from its historical role as an industrial and shipping center—and some thought a stretch too far for a city whose employment base was poorly suited to knowledge-centric services.

The first major step was the formation of an assembly of stakeholders. The Assembly became a formal institution with appointed leadership and by-laws, and by 1991 it had published its first major product, a general plan also known as Metropoli-30. Funds from Spain and the EU helped to finance the diagnostic and analytical groundwork for the plan.

Internal and external learning

The learning process in Bilbao took place on many levels. Two major forms are noted here. First is the internal process characterized by self-recognition and awareness, starting with the realization that Europe's transformation was leading to drastic economic decline for the city. Many of the agencies and institutions were already aware that their fates were tied to one another. The formation of Metropoli-30 gave them the opportunity to explore and confirm these views.

A second process of learning helped to sustain the continuity of action and conviction. Many learning events—meaning the staging of high-profile speakers, conferences, seminars and roundtables—were held in public in the run-up to the Revitalization Plan, which was published in 1992. These were widely publicized and well attended. They helped to build a community consciousness about the mission of the city and to widen community understanding about the range of possibilities for the city's future.

Box 8.1 *Timeline for Bilbao*

- 1986 Spain joins the European Community
- 1989 Formation of Assembly
- 1991 Creation of Metropoli-30
- 1992 Revitalization Plan
- 1993 Bilbao Ria 2000

  - External Port
  - Abandoibarra, footbridges, Ribera Park

- 1995 Metro System inaugurated
- 1997 Guggenheim Museum
- 1999 Bilbao 2010: The Strategy
- 2000 Airport
- 1990–2005 More than 40 seminars from world-class thought leaders
- 2006 World Forum on Values for City Development
- 2008 European Institute for City Development

The learning process became the hallmark of BM-30. Between 1990 and 2005 more that 40 seminars were held in the city on many topics of urbanism. The events featured world-class thought leaders, authors, academics and practitioners from Europe and elsewhere. Meanwhile, various city leaders were aware of developments in other cities, particularly the transformations being made in Baltimore, Pittsburgh and Glasgow. The key lesson for Bilbao's leadership was the confirmation of the very idea that transformation was possible.[1]

This heartening message helped to drive Bilbao's leaders to take a major gamble on the Guggenheim Museum. The museum was to become the flagship project for BM-30, but in the beginning both sides were anxious. Originally Guggenheim had aimed for a higher-status city, with Vienna a favorite candidate. When Bilbao sent an emissary to make its case, the idea was rebuffed. Later, many remarked that the commitment fee charged by architect Frank Ghery even to consider the site was thought to be exorbitant. But by the mid-1990s, with no suitor at hand, Guggenheim revisited other options. With the help of the European Union, Bilbao mobilized resources to meet the financial requirements of the new museum.

Bilbao's core leadership, Ria 2000 (the executive and implementing arm of the corporate arrangements in Bilbao), the city, the province, and BM-30 were aware that, had the proposition been subjected to a vote, the population would not have approved. The former chief architect of the municipal government, Ibon Areso, recalled that the strategy was to project the idea as an investment in culture rather than expense on a large new project. The accounting firm KPMG calculated that the museum would have to attract 400,000 visitors per year in order to break even financially. The city and province took a big gamble that paid off. Plenty of critical views are still heard about the museum, splendid as it may be, plunked down as if it were an alien spaceship on the banks of the Nervión River. On the other hand, the financial gamble paid off handsomely. The museum is credited with attracting three times the previous level of tourists in the first year.

Following the Guggenheim came nearly a dozen other major projects in and around Bilbao, but mostly focused on the reclaimed waterway, the former site of derelict shipyards and warehouses. In their place were built attractive esplanades, pedestrian malls, a graceful footbridge and other amenities.

World-class architects were retained to design the new airport, metro system, convention center and other public buildings along the Nervión River. In addition, the regional transportation system was upgraded and major improvements were made in university and educational institutions. A decade later, tourism had blossomed in Bilbao. Hotel usage doubled and air travel tripled between 1994 and 2002.

An important part of Bilbao's success is that the city mobilized resources and support from many quarters. The central executive actor was Ria 2000, the agency commissioned to implement Bilbao's strategic plan. Even the considerable economic and financial muscle of the city and of the Basque community would not have been sufficient to achieve Bilbao's transformation. The European Union provided both grant and credit finance. Also, the city brought a large number of organizations and agencies within the Basque region to support its efforts. More than 40 institutions and agencies have subscribed to Metropoli-30, and this organization itself represents a significant achievement.

Box 8.2 *Bilbao Metropoli-30 vision setting*

Bilbao Metropoli-30 regularly takes part in conferences, organizations and networks worldwide. Specifically, the association collaborates with the Urban Forum Network, International Institute of Administrative Sciences (IIAS), Standing Committee on Urban and Regional Statistics (SCORUS), part of the International Statistical Institute (ISI), the System Dynamics Society, the World Future Society, the International Network for Marketing and Urban Development and the Global Business Network (GBN).

> In 1999, a decade after the Strategic Revitalization Plan, the association, with the participation of its members and further support from 20 international experts, launched a study of advanced international models of urban strategy development. The conclusion of "Bilbao 2010" is that success lies in ideas and values, which set the strategy for the future of metropolitan Bilbao. It is a city capable of identifying, attracting and materializing good ideas to benefit the whole community.
>
> Source: Taken from presentation by Director
> General, Bilbao Metropoli-30 (Cearra, 2005)

Academic and policy literature has focused on many issues that arise from downtown revitalization and urban restructuring, particularly at the hands of city-regions practicing "entrepreneurial urbanism." As cities begin to enter into a developmental mode at a regional level, large projects involving wholesale reformulation of urban fabric inevitably have polarizing effects for local populations because of physical or cultural displacement. Yet only a small handful of the scores of articles written about Bilbao pay any attention to the collective learning and the formation of social capital in this process. Etxebarria Kerexeta notes that the "intense participation in strategic conversations between firms and the rest of the players from civil society has decisively contributed to creating high returns from the social formation" (Etxebarria Kerexeta and Franco Ibarzabal, 2003).

BM-30 today

In contrast to the executive role of Ria 2000, BM-30 takes the long-view, visionary and deliberative role. The website lists a running total of 64 workshops and another 50 or so forums, conferences and courses of various types covering urban topics and including urban management. Each year Metropoli-30, with others, organizes or co-sponsors investigative conferences, learning events, workshops and seminars. Increasingly, Bilbao collaborates with cities in other countries including China, Colombia, Denmark, France, Japan, Mexico, the US and the UK, to name only those involved in learning events during 2009. Singapore has represented another turning point in Bilbao's emerging vision of itself as a leading knowledge city.

Recent programs, such as OPENCities, aim specifically to pair Bilbao with European counterparts, in pursuit of specific objectives. Participating cities include

Belfast, Dublin, Dusseldorf, Madrid, Sofia and Vienna. Subsequent phases of the project will bring in Bucharest, Mitra, Poznan and others, along with consultants to develop management indicators.

These and other initiatives (Cities of the Future, for instance, also sponsored by the British Council (Clark, 2008)) are filling out Bilbao's vision of a knowledge-centric urban place. Bilbao is becoming a source of experience and practice. In many cases it acts as the teacher in urban management.

Above all, the lesson from Bilbao is that the city created an entirely new element—a conscientious agency, Metropoli-30—in the city and regional political structure. The key factor is that the structure involved a cerebral function for the city, one that was deliberate in design and concerned itself with the role of knowledge in its long-term development. This collaborative instrument was a significant, possibly indispensable, tool for the city to grow and thrive.

Seattle

In an earlier paper, I categorized Seattle as an "informal" learning system based mainly on the unofficial, though highly organized operation of the Trade Development Alliance of Greater Seattle (Campbell, 2009). Since 2004, I would reclassify Seattle in the corporate category because of the formation of the Puget Sound Regional Partnership (PSRP). In effect, Seattle has evolved a step further. Building on a long record of study missions, in fact as a direct outgrowth of several of them, the PSRP was created to be a forward-planning agency very similar in structure and mission to Metropoli-30 in Bilbao. The main difference is that the PSRP has a very strong research and internal knowledge-generation component.

Seattle's two decades of study missions helped pave the way for a regional institution like the PSRP. Recall from Chapter 4 that Seattle began its study tour program in 1992 with a visit by a small delegation to several European cities. Continuous and repeated visits over nearly two decades have created not just a leadership elite in the city, but also a moving dialogue about issues of common concern. Collective processing of central themes created a mindset in which the collective leadership began to see eye to eye on the need for a supra-local entity that would fill the gaps in data, management and vision that had been left in the breach among the individual jurisdictions and organizations below the level of the state.[2]

One theme, "process paralysis," has been a familiar one in Seattle's extensively participatory culture. The topic came to the surface during the visit to Shanghai, and it had arisen a year earlier in Barcelona. A large contingent of Seattleites took part in both visits. The Seattle delegates were struck by the consensus style of decision making by the leadership elites of Barcelona, a group drawn from all points on the political spectrum, ranging from socialists, organized civil society, conservative business, and political groups from all parties. Barcelona's emphasis on consensus is founded in part on a strong Catalan identity, reinforced by a history of open hostility toward Catalonia by the Franco government.

The impact of these observations on the leadership elites of Seattle triggered a retreat-style meeting at which the assembled group, again drawn from the city, the county, NGOs, the business community, and specialized agencies like the ports, agreed to form a working group to "get their arms around coordination issues." A year later, the PSRP was legally formed, with representation from key elements in government and business, and began laying the plans for economic options and infrastructure needs for Seattle over the long term. The legal formation of the group and pledges to it, including pledges in capital from private industry, were announced at the Munich study tour in 2004.

Many participants I spoke with referred to benefits that endured long after a study tour; for example, when telephoning a government agency or business, and having that shared experience, knowing the face of the "person on the other end of the call." All of this facilitates understanding and the speed of doing business.

Seattle's record of moving together, despite the paralysis, is built in part on its own set of shared values and identity. Some of this is the product of the study missions and all the related Chamber of Commerce and trade engagements that are formed in the city. President of the TDA Bill Stafford feels that the positive reputation of Greater Seattle for working more smoothly than other regions is due in part to good coordination with the public and private sectors and a cohesiveness of view over the long term.

That conclusion was given strong support from the results of a survey of more than 50 of some 350 study-tour veterans. The data showed that a very high proportion agreed that the size and strength of their personal networks had increased as a result of the study missions. These opinions were more moderate when it came to working with people across municipal boundaries, i.e., jurisdictions and places outside Seattle proper. Three-quarters of the respondents agreed or strongly agreed that they were put in closer touch with people in different sectors within Seattle.

Similarly, strong agreement was expressed by respondents about ease of contact and quality research (Table 8.1). These findings suggest that the bonding objectives of the missions are not only being met but that they are paying off with trusting relationships that facilitate quality information flow in the community.

The missions' success is also demonstrated by the high numbers and repeat visits of private sector participants—in effect, meeting a market test of the value

Table 8.1 Network exchange

Follow up with study tour participants	Strongly disagree	Disagree	Neutral	Agree	Strongly agree
Easier to call on someone I did not know before	0	2	7	6	15
Greater likelihood that I will get good answers	0	0	5	9	15
Greatly increase my ability to get information	0	1	4	7	18

proposition of study tours. Further, the missions open rich insights for participants and appear to facilitate high-quality information flow and personal or professional change after mission experiences. The findings also suggest that the study missions are building on their own success, and that they represent a product that is consistently reliable.

More than half the survey respondents said they knew about half or more of the participants on the study missions in which they took part; a little more than 43 percent said that participants on their mission were "mostly new." This finding suggests that mission participants are already bonded to some extent and it may reflect the fact that many participants have been on multiple missions (averaging more than five). In any case, most participants start the mission with a degree of familiarity.

Box 8.3 *A mini-case of idea penetration*

Mayor Greg Nickels became a national figure when he pledged to bring the city to the Kyoto standard for greenhouse gases. Not known for his disposition to adopt international standards as a guide to anything, Nickels was converted to shades of green by pragmatism and a long history of conservation and environmentalism in Seattle, starting with the electricity conservation program of Seattle City Light in 1977.

But Nickels began to become more attuned to the value of sustainable design when he learned of the reduced snow pack in the Cascade Mountains. About this time, Nickels met with Gordon Price, former councilor for the City of Vancouver, and Nickels and his staff grew increasingly interested in Vancouver's densification downtown. Gordon claimed that the developmental trend not only produced a high-quality urban environment but reduced traffic by 13 percent. Visiting the city, Nickels was sold on the idea. He made a presentation to the Chamber of Commerce. Already a player in city-to-city learning, the Chamber helped forge a public–private linkage with a new mayor.

The greening trend picked up steam when Nickels asked the city's chief planner, Dianne Sugimura, to inject "green" into the building code. Sugimura targeted key players in real estate development for lunchtime briefings. She found that she was singing to the chorus. Developers were already oriented to the same green parameters; dozens of buildings and facilities in Seattle had been certified by LEED (Leadership in Energy and Environmental Design).[3] When the plan was presented to the council, key private sector developers were there to endorse LEED-certified building codes. The plan sailed through to adoption.

The repeated exposure to outside ideas and the internal circulation in city dialogue—public and private, formal and informal—had paved the way toward speedy understanding of green innovations in the building code.

Tampere

The learning style in Tampere, whose population is under 300,000, has grown out of a series of deliberate steps sprinkled with opportunism and luck. While the city does not operate with the formal features of Bilbao or Seattle—particularly in written conventions and rules—the cohesive deliberation with which city leaders undertook their knowledge gathering and strategic organization could make it a candidate for a corporate model. Over the four decades between 1960 and 2000, Tampere's economy was transformed from reliance on industry, with 33,000 industrial jobs, to become a knowledge economy with 25,000 students. Today Tampere is one of the foremost knowledge-based cities in Northern Europe. The Tampere case is one of learning to adapt to global influences through tactical and strategic management of global forces and local resources.

During the process, Tampere saw its textile industry decline. But the engineering talent embedded within it and other industries became one of the pillars supporting knowledge-intensive clusters. Tampere was wise to make good use of its engineering talent. The city won the relocation of national universities, and these in turn helped to attract Nokia and other high-tech firms. But steering the process and managing international competitive forces required increasing degrees of coherence and skill on the part of public and private sectors.

During the mid-1990s, this skill was expressed mainly in terms of voluntary cooperation among networks of firms, research organizations, universities, and local and regional governments (Kostiainen and Sotarauta, 2003). The management style then evolved into a development network based on increasingly close ties, which managed to foster institutional entrepreneurship and regional innovation. Tampere's political and business communities effectively created informal corporate governance.

As knowledge-intensive clusters began to form, the city, the universities, and high-tech knowledge industries entered into mutually beneficial relationships that grew in sophistication and brought about a corporate management style. The network consisted of development agencies for economy, industry, innovation and municipalities. Furthermore, the municipalities in surrounding Tampere agreed on a coordinated strategy.

Though it lacks the same formalized, institutional personality of Metropoli-30, and has never had a guiding assembly representing elected officials and their respective jurisdictions (as formed both by Metropoli-30 and the PSRP in Seattle), Tampere's development network achieved a coordinated action plan that fostered innovation in knowledge-based industries. Systemic and continuous policies gradually formed a web-work of agencies and institutions that crisscrossed public, private and civic boundaries. Kostiainen and Sotarauta's graphic illustration is reproduced in Figure 8.1.

Kostiainen and Sotarauta depict the building process in Tampere, Finland in terms of knowledge creation with special reference to the ideas of Nonaka (Kostiainen and Sotarauta, 2003). Recall that Nonaka and his collaborators invoked the term *ba*, a place or space of learning, originally developed to describe intra-organizational knowledge creation and innovation. Tampere is an example that answers some of the questions posed earlier in the book about how a city network, being a more or less tightly coupled policy structure in an urban region, can achieve an environment of knowledge creation and innovation.

Over the past several decades, the direction of change began to merge with the emphasis on knowledge regions. This tendency has had its most visible expression in the EU's Seventh Framework Programme. Today, networked institutions in Tampere function as thought centers for research and development to feed the growth of high-tech and knowledge-based industries in the region. Policies and practices have created an operating environment that allows the city to act on the global stage with adaptive capacity.

In Kostiainen's view, the key feature in Tampere was a versatile group of specialized developers, "each established with purposeful collaboration and

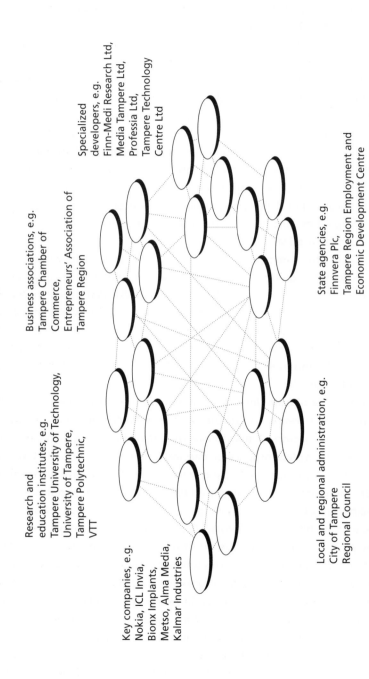

Research and
education institutes, e.g.
Tampere University of Technology,
University of Tampere,
Tampere Polytechnic,
VTT

Business associations, e.g.
Tampere Chamber of
Commerce,
Entrepreneurs' Association of
Tampere Region

Specialized
developers, e.g.
Finn-Medi Research Ltd,
Media Tampere Ltd,
Professia Ltd,
Tampere Technology
Centre Ltd

Key companies, e.g.
Nokia, ICL Invia,
Bionx Implants,
Metso, Alma Media,
Kalmar Industries

Local and regional administration, e.g.
City of Tampere
Regional Council

State agencies, e.g.
Finnvera Plc,
Tampere Region Employment and
Economic Development Centre

Figure 8.1 Tampere's network of actors

Source: Kostiainen and Sotarauta, 2003

ownership as public bodies . . . most focused on a particularly strategic cluster" (Kostiainen, 2002: 617). The city also formed CityWeb, which serves as a "loose umbrella aiming to facilitate launching and carry out projects related to improving preconditions of learning and enhancing of social capital." The Board of the Tampere Regional Centre of Expertise Programme and the Advisory Committee induce dozens of representatives from companies and the public sector to take part. The Centre of Expertise, in Sotarauta's words, has "sought to induce innovation by persuading, through conditioned resources, universities and firms to work together and thus to strengthen the foundation for variation and increased innovation activity" (Sotarauta and Srinivas, 2005). Though they have had mixed results, the policy of induced coordination more or less approximates corporate steering.

Summing up the corporate style

The spectrum of cases illustrates both common and different aspects of a corporate style. First is the reason, or motivation, to learn. Bilbao's leadership elite foresaw a pending crash and mobilized broad-based support to take action and avert a crisis. It succeeded by finding a feasible platform that reflected and in turn shaped the common interests of key stakeholders. Seattle's motivation was similarly triggered by the recession in 1993 and layoffs by Boeing. But the purpose of learning among Seattle elites was one of understanding competition.

A second common feature is that the corporate cases discussed in this chapter, as well as others like Singapore's Urban Redevelopment Authority, have oversight boards and written rules of the game (though not elected representatives, as in Bilbao) about their mission and decision making. Embedded in different ways are learning units, for instance, the Trade Development Alliance in Seattle and the International Group of the Urban Redevelopment Authority in Singapore.

Seattle and Bilbao clear a threshold of effort that serves to deepen and broaden institutional roots. All the corporate cases serve a wide geographical territory made up of many political jurisdictions, but none of these benefit from direct service provision by the entities we are discussing here. Instead, the corporate functions consist mainly of establishing strategic direction alongside gathering data, and setting rules for deliberation and decision making.

In Seattle, the initial configuration was for data gathering and research. It later became benchmarking, and later still, with the PSRP, it became diagnosis, long-term vision, and the means to make changes. Tampere followed a similar trajectory, paying close attention to global cues of price and competition and then, using the network of agencies, suggesting tactical steps to achieve its own vision of a high-tech, knowledge-intensive city.

The learning style in Bilbao and Seattle are mirror images of one another. Both city organizations search out and husband learning; both have a formally desig-nated leadership structure; both have widespread representation from public, private and civic sectors; both have a rule-making and decision-making function; and both seek to help integrate different segments and stakeholders in their respective regions. It is notable also that each city has joined forces, along with another dozen cities, to collaborate on establishing benchmark data. Tampere differs in several ways. Both research and intelligence functions are diffused among its constituent parts and Tampere has no elected members in its delib-erative body.

There is little doubt that informal circles of thinkers and practitioners, busi-nesses and academics did much to process the new ideas in Bilbao, Seattle and Tampere. But the cases are fundamentally different from those relying exclusively on informal and technical learners because there was a decision-making structure that staged learning, ratified lessons, and followed a recognized procedure. The corporate systems have an overlay that guides and moderates the process. In the case of Bilbao, this was needed to keep all stakeholders not only on the same page but in the same book. Some elements in the Bilbao region (Basque Country) might easily have diverted or slowed the modernization project, or worse. On the other hand, the institutional system of invention and agreement for city growth produced in Bilbao a solid foundation for graduating to next steps that are not so clearly evident in Tampere or Seattle.

Seattle's city-regional structure evolved to a corporate one with the formation of the Puget Sound Regional Partnership, which built on the successes of the Trade Development Alliance. This is not to say that the TDA will melt away. On the contrary, it will in all likelihood continue to be the learning and innovation center in Seattle, working in tandem with the PSRP—but increasingly the applications of learning in policy and investment will most likely be lodged in the PSRP.

Notes

1   Personal communication, Ibon Areso, a key figure in Bilbao's transformation.
2   The Trade Development Alliance has also helped purely trade development missions, separate from its study-tour mandate. The TDA organized 26 outbound missions in its 10 years of operation and assisted in the development of 14 others.
3   Leadership in Energy and Environmental Design (LEED) is an internationally recognized certification system created by the United States Green Building Council, which is a

non-profit community of industry leaders working to make green buildings available to everyone in the US, within a generation.

References

Campbell, T. (2009). "Learning cities. Knowledge, capacity and competitiveness," *Habitat International*, 33, pp. 195–201.

Cearra, A. M. (2005). "Governance and city competitiveness: the role of metropolitan economic development agencies" (presentation), OECD International Conference on City Competitiveness, March 3–4, Santa Cruz, Tenerife, Spain.

Clark, G. (2008). "Cities of the future," in British Council (ed.), *The city of the future*, British Council, Madrid.

Etxebarria Kerexeta, G. and H. Franco Ibarzabal (2003). "Reflections on urban revitalisation strategies in old industrial regions. The case of Bilbao," *European Association for Evolutionary Political Economy. 2003 Annual Conference*, Maastricht, The Netherlands.

Kostiainen, J. (2002). "Learning and the 'ba' in the development network of an urban region," *European Planning Studies*, 10, pp. 613–631.

Kostiainen, J. and M. Sotarauta (2003). "Great leap or long march to knowledge economy: institutions, actors and resources in the development of Tampere," *European Planning Studies*, 11, pp. 415–438.

Ploger, J. (2007). *Bilbao city report*, CASE repor 43, Centre for the Analysis of Social Exclusion, London School of Economics, London.

Sotarauta, M. and S. Srinivas (2005). "Co-evolutionary policy processes: understanding innovative economies and future resilience," *Futures*, 38, pp. 312–326.

9 Clouds of trust in style

Each of the previous three chapters describes a style of learning that can be found in many cities. And though the informal style is the most common, often elements of many styles operate in parallel with other modes of learning. Most of all, we have seen that learning depends to some degree on an underlying quality about relationships among those engaged in some major city project, its plans, developments and major events. Although each learning style has its stronger and weaker points, there is something more to the secret of the innovative milieu. This chapter will dive a little deeper into the clouds of trust introduced in Chapter 6 and explore how internal learning—and particularly the atmospheric chemistry of social relations—interacts with the external world of knowledge acquisition, taking Turin, Portland and Charlotte as examples. Let's begin with a review of how learning got started in these places.

Origins of style

The cities started at different times and took quite different routes to success. Recall that Turin accomplished a wholesale turnaround in its political life, impelled by the momentum of the national decentralization policy coupled with strong support for reform at the local level. One pair of authors call Turin the most innovative of the cities covered in a recent study of urban change in Italy (Dente and Coletti, 2009).

Portland established a landmark growth boundary in the 1970s and became a bellwether for US cities by shunning additional freeways in favor of light rail and later in its evolution establishing a growth boundary and emphasizing biking and walking in urban transit. Charlotte also has made wholesale changes in city-center urban form, complemented by light rail and improved bus transit, attention to neighborhood relations, and efforts to resolve social tensions. Charlotte is also more deliberately engaged in the search for future leaders than any of the other cities covered in this book.

Note should be taken that these cities started at quite different historical points in their respective experiences of political, socio-economic and urban evolution, in the sense that each started with a fresh break from the past. Portland is the most advanced in modern strategic planning. It started with a new land use law in 1973. Charlotte launched wholesale reform of its downtown area in the 1970s. These initiatives put the two cities a decade or more ahead in the modern phase of strategic planning in comparison to the other cases discussed here.

Charlotte's single-minded drive toward modernizing its downtown was guided at first by the 1966 Odell plan, an effort that was later modified to create an urban center suited to the city's ambition to become a global leader in the finance sector. This drive ultimately led to major changes in urban form, but the wider and longer-term impacts of changes in Charlotte's land use, transit and social issues came decades later as logical sequels of the Odell plan rather than premeditated elements.

Turin has experienced the most recent clear break from the past. In 1993, the national government promulgated decentralization (in elections, and later in finance and decision making), triggering a political sea-change in participatory governance in Turin that paved the way for its two strategic plans and a successful Olympic Games in 2006.

Clouds of trust

Actors in open urban systems take part in collective learning, even when no explicit, formal arrangements govern the system. Further, trust and value sharing, seen in many doing academic work, have played an important role in the case material in earlier chapters. How is an innovative milieu—the soft infrastructure, or Nonaka's ba—formed in a creative city?

The cases have shown that many interconnections link individuals and their trust networks in each city. We note that all three proactive reformers for which we have detailed network data are categorized as informal. We have yet to gather data on cities that do not fit the reformer category.[1] Still, we can learn something from the evidence we do have and make some educated guesses about the non-reformers.

The extent to which the informants were linked to one another gives some crude snapshot of the environment of trust for that particular time, in that particular domain of planning work. But it is important to note that we are limited in the extent to which we can compare the three cities. Turin and Charlotte are most alike in that the persons interviewed in these cities were members of a well-defined group of activists taking part in a common endeavor at about the same time. The case of Portland is different. There, the network data intentionally sampled a number of distinct groups, who were taking part in activities with differing objectives. The aim in Portland was to examine the extent to which the various domains had interconnecting bridges among them.

The role of informal networks

With these distinctions in mind, what can we say about environments of trust? In each case, interviews revealed instances in which internal networks processed, discussed and absorbed new knowledge and lessons from other cities. For instance, bicycle use in Amsterdam excited the biking enthusiasts in Portland and fueled their inputs into their own city's planning. Light rail seen in Denver and Portland filtered into many discussions held by the leading figures in Charlotte's planning. Similarly, Turin learned from cities like Glasgow and Barcelona and debated openly the specifics of local economic development and strategic planning processes. These instances are not the only knowledge brought into the respective cities, and perhaps not the most important. But in each instance, outside lessons were clearly identifiable reference points brought into the discussion and debate by interviewees as they reflected on their own networks of trust.

The graphics from Chapter 6 are a sample from a small subset of actors in the respective civic processes in each of these cities. But in each case the cities went to lengths to tap into sentiment across a broad spectrum of social groupings in the community. For instance, Portland and Charlotte had a deliberate practice of mobilizing many clearly delineated but overlapping interest groups. Over time in Portland, park and open space supporters forged ties and alliances with cyclists, urban trails advocates, and public transit enthusiasts and have either been invited or have otherwise made their way into the city's decision-making circles.

Charlotte was somewhat more deliberate about assembling networks, beginning with "The Group," formed with reference to a similar arrangement its members had observed in Pittsburgh. The Group expanded and for several decades was a central actor in plotting Charlotte's future. With retirements and the rapidly changing financial sector in recent years, Charlotte is now developing a new generation of leaders.

Features of informal clouds

Although the city clouds resemble one another in general form, each city presents a distinct overall pattern. And because of the small sample size, they cannot be compared in any strict sense. On the whole, Turin and Charlotte are both rather tightly knit. They differ very little in arithmetic indicators that measure networks, for instance overall density and average distance (Table 9.1). Density refers to the number of connections present as a proportion of the total connections possible, the range of which is 8.5 percent in the case of Charlotte and 10.5 percent in the case of Turin. Average distance between any two ties is also small, less than a half a tie, 3.57 vs 3.98.

What do these figures mean in practice? Let's take Profumo, the University Rector in Turin. He would be less than four links away, on average, from any of the more than 100 people named in the Turin network. Average distance, for instance 4.43 in Portland, means that, taking all linkages into account, any member of the network is a little more than four links away from any other. Diameter, another reflection of coherence, is the number of nodes across the entire graph. In short, one might say that the informal network in Turin is tight, and that of the other cities less so.

Several other features of the networks bear scrutiny: the power positions and the isolates. In all the cases, several people were named repeatedly. They are what social network analysts call "power nodes," because these persons gather information from many sources and can exercise discretion about when, with whom, and how to divulge what they know (Borgatti et al., 2002). They may also be latent leaders. Network members interviewed for this study did not always recognize the degree to which popular figures were interconnected with one another, nor did interviewees always recognize the extent to which specific individuals had the trust of their peers, or conversely were isolated, sometimes completely, from their peers. The discovery of this information proved to be surprising for many of the interviewees.

For example, in Turin, though the current mayor is an obvious and well-recognized political leader in the community, the most frequently named trusted

Table 9.1 Coherence measures

City	Density	Av. distance	Diameter
Portland	0.085	4.432	8.000
Charlotte	0.085	3.976	6.000
Turin	0.105	3.569	6.000

Charlotte

Portland

Turin

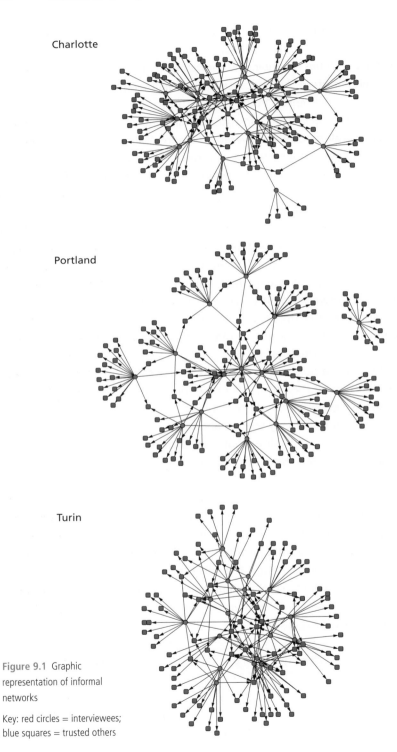

Figure 9.1 Graphic representation of informal networks

Key: red circles = interviewees; blue squares = trusted others

persons were not in the public sector at all. That prize went to people in the business and academic communities. Charlotte offers a different picture. That city is going through a serious transition in its leadership. The older "benevolent dictators" have passed, and trust is directed most often toward the CEO of a major foundation.

As for isolated characters (good examples are the two circles in the lower right of Charlotte in Figure 9.1), these represent interviewees whose references coincided with no one named by any of the others interviewed and to whom no other interviewee made reference. These may merely be the anomalies of a small sample, but they nonetheless illustrate a real concern because they are like sink holes in a community of trust.

Other findings relate both to the growth of new edges and the durability of networks of trust. Data in Portland and Turin showed clearly how new members not previously linked to traditional power elites were inducted or welcomed into established networks during the planning process. A common theme heard in the speech of young persons interviewed in Portland—"it's not done yet," "you get heard"—reflected an openness to young people and new ideas. Participants involved in strategic planning in Turin found the new openings created by Mayor Castellani both unexpected and unprecedented. Several interviewees explained that they had not anticipated being a part of the deliberative efforts in strategic planning in Turin, since they were not connected to "the right family," the "right industry" or the right "social patron."

Looking a level deeper

We can weed out many of the connections shown in the city clouds and drill down to connections only among those interviewed. The rationale for doing this is that the lists of trusted others provided by the interviewees contain no information about whether any of the trust avowed by an interviewee is reciprocated by the other. Looking specifically at the reciprocal directions of trust tells us a little more about the trust value of the cloud. Figure 9.2 illustrates these mutual trust ties.

Here, a somewhat different character emerges from what we might call the internal part of the clouds. Turin's internal cloud is composed of five individuals (each with four or more ties, and a density of 0.1838—see Table 9.2). These individuals are clearly leaders, operating in the core. For Portland, core individuals are named less often than in Turin, reflecting the wider sample that we saw in the complete cloud (density 15.7). In other words, the inner core of trust in Portland is more spread out. At the same time, both Turin and Portland have one isolated character not included as a part of anyone's trust group.

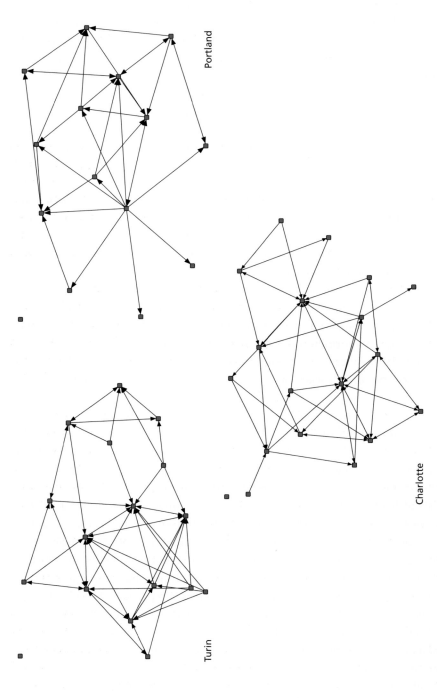

Figure 9.2 Reciprocal ties of trust in city clouds

Key: blue = interviewees; isolated blue squares = no reciprocal relationships with others in the cloud of trust

Table 9.2 Cohesiveness measures in three city clouds

	Charlotte	*Turin*	*Portland*
Density	14.6	18.4	15.7
Distance	2.4	2.4	2.3
Compactness	0.38	0.36	0.33

Though Portland is not the least dense of the three sampled networks, the overall structure (especially diameter) connects a wide range of subgroups, about a dozen of them surrounding the perimeter of Portland's "core." Peripheral groupings could all be considered something akin to Granovetter's loose ties (Granovetter, 1973), in the sense that they are not directly connected to many others elsewhere in the network. These small clusters represent sources of ideas that are likely to be different from the consensus ideas that are manufactured and circulated in the core.

Granovetter theorized that loose ties of roughly this kind are "bridges" to sources of fresh and out-of-the-box thinking. In contrast, strong ties, bonds of family and close friends (ties that also entail reciprocal obligation), are less likely to provide new or fresh information. Strong ties therefore offer less chance of a bridge to new resource connections. Loose ties in Portland's case might mean that it has more access to that key idea from out of the blue that just might solve the problem at hand.

Conversely, the comparative advantage of tighter coherence in Turin would be the speedy transfer of ideas between and among members in the network, perhaps with the fillip of being able to reach a consensus more quickly. But though they are fast and coherent, Charlotte and Turin might not have the range of options that Portland could develop with its links into many peripheral interest groups. Charlotte falls somewhere in between these "extremes," with a distance equivalent to Portland but a tighter overall grouping.

In short, the internal networks of the three cities offer insight into many aspects of processing and exchanging planning information. Tight networks offer some advantages, e.g., speed of circulation, which is the obverse to the advantages of loose networks, e.g., access to a variety of ideas. Arguments can be made about how each can serve the planning process. One area of interest is whether a few adjustments in key linkages within a network would be sufficient to increase both speed and diversity, an idea that has been raised by some scholars (Lazer and Friedman, 2007). Also, data of this kind offer insight into possibly "hidden" leaders or information power centers. Another story emerging from this analysis is about the openness and growth of networks, a point that is of potential importance in meeting new challenges posed by groups of foreign and immigrant talent taking up new positions in cities.

Forming a "ba"

The cases suggest that new knowledge in general, and being proactive in acquiring new knowledge in particular, are associated with successful outcomes in terms of urban transformation. Learning appears to be both acquired for purposes of, and associated with improvements that enhance, competitiveness, at least in the eyes of interviewees. It remains to be shown whether this association can be demonstrated with more objective rigor.

The questions posed here, and the data generated, suggest a new window of inquiry in urban development. The findings also suggest that external and internal learning constitute a kind of soft infrastructure and are intricately involved in transformations. To the extent that this is true, city and national policy may wish to look more favorably on learning and seek to facilitate the process rather than treat it with indifference, as is the case in some cities.

More evidence is needed at both macro and micro levels to establish more clearly the importance of external knowledge gathering as opposed to other forms of learning and to map out the translation of new knowledge in competitiveness. For one thing, further observation will help to understand the processes of absorption and adaptation and may have useful insights in terms of the speed and coherence of city development policy. Further analysis along these lines would also help to establish the overall scope of exchange currently ongoing, to document the scale of demand as well as the costs and benefits of this and other, complementary or competitive, forms of learning.

The findings also suggest that informal trust networks may be a useful indicator of soft infrastructure, although much additional work is needed to clarify and understand these ideas. The tools of social network analysis promise both to describe and quantitatively to measure variables of connectivity and trust in a way that can be compared both over time and across space. One area of work that could be researched further relates to the fact that cities achieve knowledge processing by different routes, perhaps trading off speed of reaching consensus against richness and diversity in potential solutions.

A second area of interest, one that concerns many cities coping with the management of global talent, is that of attracting new social capital or managing the stocks already in town. The three cases here have shown quite distinct styles of incorporating new blood into informal planning networks, somewhat aligned with the styles of diversity and speed, discussed earlier. The findings also suggest that the shape of networks may matter as much if not more than their size.

The analysis of these case cities has attempted to reveal the tissue and features of a city's ba. The networks tell us part of the story; leadership and participation another part; the learning style itself yet another.

Learning from abroad

Fluid social relationships internal to the city form the glue of ba. What about the knowledge, the second aspect of milieu? Right off the bat, it's useful to recall that all the cities exhibited most of the characteristics of "proactive reformer cities" mentioned earlier. Proactive reformers are deliberate in having learning strategies, they sustain an effort to acquire and store knowledge, they are committed to allocating substantial public resources for learning, and they believe in building capacity to manage knowledge. Though wide variations can be seen in the degree of use and importance accorded to one mechanism or the other, both fluid social relationships and knowledge were amply evident in each of the cases.

> **Box 9.1 *Barcelona mini-case***
>
> Barcelona is often cited as a benchmark for achieving innovative reform. Catalonia, the region of which Barcelona is the capital, moved most quickly of all the Spanish regions after the 1975 death of Franco to strengthen regional identity and political autonomy. The city then stood at the center of a political renaissance in Catalonia.
>
> Barcelona has benefited from many resources for learning not readily available to the other cities considered in this analysis. Barcelona's early (1980s) drive to establish a regional identity, then to bid for and hold the Olympic Games, and form a metropolitan organization all benefited from extensive exchange. For instance, the Barcelona Metropolitan authority (now defunct) organized many targeted visits, among them trips to Warsaw to study labor relations, Helsinki for health and education, and Stockholm for waste incineration. Each of these cities was chosen with care, and delegations of metropolitan representatives participated in order to facilitate consensus on how to move forward at home.
>
> In the late 1990s, Barcelona began to transform its economy by emphasizing knowledge-intensive industries in the form of biomedical and life

sciences and university education, and created a specialized innovation district known as "22@Barcelona." This push for knowledge intensity, combined with expanded facilities in international conferencing, put in place the foundations for a self-reinforcing process of city learning. Barcelona's leadership was aware that Bilbao and Madrid were pursuing similar strategies. Bilbao eventually proclaimed itself a "learning center with the institutionalization of knowledge management." Partly because of this competition, Barcelona's learning effort reached a wider array of global destinations than did the smaller cities considered in this study.

Exposure to outside influences

The cities recognized that applicable lessons could be found in other cities. No matter what their starting point or area of interest, each city has engaged in a serious, conscientious and sustained effort to seek out knowledge from other cities and bring back lessons for application to problems back home. Table 9.3 presents a few of the many features—organizing sponsor, delegation size, themes

Table 9.3 City-to-city exchanges: typical features

City	Routine sponsor or organizer of visits	Typical delegation size	Sample themes	Example of city visited
Barcelona	City, Chamber of Commerce and LED* agencies	25–75	Partnerships with private sector; venture capital	Seattle, Silicon Valley
Charlotte	Chamber, LED agency, GMF*	40–75	Land bridges, light rail	Amsterdam, Portland
Portland	Chamber, GMF	45–70	Land use, bicycles in transit	Copenhagen, Brussels
Turin	City, LED agencies, Chamber, GMF	25–50	Strategic planning, land use, economic development	Barcelona, Stockholm, Glasgow

* Note: LED = local economic development; GMF = German Marshall Fund

and hosts—typical of learning from external sources. Barcelona is included for comparison in Table 9.3.

All the cities engaged in a program of visits, some of which have been sustained over decades and involved multiple and direct exchanges covering a diverse set of issues. The cities were deliberate in their searches and acquisitions of lessons. They identified specific objectives, selecting cities that were experienced in similar issues of policy and practice in infrastructure, services or social issues.

Figure 9.3 presents a schematic diagram of some of the cities cited by interviewees as study destinations.[2] On the whole, each of the cities conducted at least one visit per year—almost certainly an undercount, given the limitations of this inquiry. The graphic shows that Barcelona has connected with a wider geographic array of cities (as is the case with most cities in the population range of five million or more). The other three case cities, all smaller in population, stayed mainly in Western Europe and the US. A handful of cities attracted visits from both sides of the Atlantic.

At the same time, many differences distinguish external learning in these case cities. As we shall see in the ensuing discussion, visits organized by business and trade interests often, but not always, operate on more commercial criteria with a somewhat narrower focus than those organized by the City Hall or city development agencies. For example, Barcelona's visit to Silicon Valley (indicated in Figure 9.3), organized by the Development Agency and the Chamber of Commerce, was aimed at exploring the robust system of venture capital in the Valley. No such system has been developed anywhere in Spain, and many businesses were vitally interested in supporting high-tech startups being launched in Barcelona. In contrast, Turin's visits organized by the City Hall and Portland's sponsored by the Comparative Domestic Policy Program of the German Marshall Fund of the United States aimed at issues more in the public realm—for instance, strategic planning and democratic participation in Turin, and bicycles and open space in Portland.

In the case of Turin, specific and well-targeted connections were arranged to help the city guide its own work in two strategic planning cycles during the period 1993–2005. During each period of strategic planning, Turin arranged for guest presentations to be made by visiting delegations from European cities. Recall that in Turin's first planning phase, when the idea of a strategic plan was novel there, five cities with well-known achievements in strategic planning (Barcelona, Bilbao, Glasgow, Lyon and Stockholm) were invited in sequence to present their experiences to a local audience of planners and the public. The audience included a wide cross-section of Turin's political leadership, its technical professionals, and business groups, as well as the broader public.

Charlotte was similar to Turin, though on a smaller scale and with the Chamber of Commerce taking a more active role, for instance, focusing on downtown urban

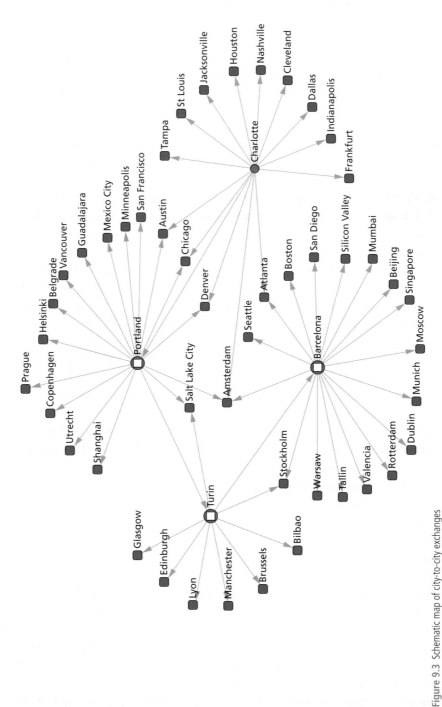

Figure 9.3 Schematic map of city-to-city exchanges

Key: circle = sending city; square = receiving city; square over circle = both design and infrastructure. Charlotte's visit to Portland studied practical and financial issues in the light rail system. Chamber of Commerce visits to Amsterdam and Denver were cited in interviews as being helpful in understanding issues about moving people in higher-density, downtown spaces. In the latter half of the last decade, the focus in Charlotte began to shift toward its fast-moving demographic picture and a variety of other issues connected to the city's changing economic fortunes brought on by the globalization of the financial sector and the recent financial crisis.

These learning experiences triggered an intensive, introspective approach to civic and racial relations in Charlotte, covering issues such as inter-neighborhood equity, quality of education, and civic leadership. These fundamental changes provoked the city to conduct a "self-visit"—organized by the Chamber of Commerce with good reviews from participants—to focus internally on the economic and social issues affecting Charlotte.

City-to-city learning in Portland was pursued explicitly as a source of new knowledge, and recently, in contrast to Turin's concern with strategic planning, Portland has focused on what might be called second-generation public-goods issues arising from earlier innovations in land use regulation. Many complicated ramifications flowed from the imposition of the physical growth boundary put in place in the 1970s. The planning focus fell onto the integration of land use with transit, and in particular with light rail, streetcars, walking, bicycles, and the connections between mobility, green space and livable neighborhoods.

Many respondents from Portland spoke of "eye-opening" insights about the use of bicycles and walkways in Amsterdam and Copenhagen. These cities view pedestrian modes as functional elements in the overall transit network. Portlanders learned that paths for biking and walking have "to have a destination." The European cities taught Portland that bicycles and walkways were not merely aesthetic or recreational elements, but legitimate, even essential parts of the urban transit system.

Summing up external ties

In sum, the cities shared a strong interest in city-to-city learning, but differences are evident in agency, sponsorship, purpose, and destination of learning. On the whole, US cities tended to be led somewhat more by business groups, while European cities were led by City Hall and economic development agencies. Portland and Charlotte relied mostly, but not entirely, on city visits driven by the Chamber of Commerce or other local business groups in annual, well-attended and productive events. Interspersed with these were specific visits organized by outside groups such as the German Marshall Fund. Somewhat in contrast is Turin, where the city and its agencies (economic development and *Torino Internazionale*, an agency whose mandate is to implement strategic plans) took the lead. Turin's business groups were involved, but were secondary or at least were not alone in driving the process and shaping the agenda. Similarly, in Barcelona the metro agency planning unit designed learning visits, and these were complemented by other development groups as the city's global intentions began to gain momentum.

Comparing organizational styles of learning

What about the other styles of learning, the technical and corporate? How do these stack up in terms of acquisition of knowledge and internal relationships? The styles of proactive cities have advantages and drawbacks and they can be compared in relation to four factors. These are:

1   their relative flexibility of change in response to new circumstances;
2   the degree to which they are participatory;
3   the extent to which newcomers must overcome barriers to enter the planning
    elites.

The modalities also vary in

4   the way knowledge is managed and stored and how it is converted to reform
    and innovation.

We look at each of these in turn.

Flexibility in structure

The informal operating style in Turin and Charlotte allows the cities a freewheeling ability to deploy the mechanisms of learning flexibly. Indeed, some of the learning in Charlotte—by the Chamber of Commerce, for instance—was conducted separately and independently from others in the central core of planners. Seattle is a case where exactly the opposite is true. The large and evolving central core shapes the agenda and point of view of the Puget Sound Regional Partnership. On the other hand, the Charlotte group could shift focus in rather short order without losing its overall sense of direction. For instance, city leaders showed a long-term drive toward reshaping the downtown area, but also made many short-term forays into issues such as race, schools, community development and inner-city commercial success, all related but not central to the downtown reformation.

Turin's focus was held to a narrower scope by the discipline of strategic plans and later the Winter Olympics. But the airing of opinion and processing of ideas in informal sessions, like the Mayor's Friday tea and innumerable public planning meetings, allowed for consideration of a wide array of ideas.

Opening the door to new issues was more restrained in cities with relatively technical and corporate learning styles. Amman and Curitiba operate with more narrowly defined agendas which, once analyzed internally, are put before a wider audience. Portland, though categorized as an informal learning city because of its many interest groups, and particularly the young who find a way to be heard, sometimes has the airs of a technical learner because of the institutionalized and professional mandate of Metro.[3] If a technical meeting is not scheduled, cyclists might be expected to organize a breakfast on bikes on one of the city bridges to grab headlines and make their point. Bilbao's heavy system of ordered meetings and structured agendas makes the process of discovery and deliberation much more predictable, but also more cumbersome. If Bilbao and Seattle did not have executive bodies or boards, they would need to invent an action figure to carry business forward.

Furthermore, styles have evolved. The learning style of the Trade Development Alliance (TDA) in Seattle began perhaps as the most informal and in many ways the most inward of the cases reviewed here. The intense interaction among participants on a study and other missions (trade and special visits) served to break down barriers and forge new bilateral and multilateral understandings among public, private and civic groups. This laid the groundwork for a complementary and more corporate style of learning in Seattle today. Curitiba demonstrated great flexibility in the way its technical resources were deployed and Tampere's loose corporate style allowed for great flexibility by accommodating inputs from many directions.

Participation and barriers to entry

Whether corporate, technical, informal, or a hybrid like Barcelona, all the cities brought a large variety of stakeholders to the table and incorporated them into a formal structure with a balance of power that accommodated deliberation and decision making. Each learning style—loose, technical or formalized—finds a way to identify and incorporate business and civic leaders and other stakeholders into the process of knowledge discovery and validation. Curitiba and Bilbao use highly structured agencies; Portland and Turin used more open, even ad hoc methods. Portland and Charlotte were perhaps most disposed to allow newcomers to break into the conversation.

The structure of the learning group inevitably affects the ease and quality of participation by a wider public. Recall from the Portland story the exclamations by young newcomers in Portland—"you get heard" and "it's not done yet"— which contrast somewhat with the surprise expressed by newcomers in Turin that invitations were received out of the blue. Both systems found a way to get young people into the processing of ideas, but the tight internal connections in Turin contrast with the wider, heterogeneous structure of Portland's cloud. Bilbao, Amman and Seattle, while all professedly open to incorporating public opinion, do so by more structured means. There is a sense that as the cities move "up" the ladder of official representation, the doors of access close a little further. Keeping the doors freely swinging becomes a topic of managerial challenge, one that we address in the next chapter.

Learning and knowledge

The technical group, Amman, Juárez and Curitiba, were especially good at building and storing data. Our global survey showed that having a responsible unit in charge and following up with seminars were generalizable for all the proactive reformers, but think tanks do this best. Corporate models also foster deep reservoirs of knowledge, not just data and statistics but analytical material as well. Seattle and Bilbao have built up a large stock of institutional knowledge. To some extent, the knowledge base in all cities floats around in clouds of trust. But what about the informal style? Are they at a disadvantage by not having more institutionalized storage? Can the knowledge outside relatively shallow working memory in clouds of trust be converted to long-term memory and accessed over time? Informal styles may be flexible, but do they risk tradeoffs of losing access to knowledge over time?

Storage and access are not the only management issues. Turning back to Granovetter's (1983) loose ties, we are reminded that those occasional ad hoc, sometimes accidental encounters are those that are most likely to provide the source of break-out ideas. Certainly all cities can benefit from off-hand discoveries, but few cities can expect much in new knowledge and even less in soft infrastructure by engaging only in casual learning. Accordingly, cities need to manage two types of learning modes, one loose and the other strong.

Getting from knowledge to innovation

Assigning value to knowledge and making efforts to obtain it achieve only part of the formula for innovation. Each of the styles demonstrates a way to achieve the second, innovative, step. The informal cities establish ties on the fly and in specific projects or challenges. For example, the challenges of the Olympic bid in Turin or the change of the guard in Charlotte were met using the capital of trust stored in the network relationships. The innovation involved in winning the bid for the Olympics or creating an interim leadership depended on a central figure or group who could draw the elements together, as the Mayor and the University Rector did in Turin, and as foundations did in Portland. Distributed trust then relied on a point person to act.

Technical cases work differently. Knowledge developed in focal places—the think tanks in Amman, Curitiba and Juárez—and relies on distributed actors to make use of it in innovative ways. Technical strength builds knowledge in a confined way, within their technical cadres, and think tanks relied on their reputations to have good answers for rights of way or land use suggestions.

Corporate bodies draw on both concentration and distribution. Knowledge in Bilbao, Seattle and Tampere is fed into a corporate body from many sources for deliberation, and decisions about innovative uses are taken by representatives of the community both individually and collectively.

Notes

1   The next chapter will delve more deeply into why cities do not learn, or if they do, why they fail to innovate.
2   The cities named in Figure 9.2 are only a partial list compiled from information in interviews and complemented by other sources to reflect activity during a representative span of time, for instance during strategic planning 1993–2005 in Turin, or during 1995–2009 in the other cities. Accordingly, the cities listed here will not coincide necessarily with those appearing in the web-based survey reviewed in Chapter 5. Also, outside agents, such as the Transatlantic Cities Network of the Comparative Domestic Policy Program, have sponsored visits or exchanges involving Turin, Portland and Charlotte. Other programs in the German Marshall Fund have sponsored exchanges, but not always related directly to city issues.
3   Portland Metro refers to the elected metropolitan government of the Portland urban region.

References

Borgatti, S. P., M. G. Everett and L. C. Freeman (2002). *Ucinet for Windows: software for social network analysis*, Analytic Technologies, Harvard, MA.

Dente, B. and P. Coletti (2009). "Measuring governance in urban innovation," *International Research Society for Public Management*, 6–8 April, p. 17.

Granovetter, M. (1973). "The strength of weak ties," *The American Journal of Sociology*, 78, pp. 1360–1380.

Granovetter, M. (1983). "The strength of weak ties: a network theory revisited," *Sociological Theory*, 1, pp. 201–233.

Lazer, D. and A. Friedman (2007). "The network structure of exploration and exploitation," *Administrative Science Quarterly*, 52, pp. 667–694.

Part IV
Secrets of a knowing and accelerating change

10 Taking stock: why some cities learn and others do not

City learning is about the creation of a certain type of social capital. It is not just the novel practices or hot technologies. Learning is about the shared values held by people from all walks of life who care about the city where they live. The day-to-day cross-currents in political interests and economic forces, the interruptions in political terms, the occasional calamity—all make the continuity of management or mayor leadership difficult to sustain in most places. Proactive learning cities are able to count on networks of individuals who learn for and on behalf of their cities. This takes place even in cities like Juárez where civil strife reaches a level of lethal conflict equivalent to wartime. All of the cities that have achieved reforms or innovations have also, as an organized collective, proactively pursued new knowledge as an explicit or implicit part of the change process and managed to convert individual and private learning into a collective capital that benefits the public realm.

One of the chief aims of this book is to bring this learning side of urban development into the open. The learning discussed here is not merely a matter of a mayor bringing home a great idea and issuing instructions to make it happen. Proactive learning cities have a much thicker and better-connected institutional character. Gathering and managing new knowledge in this way is an important aspect of urban development that has been largely overlooked. At the same time, many counter-factual cities need to be explored. Some cities learn, but don't reform. These varying outcomes are explored later in the chapter.

The book has focused on those cities that have proven to be the most ambitious—the proactive and reformer-learners. The aim has been to glean what we can from their experiences, recognizing the many learning channels that operate everyday, ranging from the individual civic-minded neighbor, to the profit-seeking entrepreneur, to burgeoning and proven programs in city twinnings and clusters, and even "grazing." And while cities can benefit from all of these learning channels, the focus has been on spontaneous movement within cities because it shows effective demand and sustained effort. The self-organizing nature of proactive learners helps us to see distinctive features—for instance, in the targeting of learning and the mechanisms for processing and storage—that might help to improve other, conventional forms of assistance, such as, twinning, working in clusters, and conventional technical assistance and institutional capacity building. For instance, twinning and clustering generally impact a narrower community of practice. More important, they must negotiate the objectives and terms of learning in what are almost always asymmetrical relationships in terms of finance and technical knowledge. Of course, the proposition is not either one or the other, twinning or full-blown proactive learners, but how the many kinds of learning are fitted into a strategic pattern as seen in proactive cities.

Taking stock of cities

If we could imagine collapsing global space over the past 50 years, we might see cities as cells under a microscope, their Brownian-like motion directed at intercell buffeting. We would recognize something peculiar in this frenetic interaction. The buffeting is not random, but patterned. The cells visit one another and exchange some mysterious substance. Unlike material exchange, most of which is packaged and shipped at arm's length, knowledge is exchanged personally. Most of the critical knowledge brought into innovative use for the cities discussed in this book has been exchanged within and among networks, but in a face-to-face mode.

The book has argued that there are two reasons for this. First, working policies and practice are complicated and strongly dependent on context. The trained eyes of city practitioners can immediately detect the gravity of contextual differences and gauge whether adjustments can be made to import and adapt the idea successfully. A second reason for face-to-face exchange is that the most experienced learners and wisest organizational gurus realize that bonding internally, among the learning team, is critical to success back home, even if an idea is not picked up on a study tour. The interpersonal exchange of values is vital to the establishment of a free-trade zone of ideas and the creation of an innovative atmosphere.

Perhaps the single most important observation from this review is that, though cities learn in many different ways, a significant part of their learning comes from other cities. It is already evident that achieving urban learning is much more complicated than a straight technology transfer. The learning process and institutional capacity building will run over many years and entail multiple layers of learning.

But the findings in this analysis suggest that cities are making the market. They are not waiting for national or international agencies to set things up for them. They seem to be engaged in learning because gaining well-defined knowledge cuts the risk of loss or failure. Visits on the order of thousands per year suggest that cities are making use of this risk-adaptation model. Policy makers should be thinking about ways to make that market work better, to provide assistance to early adopters, and explore ways to reduce barriers for others to take part.

The approach in the book is to divide the world of cities in several ways. First is to group them by the effort they exert in learning. Recall that my typology ranges from "proactive" to "grazers." They all learn, but the highest pay-offs take place in those cities, proactive learners, that dedicate an agency and spend money on the process. At the middle of the spectrum are cities that share special features, like those that cluster around issues of heritage, health, environment or ports, where learning is focused on specific topics. Close to these in practice are cities engaged in twinning or one-on-one exchanges. At the opposite end of the spectrum from proactive learners, a point where any city might be represented at times, are those that merely window-shop at conferences and expos. Though outside assistance and policy change could help cities all along the spectrum, the focus in the analysis was on the proactive types.

These in turn were further scrutinized in terms of reform and innovation, and we can be confident that proactive cities are also reformers, and that reformers are more likely to document lessons, have an office to manage information, conduct follow-up activities to process knowledge and deepen learning, and above all have well-connected networks to test knowledge and act coherently. These are all mechanisms for discussion, processing ideas, storing information, and converting good ideas to innovative uses.

Frequency of city-to-city visits doesn't appear to predict anything about reform. Rather, if we are to generalize from the reports by survey takers, reform and innovation seem to be more about the time spent on learning—both away and at home—and not about the total numbers of trips made.

Proactive reformers spend more time on learning, visit often and longer, and tend to go after more analytical topics than their cousin non-reformers. Reformers are seeking knowledge on metropolitan governance and local economic development, two of the most pressing and complicated urban issues of the day. Non-reformers tend to be looking for tools and practices of day-to-day business. Cities of both kinds are seeking information on urban transport. Climate change is on the mind of some cities, but this topic was not very much emphasized; certainly it was not given the priority that development assistance agencies would accord to it. An even wider gap in priorities appears to separate cities and development-assistance agencies in connection with gender and HIV issues.

It's also notable that cities are visiting in a pattern that is not exactly in line with trends and policy orientation of nations and the international development community. We have to assume that cities from the South are visiting the North for good reasons, unless we can find evidence to the contrary. But Southern cities are also visiting their Southern neighbors. All directions in this exchange need to be scrutinized further to understand how much travel to the North is linked to shopping in Paris and how much to earnest and legitimate capture of new knowledge about, say, cultural heritage or public–private arrangements in Parisian land use planning.

Why cities do not learn

Despite notable successes here and there, on the whole, a large number of cities, especially in the developing world, are not engaged in learning to be smart. If gaining new knowledge is a risk-reduction strategy, why are more cities not following this path? Why did it take more than three decades for Curitiba's bus rapid transit scheme to spread to other cities in Latin America? Why do successes in a few places not spread more rapidly? We need to ask: why don't cities learn?

The premise of this book is that many cities that succeed have a learning system, even though some of them might not call it that. The book has tried to show the mechanics and processes of learning and how learning plays a role in creating an innovative climate. No cities were found that were proactive learners and were not engaged in innovation or change. But what about cities that cannot meet the requirements to be learners? Some of these have pieces of whole assemblies of learning systems. Others seem to be stuck, and still others phase in and out of learning periods. Table 10.1 summarizes the relationship between learners and reformers.

Table 10.1 Conceptual map of learners and reformers

	Learner	Non-learner
Innovator	Cases in Part III	One-shot wonders Colombo, Dakar, Surabaya, Naga City
Non-innovator	None found	Half of the survey (see Table 10.2)

To sharpen the question, we can take a closer look at some cities that categorize themselves as having made few or no reforms—the non-innovators in Table 10.1—but do not meet the criteria of being learners. Some of these—Colombo, Dakar, Surabaya and Naga City—were reported as having made few reforms, yet each has one or more of the features—but none has all—of making visits, having an office, tracking outcomes, or documenting lessons. Unfortunately, we have no information about the critical component of clouds of trust in these cities. And though our database may be small, let's assume for the moment that the data and the methodological factors in gathering data for this book are not themselves at issue, or at least are not the only issue. What other explanations might account for cities—those in the bottom-right half of Table 10.1—that are not proactive and do not change? Around half the cities in the survey, those listed in Table 10.2, fit in this quadrant. Exploring some of the reasons why they do not learn will put us in a better place to draw conclusions and suggest steps to improve the harvest of learning and the prospects for reform.

Table 10.2 shows those cities according to the extent to which they have achieved one or more of the learning factors. It's worth remembering that this measure is subjective and the judgment of only one person, the survey respondent.

Table 10.2 Institutional attributes

City	Institutional elements						
	Pop (mlns)	Has office	Documents	Follows	Tracks	Holds sessions	One or more
Turin	1.2	Yes	No	No	Yes	Yes	3
Kobe	1.5	No	Yes	No	No	No	1
Melbourne	3.9	No	Yes	No	No	Many	2
Pateros	0.75	Yes	No	No	No	DK*	1
Masbate	0.55	Yes	No	No	Yes	Few	2
Stockholm Metro	1.9	Yes	Yes	Yes	No	Some	3
Surabaya	3.0	Yes	No	Yes	Yes	Few	3
Tabriz	1.4	Yes	Yes	No	No	Many	3
Tehran	12.7	Yes	Yes	No	No	Many	3
Ulaanbaatar	1.1	Yes	No	No	Yes	Few	2
Hanoi	0.7	Yes	Yes	Yes	Yes	Few	4

*DK = Don't know

Six reasons for failing to learn

We can identify numerous reasons why cities do not engage in learning in any systematic way. Not all of them are simply the mirror-image opposites to those we have identified as features of proactive learners. The reasons fall into three broad groups. One group relates to external factors, one intermediate, and another more internal. Each will be discussed in more detail below.

In the external set, the first reason is calamity: the disruptive forces of natural and man-made disasters, such as those that impacted Kobe, Japan and, more recently, Juárez, Mexico. Another set of reasons is that some cities, like Surabaya, Tabriz and Tehran, are subject to forces such as centralized national policy or a political environment—macroscopic factors—that block free and open exchange and are cautious about innovation.

The intermediate group consists of factors that push a learning city off course. Some cities—Turin is a good example—can point to learning in the past, but have fallen out of the rhythm of learning. They are in a phase transition. After very impressive results over a period of more than a decade, some of the city's elements of learning have atrophied.

The third set of reasons concerns the internal capacity of cities. Many cities are simply too small to muster a critical mass of institutional and social capital for sustained learning. Pateros, Philippines provides an example. Fourth among all is that some cities have institutional capacity, but have not gone the extra mile to gather sufficient knowledge in order to shape clear options. Fifth, still others have plenty of knowledge, but no coherence of action to keep them moving forward. Tarragona and Mumbai are introduced as new cases to illustrate these last two reasons. Let's take each of these reasons in turn.

Calamity

Kobe, Japan is an industrial port city of less than two million. Kobe has achieved notable innovations—for instance, in the staging of the Kobe Arts Biennial, solid waste management, and Kobe Luminaire, a lights festival in commemoration of the loss of life following the 1995 earthquake. Recent innovations are few. One factor is that the city has experienced long-term ripple effects from the devastating earthquake in 1995. A recent report on the difficulty in progressing forward with planning for the city cited reverberations from the top-down actions of Kobe's strong mayor in the immediate aftermath of the quake. Decisive actions taken at the time helped Kobe to speed its recovery, but also underscored the importance, magnified during times of disaster, of community participation and social organization in advance of planning for recovery (Shaw and Goda, 2004). The effects of natural and man-made calamities—such as Hurricane Katrina in New Orleans, the drug wars in Juárez, or the tsunamis that have devastated communities in Indonesia and Japan—create tremendous disruption in assembling the social capital and institutional wherewithal to undertake (and in the case of Juárez, to continue) learning on a systematic basis.

Macro factors

Surabaya has accomplished notable reforms, but according to a case study, it was capable of many more. In one documented case, the city converted 400 of its vehicles to biogas fuels. In reviewing the project experience, Nakamura notes the strong local (i.e., endogenous) political reasons why adoption of more new ideas may be difficult (Nakamura, 2010). Among these are the tradition of central control in Indonesia, even though the country has been undergoing rapid decentralization since the "big bang" transformation of the late 1990s. Moreover, city leaders, particularly mayors, have little incentive to adopt pro-grams for long-range effect, like those relating to climate change. In contrast, Nakamura correlates adoption of environmental change with that in other cities —Chiang Mai, Rayon and Muangklang, all in Thailand—where greater local government autonomy was coupled with NGOs and a proactive stance by the mayor.

Cities that failed to achieve milestones in ICLEI programs for climate change shared features which are similar to or complicate those of non-learners, i.e., absence of institutional capacity. Nakamura found that professional staff mem-bers were unwilling to pursue change without a clear-cut signal from local political leadership. Other issues include questions, real and perceived, about autonomy of local governments to act; limited availability of finance; and whether or not active NGOs were in the picture.

Phase changes

While conducting research for this book, I asked the CEO of a high-tech area in Barcelona to address the topic of leadership in the city. "There are about 100 individuals who run the city," he said, in a matter-of-fact way. Asked to name some of them, he replied: "It would have to be one list before the year 2000 and another list afterwards." By this he meant that one leadership group worked in unison when the city was enjoying soaring success in the 1990s, and another group was in power, so to speak, afterwards, when the city began to struggle following a recession and rapid onset of technology change early in this century.

I noted that a few individuals crossed over the two periods, but not many. Other informants corroborated this observation. The point is that like all city organizations, maybe more than corporations, leadership changes, and with the changes comes the risk of interruption in the continuity not just of political power, but also of understanding and values shared by those in the inner circle of managing the city's fortunes. Juárez, Charlotte and Turin are also indicative of these circumstances.

Juárez and Charlotte can be seen to be weaving in and out of learning phases, because of leadership, external conditions (as in Juárez), or macro-economic or political change in the cases of Charlotte and Turin. Both of these cities accomplished multiple innovations over decades. But central leaders in Charlotte's success have faded out of the picture with age or external circumstances (the collapse of the financial industry in the US). Turin's innovative energies have fallen into decline after four successive administrations capped off by the Winter Olympics. Recall that the build-up of institutional capacity is a process of decades, not years, and we see hints, if not clear evidence, of how easily a learning system can be disrupted.

The third group of reasons for failure to learn consists of cities that for one reason or another have not met the threshold of motivation and critical mass of ingredients to make learning a part of development. Three cases help to illustrate these conditions. One of them, represented by smaller communities like Pateros, Philippines is representative of a threshold issue. Tarragona, Spain and Mumbai, India exhibit internal dissent and a failure to take off or stumbling along the way.

Below the threshold

A small municipality nestled in Metro Manila, Pateros, population under 100,000, was classified as a non-reformer and had few of the attributes of a learning city. The average income for Philippine cities is just over US$3,000 per year. Limited budgets and the proverbial weakness of institutional capacity in the first place makes systematic learning difficult for hundreds if not thousands of small municipalities like Pateros. Cities in this category are often unable to clear the thresholds of enlightened leadership, political motivation, financial clout, or institutional strength necessary to get started on learning. Numerous programs of national and international assistance, such as twinning, cluster learners and lending, can help to clear some of these thresholds. The problem is that the sheer number of cities in the size range of Pateros—more than 4000 around the globe—represents an issue of scale that is difficult for outside agents to address.

Limited knowledge—Tarragona, Spain

Tarragona is a city of under 200,000 inhabitants located to the south of Barcelona, where hills of several hundred meters overlook a natural harbor. These features attracted the first Roman settlement on the Iberian Peninsula. Roman legions were stationed there for several centuries and built fortifications and splendid civil works that still stand today. Tarragona now trades on its strong tourist appeal, which involves its beaches and the ruins, now restored and integrated into the urban fabric. But it wasn't always like that.

Three decades ago, while many cities in Spain were pondering their own pathways toward greater independence from Madrid, Tarragona staged a planning exercise complete with public debates. The issue of economic direction was central: one option was to maintain and develop the fishing and related industries, which had evolved over decades, particularly after World War II. A second option was to head in the cultural, touristic and educational direction, building in part on the city's handsome architectural heritage from Roman times.

A vote was put to the population, which, like the leadership in the city, was divided on the issue. The referendum resulted in a decision to stick to an industrial strategy, despite the many assets in cultural heritage. Industry was something the populace knew, a sector that had employed voters and their parents' generation. The moment of decision came at the same time that Bilbao and Barcelona were about to adopt outward, cultural and touristic strategies.

Had Tarragona's leadership taken greater measure of the direction in neighboring cities like Barcelona and Valencia, it might have been able to build more confidence in a non-industrial strategy. Several decades later, Tarragona, realizing the mistake of the referendum, reversed its course, but had by then lost decades of higher growth. With a stronger sense of vision, clearer ideas about how alternative pathways might have been formed and where they might have led, Tarragona's voters might have reached a different decision.

Adequate knowledge, limited cohesion—Mumbai

A world away from Tarragona is Mumbai, one of India's largest population centers (population of the core area around 12 million) and its pre-eminent economic powerhouse. Financial, trade and entertainment industries have driven the city's per capita income to among the highest in Asia. But deep cultural, economic and political divisions have impeded its development.

One of the most glaring obstacles is the yawning gap between rich and poor. Financial and Bollywood millionaires share a metropolitan area with a poor majority. The respective living circumstances give expression to the acute economic divergence. Dharavi, the city's most famous slum and home to 800,000 people, occupies a large quadrant of the city. Despite its well-known industry of small-scale producers and recyclers, the residents in this settlement live on less than a couple of dollars a day. Nearby, gleaming high-rise towers are home to the rich.

For decades, the business and commercial communities, organized as "Mumbai 2020," have worked to form a vision of the future. One objective was to make Mumbai a world-class financial center. But clogged transportation and incomplete infrastructure, both partial derivatives of irrational land use, have driven property prices to reach a level with those in Manhattan. Dharavi grew up in Mumbai for the same reasons that slums develop elsewhere in the world. Often at the core of the problem is a sluggish or dysfunctional system of land allocation and taxation, opening the door for speculation and leaving the poor in desperate straits as the rich bid up the prices of residential and commercial space.

In each of these last two cases, many deep-seated problems—ranging from demographic and economic change in Tarragona to historical and cultural divisions in Mumbai—complicated the formation of a coherent and dedicated effort to learn and convert learning to innovative policy break-throughs. In each of them, some aspect of learning might have made a difference. Tarragona had alternative models at its doorstep. Barcelona, Valencia and Bilbao were each busy developing ideas about city growth. Leadership in Tarragona appears not to have extended first-order learning into wider circles. Voters and stakeholders in the city's future economic success might have made different choices had they possessed a clearer idea of alternative pathways to the future.

Mumbai 2020 worked to develop alternative ideas, but the critical breakdown was at the deeper level of what I have called third-order learning: the creation of a coherent body of thought and values. Clearly a strong unifying force was needed—probably one that would involve change in property rights and land use—and this still eludes Mumbai. Yet the city, and particularly Mumbai 2020, has never lacked the means to learn about solutions in financial centers elsewhere, in places like London, New York and Shanghai.

In fact, Mumbai 2020 sponsored many forays outward to gather ideas and shape plans. But the business-minded constituency of Mumbai 2020 did not extend into public sector domains, where a very different set of values prevailed. The two worlds are still separated by a wide chasm of uncertainty and suspicion. A coalition of interests in Mumbai has recently pressed to reform state laws that keep land locked away from the market. But these initiatives are being challenged in the courts. Mumbai seems far from reaching a ba.

Orders of learning and context

Many other cities could be placed in one or another of the groups of non-learners. The purpose of documenting a selected few is not to argue that learning is the root cause of breakdown in reform. It is certainly not the main factor in innovation and change, but it is quite possibly one of many factors that deserve more attention.

One set of factors can be inferred from the preliminary evidence gathered for this book. The answer lies somewhere in the range of second- and third-order learning. Recall from Chapter 1 in connection with Seattle, and again in subsequent chapters: first-order learning refers to finding ideas; second-order learning is dissemination internally; and third-order learning is the reaching of a ba, where leadership communities achieve a level of self-identity and self-confidence that allows them to take chances, to share values, and above all to think and act coherently and relatively quickly. Reaching a strong cloud of trust at the core of the ba requires intensive commitment.

Deep dives into individual case studies gave us some clues about the way to help cities learn. For one thing, we saw in Part III of this book organizational styles that range from loosely ad hoc in Portland to tightly formal in Bilbao. Yet all the cities were successful learners and innovators. It is no surprise that contextual and historical circumstances play a role in how the organizational arrangements are formed. But it is worth taking a fresh look at how contextual circumstances have been managed and how some cities have cobbled together a learning system that includes an innovative milieu.

The signal feature of third-order learning is that learning arrangements help to create an atmosphere that is conducive to innovation. Further, in some cities, new linkages in that organizational tissue are put together on the march, as the work is being done, as in Turin. In others, the ties have evolved over time and are reinforced where needed. In still others—Portland, for instance—the issue is bridging between already well-established groups. In essence, these three approaches give us further clues about how to stimulate and manage the elemental units of soft infrastructure.

What about content? What has been learned?

In Chapter 2 we reviewed 10 issues that have emerged on city agendas over the past decade, and saw later in Chapter 5 that only three or four of these are high on the list of priorities for learning cities. At the same time, some cities have indicated areas of vital concern that were not in the top 10. Several points are worth bringing to light about the content of learning.

The survey results are remarkable in revealing an agenda of topics *not* focused on the day-to-day machinery of running cities, for instance, land registries, accounting practices, basic plan-making, project evaluation, personnel management, and more. And yet, arguably, the great bulk of city learning in twinning and one-on-one exchange of the kind being perfected in Europe takes place precisely around these kinds of issues. For instance, British, Dutch, French, German and Swedish municipal assistance programs grapple with the bread-and-butter issues of democratic decision-making processes, such as participation to improve demand detection, improved connect under-serviced communities, and systems to record and manage data, services and pricing.

On the other hand, survey takers and respondents in case study interviews were more focused on what might be called special problems as opposed to routine management and professional skills. They are concerned with the start-up and institutional design of relationships between public and private sectors in bus rapid transit systems or solid waste transfer, economic development and project finance. These differing views undoubtedly reflect a segmented market in the demand for learning, and any policy approach to improve sponsored learning as a part of institutional capacity development should begin with a clear picture of the objectives and audience.

In the wider scene of policy and practice, we might ask whether cities as a collective—city leaders and national policy makers—are reaching a new global understanding about policy issues that have long been debated over the past four or five decades. Some of these issues include the role of cities in national economic development, the advisability of promoting or retarding rural to urban migration, the presence and long-term persistence of poverty in emerging (and some post-industrial) nations, the pace and depth of change in democratic decentralization, and the proper place for the private sector in public goods. All these have been central to the policy debate about urbanization.

The sources of data and insight developed in this book can provide only partial answers as to whether cities are gaining any new perspective or wisdom about a general understanding or consensus. We cannot say and indeed have not attempted to determine whether any new consensus has been achieved. What is clear is that cities feel the impacts of all of these major issues, and many are moving ahead to address them with actionable tools at the micro-scale.

It is evident from the cases, however, that the most successful proactive cities have moved the needle quite far to incorporate a wider group of stakeholders into the learning and planning process. Informal and corporate styles of learning show this most clearly. Turin, Portland, Seattle and Bilbao, and to a lesser extent Curitiba, Juárez and Amman, have developed mechanisms to raise the common denominator to include business interests in active exchange and often working partnerships in connection with managing land use, transport and economic development.

As for the 10 emerging issues identified in Chapter 2, the survey suggested that cities have focused tightly on a few key areas (metropolitan governance, local economic development), are still grappling with many long-standing issues (urban transport, project finance), and have shown concern for some topics that are not on the consensus list of global institutions at all, such as attracting and retaining the young for economic development and management elites. Let's start with how that young talent gets into the mainstream.

Portland, Turin and Barcelona are deeply concerned about attracting and retaining young global talent. The concern over young talent goes beyond the insights raised by Richard Florida, whose seminal work on creative cities first drew attention to the three "Ts," talent, tolerance and technology, as central to com- petitiveness (Florida, 2002). Whatever the degree of truth in Florida's insights, it is clear that cities with young talent share a common challenge of refreshing the cadres of city leadership. Achieving a vibrant and responsive city requires sustained leadership and a steady course over many years. Inputs from a wide range of actors are vital to the process of collective understanding and coherent responses to challenges. Learning cities must be engaged in a continuous effort to keep fresh ideas flowing into the community.

Turin found ways to integrate new and younger elites in the governance and planning process, but not in a systematic way. Accretion happened in a way quite true to network theoretical ideas: attachments took place where network members found the most appealing new links—for instance, in someone whose message had been heard in public or by whom an article had been written. A signal was picked up and someone in the network moved to incorporate the author into it. Still, the results were surprising for the city and more surprising for those invited to join the standing elites.

Young Portlanders found it easier to get heard, as many of the interviewees attested in the Portland case study. Portland's elite networks are well identified and share among them a common underlying set of values like environmental quality and greenness in cities.

Much like Turin, but on a larger scale, Barcelona has long been bidding for global talent that is critical to success for its knowledge-based economy. Attracting young professionals is only part of the battle. Keeping them requires accommo- dating a different life and work style. In the words of one quipster in Barcelona, the new global talent "is in love with the Blackberry, not the car." This apparently superficial reference actually has deep roots in cultural and generational change that applies to many cities.

In the past, those moving up the ranks of power and the ladder of the elites carried with them sets of values that prized sleek material assets. In the words of one interviewee: "The old guard likes flashy cars; the young entrepreneurs prize electronic gadgets." Previous elites also understood that organizations run in hierarchies. The younger generation of talent sees things differently: besides spending a lot of time in the virtual world, newcomers are entrepreneurs and see their social scene and business life on a flatter, less hierarchical, and more decentralized landscape.

A second problem found in every city was that of metropolitan governance. Many of the thousand cities have grown slowly to the realization that growth in communities on the periphery was creating a burden of governance for which most municipal legislation and governance tools were no match. Portland is perhaps the most advanced of the cases examined in the book.

Portland's growth boundary sets a solid framework, within which contending groups can debate policy positions. A technical focus on demographic data and land use, together with a limited array of clearly regional services, give Portland's Metro a role that for the most part has been managed successfully. Twin Cities Metro Region in Minneapolis–St. Paul has taken a similar approach. The Portland boundary and its limited services mandate provide a framework for growth strategies and a focus for learning, for instance, around integrated land use, parklands, open space, and transit strategies.

But for most cities, the widening scope of the city-regional economy and the growing interrelationship in large-scale physical infrastructure makes inter-jurisdictional arrangements even more important than they were in the past. Many cities are most probably paying a price (a kind of self-imposed tax) on their respective gross regional products by not capturing economies of scale in the development of services like regional transport, solid waste and environmental management and protection. Seattle and Bilbao are both making efforts to fill this gap by having structured a deliberative governance and decision-making system. The fact that every city is facing some version of this problem, especially in the emerging nations, elevates the issue to a learning topic. At the same time, scores of cities have tried many experiments—from economic development agencies in India, to limited service responsibilities in Mexico, to several tiers of government in Seoul. The harvests of learning from these and other cases should be packaged and made more easily available to the many cities looking for answers.

A third common issue is that of building a regional economy. Hand in glove with area-wide governance is the prospect for fusion of nearby centers. For instance, in the Turin–Milan corridor, with the decrease in transaction costs that will come with high-speed rail, trade will increase between the two nodes, meaning greater movement of goods, professional skill and tourists. Increased rail service between similar nodes in OECD countries—Lyon, Toulouse and central Europe, and south to Barcelona and Valencia, as well as numerous cities in the US, Japan, China and India—all offer many examples of living laboratories from which each could learn lessons and prepare for inevitable change.

Summing up

The proactive learners represent a kind of idealized template, and no one should underestimate the difficulty of replicating any one model. It requires an open democratic process, enlightened leadership, a community of trust that few cities—few communities anywhere—can claim as their own. And yet we have seen numerous cases where pieces or whole assemblies have been put in place and thrived over decades. Each of the groups of learners discussed in Chapter 4 can be related to one or more of the basic elements of learning cities as a guide to improving the yield of acquired knowledge and setting the stage for innovation (see Box 10.1).

Box 10.1 *Elements of learning*

- *Learning modalities.* Previous cases each exhibited a style or mode of learning—corporate, informal or technical, as described in Part III. Evidence from those cases suggests that research organizations of some kind (private or public, sometimes universities) may be important building blocks for city learning, and that learning may take place in phases. Field analysis will explore questions of "agency"—the presence of high-level technical excellence in nearby firms, facilities and universities is important—and whether distinct phases are identifiable. Additional questions concern digital means of learning, and whether and to what extent digital capacity plays a role in learning, for instance, in face-to-face modality.
- *Agency, storage and networks.* A growing body of literature has begun to focus on networks, seeing them as mechanisms of social and technical bonding between and among professionals in a city region. Interactions between members of the learning community can be seen as part of

the "soft infrastructure" in regional competitiveness. Scholars of social capital have suggested that "tightness of bonds" (strong ties) in a network consisting of like-minded players produces a coherent response to meet new challenges. "Weak ties," on the other hand, help to generate "out-of-the-box" breakthroughs. Strong ties require focused investment; weak ties are often haphazard. How do learning cities manage this tension? Also, networks can be seen as a form of storage—the living memory of learning experiences.

- *Trust and openness.* In addition to organizational aspects of learning, previous work of many kinds has suggested that trust is an important aspect of the learning process. One possible operative mechanism, which I observed first hand in the case of Seattle, can be seen on those occasions when city leaders share a deep knowledge-related experience, one that lasts many days. When experiences of this kind are reinforced by subsequent and multiple interactions among the same players, they form bonds of trust and these facilitate sharing and cooperation.

With a deeper idea about how learning takes place, we can modify slightly the gamut of learners that I first introduced in Chapter 4. Let's start from the "bottom."

Threshold cities

We recognize the very large number of cities that do not have the institutional wherewithal—financial, technical or managerial—to get started on learning in a collective sense. Small cities and towns (populations of around 100,000) are often stuck in an institutional resource valley from which they cannot escape.

Grazers and "NEK" cities (not enough knowledge)

These have no system of learning, or only the rudiments of such a system. They often need to define a purpose, a plan, an agency and an ongoing system just to beef up the learning yield, so to speak, and to achieve first- and maybe second-order learning. Learning is somewhat catch-as-catch-can. The purpose of learning may or may not be recognized as important in and for itself. Even if it is recognized as such, the objective of learning is not defined and new knowledge is not adequately vetted.

"Twinners"

Those cities in twinning relationships, like those cities learning in clusters, have pieces of the system in place in the sense that the learning topics are pre-defined, either in the twinning arrangements or in the voluntary association with peer communities of interest. Twinning has proved its worth and is making improvements in the various aspects of exchange, such as taking ownership of the design and scope of a program. Questions remain about the exercise of control, especially of the financing and selection of activities. These questions are intrinsic to asymmetrical relationships, as twinning almost always is. South–South twinning improves these terms of trade, but can still be stuck on financing and over the issues of who calls the shots. In most cases also, the terms of twinning relationships are usually time-bound, as compared to proactive learners, whose programs are continuous and wider in scope.

Special-purpose clusters (healthy cities, Agenda 21, heritage sites, C40) also provide a rich, but in the greater scheme of things a narrow, channel of learning. Like twinning, clustered learning can serve as a basis for a broader and longer-term program. The definition of problems and objectives needs to reach beyond the specific ones of, say, carbon footprint or preservation of heritage sites, to affect direction and pace of growth in ways that involve additional stakeholders—business groups, leadership elites—and maybe even to allied or complementary long-term objectives about the future of the city.

Proactive cities

For all of these groups to reach beyond smart cities, they must put in place a fluid system in which many stakeholders can interact in a common matrix of relationships. Learning in proactive cities is self-defined. It is purposeful, geared to the needs of the city as a whole, even if the particular subject in any given period might be focused on transit, or parks, or specific neighborhoods. The important thing is that agreement is reached on what to learn and on a process of storing and applying knowledge locally. The clouds of trust represent a collective council, an informal governance system, composed of people who believe in and care about the place where they live. The ground needs to be laid so that the process of learning and exchange is embedded and continuous.

To synthesize these patterns, I have used the term "order of learning" to refer to stages of increased involvement and commitment (see Table 10.3), ranging from registering new facts, to spreading knowledge, to reaching a ba where leadership communities achieve a level of self-identity and self-confidence that

Table 10.3 Learning types and orders of learning

Learning type (example)	Activities and orders of learning		
	Knowledge acquisition (first order)	Agency/ institutional (second order)	Trusting milieu (third order)
Under threshold (Pateros)	NA	NA	NA
Not enough knowledge (Tarragona), grazers	Undefined ⟶	? ⟶	?
Twinners	Pre-defined		?
Knowledge, no cohesion (Mumbai)	⟶ ⟶		?
Proactive (Seattle)	Self-defined		

Source: Author

allows a city to take chances, to share values, and above all to think and act coherently and react quickly.

Cities at or below the threshold of learning must either define their needs for learning or, in the case of twinning, mentoring and clusters, their needs must be pre-defined in conjunction with their partners. The proactive cities reviewed in earlier chapters defined their own needs, usually as a function of an oncoming crisis such as economic collapse or political reform, as in the cases of Seattle, Bilbao and Turin. An executive body and institutional back-up help to achieve second-order learning, so that something is done with the knowledge. Question marks in Table 10.3 indicate these as the points of challenge for learning cities. Only the proactive cities reach the point of developing an innovative milieu, where these steps are replicated and continuously refreshed.

Reaching a ba with strong cloud(s) of trust requires intensive commitment. Few cities have aimed to create a ba deliberately, but many can improve or accelerate learning once the mutual payoff is demonstrated and learning exercises are undertaken to begin building trust. We shall look at ways to achieve these steps in the next chapter.

References

Florida, R. (2002). *The rise of the creative class,* Basic Books, New York.

Nakamura, H. (2010). *Political factors facilitating practice adoption through Asian intercity network programmes for the environment,* Institute for Global Environmental Strategies, Hayama, Japan.

Shaw, R. and K. Goda (2004). "From disaster to sustainable civil society: the Kobe experience," *Disasters,* 28, pp. 16–40.

11 Turning the learning world upside down— pathways forward in policy and research

Information and communications technologies have made a tremendous impact already to change our world. One of the most promising new developments is the diffusion of sensors and the embedding of trillions of transistors in global cityscapes around the world. Advanced devices like these can do a lot to help manage cities, but ICT can go only so far in helping cities learn. The material in this book has pointed strongly to personal relationships among city leaders— tycoons, mayors and neighborhood activists—who lie at the center of change. Bonds of trust in these relationships are the indispensable elements in forming a ba and vital to getting beyond smart cities.

Drawing together strands from the previous discussion suggests some directions for a design of urban learning. It is important to note that we are basing our conclusions on case data drawn mostly from intermediate and upper-income cities. Translating lessons to the lowest-income cities requires care. It requires making sometimes heroic assumptions about context and conditions. Case data from Amman, Curitiba and Juárez, along with the survey data, provide some rationale for assuming there is some applicability from post-industrial to emerging cities.

The lessons apply in several ways. First, some will help to reformulate old pathways or create new ones to advance learning. Second, the discovery of secrets about proactive reform helps to set criteria for the identification of cities that are good candidates for assistance. Third, the modalities of learning offer some suggestions about the sequence of programmatic activities and the relationship among learning events. Finally, the evidence suggests areas of management attention—for the cities, project managers and helping institutions, and in policy, program and research.

Getting right-side up in emerging cities

Hundreds of cities are showing the way towards a better future, and they suggest an entirely new approach to solving urban problems in the global South. The core concept is that solutions, or knowledge that is key to finding solutions, already exist for many problems, but many high thresholds—conceptual, bureaucratic, cultural and physical—block them from reaching more widespread application.

The entire post-war model of development assistance to cities is predicated upon a different approach, one that flows in the opposite direction. National policy, economic adjustment, and conditionality require cities, lying at the tail end of a long chain of institutions, to synthesize the often separate policy and reform agendas of national authorities. This process often results in what Lloyd Rodwin used to describe as "apoplexy at the center and anemia at the periphery." Cities are expected to meld policy reforms and exercise powers of implementation that ministries themselves are often unable to achieve for them.

City exchange of knowledge constitutes an initiative that turns this paradigm on its head, focusing on the horizontal dimension of exchange at the base, not the apex, of the policy and implementation pyramid. Localities are the sources of solutions. Exchange at this level has proven to be productive. It might be more productive if some of the barriers to exchange were cleared away or overcome. Cities face high thresholds—institutional, conceptual and cultural—that slow the uptake of proven knowledge. Ironically, the transition to an urbanized planet has come with a large surge in creative solutions by cities themselves. We are not pretending that solutions are at hand everywhere. But solutions of some kind can be found almost anywhere.

Hundreds of cities are now engaged in inventing or searching for solutions. They operate today like so many disconnected laboratories of practice. Below the mega-city range are around 400 cities that get less attention in policy and marketing. According to McKinsey Research, these are the places that will be generating 40 percent of global GDP growth in the next 15 years. Middle-class families are being formed with the promise of new economic and political demand (Dobbs et al., 2011).

Partly in anticipation of these changes, local, national and international city-based associations have been formed and are growing more active. Among other functions, international membership and technical organizations aim to facilitate knowledge exchange among members. At the same time, global private corporations like McKinsey, IBM, Cisco and others are beginning to see cities as constitutive of a new customer class, and are finding novel applications for advanced and ubiquitous technologies in information and communications.

We see that many cities in the laboratory are energetic, but disorganized; productive, but not still not efficient; promising, but lacking channels to reach application more widely where they are needed. Above all, the barriers of institutions, distant policy and isolated practice can be cleared away by activating one of the most potent but underutilized resources available to address urban problems: knowledge already invented in or possessed by other cities. The way forward is to sharpen existing tools, create new ones, and open pathways to focus on learning. In making these suggestions, the ultimate aim is not only to help cities enhance the basis for forming a vision and guiding development. The larger prize is to work toward *embedding* knowledge in the city culture as part of the ba, an innovative milieu that allows urban communities to make coherent decisions.

Approaches to learning

The approach proposed here focuses on the many barriers to getting started and transmitting ideas, the misplaced incentives and blurry focus that cities and facilitating institutions have with respect to knowledge. Knowledge sharing is at a primitive stage. Institutional and personal incentives necessary to create a market for exchange are smothered by national prerogatives or never activated by cities operating on chronically anemic budgets. Players at all levels, local, national and international, have roles to develop.

The three orders of learning discussed earlier lay out a framework for developing learning approaches in cities. Learning entails setting up a system to acquire new knowledge, to process it and verify that it has validity for the city in question, and finally to float it in a cloud of trust so it gets the acid cynicism and passionate support it deserves. Initial conditions and contextual circumstances will dictate how a city might start. The central idea is that learning must be useful for the cities, a tool for cities that must "advance their purposes," as Peter Marris put it in connection with the adoption of new technologies (Marris, 1974). This means learning and helping agencies must start where the cities are, in organizational and managerial terms, and not blindly offer one or another best practice without tailoring it to local circumstances.

In general, each of the activities involved in learning makes a contribution. Many help discovery in city business, some toward processing and validation across silos. Proactive reformers make use of exercises of collectives. Actions of acquiring knowledge can be mixed and matched in many ways for many purposes, and the categories in Table 11.1 are not to be understood as tidy and mutually exclusive.

Table 11.1 Sample tools for orders of learning

Tools of first order: finding new knowledge	Tools of second order: processing knowledge	Tools of third order: clouds of trust; internalizing knowledge
Research	Responsible office	Inter-group exchanges
Outbound city visits	Own documentation	Systematic study tours
Inward seminars	Dissemination	Team exercises and retreats
Follow-up studies	Follow-up studies	Civic partnerships
Monitoring	Monitoring and evaluation	
Sessions at home		
Twinning and mentoring		

Who does what?

An important part of work on urban learning will be to help the participating cities develop a long-term learning process that allows learning to be built into management culture, i.e., "embedded," to employ (for purposes of connecting to other disciplines) an already overused term. Not every community either can or is willing to commit to the long term.

What can cities do?

A first step for cities is to *make learning part of the mission of governance.* Make somebody responsible, set up a point person or documentation office, like London's intelligence unit. These are city-knowledge managers in that they are the city scribes, who keep track of the most important lessons and objectives of the city, manage an internal website for learning, identify and track the LUKAS (local urban knowledge arenas) and keep an archive. This approach and these tools are the bulwarks for getting past the breaks in continuity created by political turnover.

Self-diagnosis may be needed once a learning initiative is established. Cities small and large will need to take stock of how they stack up in the orders of learning. Often, cities with few resources and low institutional capacity will be hovering in the left-hand column of Table 11.1, acquiring knowledge, but not really making the most of it. Individuals and small groups are learning every day, but the silos and organizational entropy, the chasm between business and bureaucrat, can slow transmission or block the processing of ideas. Taking stock of elements in learning, such as those tools in the table, is a step most cities can take without much outside help. Rich and poor, those recovering from calamity and those in phase transition, all can benefit from canvassing and mapping out the sources of knowledge inputs, as part of recovery as well as for long-term development.

Choose and develop a style

The style can be technical, informal, corporate or some other: choose one and begin to build on it. All of the modalities discussed in Part III have been shown to work, but each has drawbacks. The point is not to fit some category, but to commit to a degree of activity, whether intensive, proactive or moderate, but consistent, to address the areas of reform or change that are most pressing in the city. Learning is not for learning's sake, but to solve problems. An informal style is probably the path of least resistance, noting that whatever the modality, certain elements—written responsibilities, a mission, a staff—need to be in place.

Engaging private business and commercial interests stands out in all the cases. The public sector cannot do learning alone, at least not the kind that leads to good prospects for innovation and reform. To achieve this, the city's political, business and civil societies have to work together. This often means forging new alliances, or changing the terms of present relationships, in order to enter a compact that enables several world-views and sets of assumptions to be exposed to and challenged by others. Leadership is a plural noun in learning; it is critical to the collective creation of an innovative milieu.

Organize a learning program

Cities learn from other cities, so they should go to other cities; and if they go, they should make it count. Learning is partly about knowing what needs to be discovered. The learning program should pick those places or events—city visits, intermediary knowledge centers, twinning, and conference grazing—to fit the strategy. This means that the learning program should be organized in advance, following the best practice of Seattle, and systematic in its strategy, so that documentation, capturing the value added, and spotting opportunities can be moved toward institutionalized form. Further suggestions about activities and events are made in a subsequent section, below.

Institutionalize knowledge

Both case and survey data show strong linkages among having an office, department or unit on the one hand, and on the other, documenting lessons and following up with learning events back home. Home meetings—seminars and conferences organized specifically to discuss and explore learning—offer the opportunity to deepen absorption and test new ideas. Organizational units and internal learning activities are important mechanisms in building a consensus of understanding on technologies, practices, issues and policies. Cases showed time and again that invited guests from elsewhere with relevant expertise on the topic at hand can enrich the process.

Work on the social capital

Building social capital may require outside help and some cities will need long-term support, but it is a task that is within the reach of many cities, especially if the initial task—the reason for learning—is tied to a project that is modest in scale. Still, leadership of many kinds is needed. The case examples showed that political, civic, business, university and neighborhood leadership all made contributions. The key is that community actors must see their self-interest served and feel they are connected to a larger endeavor.

For cities with more institutional capacity and deeper social capital, the challenge focuses on the capacities and mechanisms involved in collective learning, i.e., the area closer to the right-hand column in Table 11.1. The diagnostic work centers on the inter-organizational and inter-network relationships that make up the modern city. In many places, the first task will be to find ways to overcome suspicion and sometimes ideological barriers that separate public from private sector mentalities.

The linkages of learning and application must reach across many jurisdictions and areas of interest in the city, as was illustrated by Bilbao. Many other divides can impede the move to an innovative milieu. In working on its ba, cities have a plethora of organizational, leadership and institutional literature from which to draw. Van de Ven and Hargrave offer a synthesis of the literature and an organizational framework that relate various bodies of theory to one another (Van de Ven and Hargrave, 2004: 293).

Business, commerce and civil society

Just as cities must engage the business community and civil society, each sector needs to reciprocate. For the corporate and business sector, the engagement cannot be merely a matter of corporate social responsibility or community good will. The cases have shown that enlightened self-interest was the motivation that drove the private sector to connect with city leadership. Cities have daily contact with business interests in a myriad of ways; licensing, building, regulating, and working on attracting investment. But too often these are conducted formally and at arm's length. One city manager told me with some pride that the city met "at least once a year" with the Chamber of Commerce and business. These channels need to be both more frequent and more varied, including joint activities to discuss problems, engage in alliance-building exercises, and take part in searching together for solutions.

Businesses, like individuals, have to see themselves as part of the community. They should be asking themselves: What should my corporate action be to make my city better? What can my company do to increase capacity? Often the barriers of mutual mistrust or suspicion keep genuinely civic arrangements from being formed between public leaders and the private sector. One step could be that enterprises partner with a neutral third party, an independent actor such as a university, foundation or neighborhood organization. Depending on the place and circumstances, a neutral, "friend of the court" partner organization can straddle the divide and help ease the natural tension between public and private sectors.

Global corporate world

The recent McKinsey report (Dobbs et al., 2011) showing middleweight cities outpacing all others in terms of growth in purchasing power over the next 15 years underscores the reasons why we see corporations like Cisco, IBM, Philips and Siemens investing in technologies and practices aimed at emerging city markets. Designing better sensors, bringing information to consumers, allowing managers to see a bigger picture to manage energy loads and traffic—all of these contributions are just a beginning. Helping cities learn, and particularly bringing new devices onto the market that help to build or reinforce the glue of trust in learning and innovation, is a frontier that needs to be explored.

First, global and local business can focus on a place, a neighborhood, district or development zone—as Cisco has done in Baltimore's low-income neighborhood near Johns Hopkins or in Barcelona's innovation district, or IBM's pilot in Dubuque, or Google in Kansas City—where actions and discussions can focus on a wide variety of needs, but actions can be concrete. Second, contributions can often be made in connection with hardware and software that service that place—water, transport, fiber optics or businesses. Third, make the commitment a long-term one. Learning takes time, and partners have to stay engaged across political administrations. These are endeavors that require triple and quadruple bottom lines.

Nations

Only a handful of nations have focused on horizontal exchange as a matter of policy. India is a bellwether. Its PEARL (Peer Experience and Reflective Learning) program, put together as a part of the Jawarhalal Nehru Urban Reform Mission, makes financial resources available to foster city-to-city exchange in a variety of specific topical areas (see box inset). Swedish SIDA developed a focus on intermediate organizations (LUKAs, or local urban knowledge arenas).

Box 11.1 *Structured learning in the Jawarhalal Nehru Urban Reform Mission (JNNURM)*

In 2004, the government of India launched one of most ambitious urban and municipal development financing and reform programs in the history of the country. The program allocated a budget of US$16 billion to be matched by state and local governments. Funds are contingent on certain policy reforms and are to be dedicated to basic infrastructure, but significant amounts are also included to bolster planning activities. More than 60 cities were made eligible to apply for funding. Perhaps the most novel of the activities under this program is the Peer Experience and Reflective Learning, called PEARL. The JNNURM cities have been grouped into various categories, such as industrial cities, heritage cities, trade and commercial cities, mega-cities, etc. The experiences are to be compiled by one of the cities or a designated institution as a knowledge manager and disseminated amongst the others. The objective of the PEARL program is to create networks between JNNURM cities for cross-learning and knowledge sharing on urban reforms and city governance. JNNURM cities have been formed into several subgroups according to the similarity of their socio-economic profiles, complexities of urban problems and issues, size, and urban growth patterns.

Source: Sivaramakrishnan, 2011

Intermediate membership organizations

Membership organizations and professional associations can play very important roles in helping members and constituent cities to learn. Most membership organizations for cities already conduct learning programs and conferences. But none to my knowledge has formed specific programs for learning cities. There is ample scope to develop a focus on learning, good learners and typical lessons. Twinning, mentoring and cluster exchanges all help to build basic tools and skills. But these programs rarely focus on the critical nexus of public, corporate, business and civic groups that need to work closely together to achieve a collective, common understanding. Together, they must formulate a vision, develop and strengthen alliances with partners, shape a learning strategy, and conduct knowledge acquisition and management.

A supporting role of this kind complements the developmental agendas of most intermediate organizations. Further, intermediate organizations can add city learning to the agenda for lobbying national governments and international organizations.

Intermediate organizations and development assistance agencies are also well positioned to match up learner and teacher cities. United Cities and Local Governments has begun this process with its mentoring cities program. The World Bank Institute (WBI) launched a program called City Round, a series of sponsored knowledge exchanges between cities. It quickly became apparent that matching cities was a critical issue. Later, other parts of the World Bank picked up on the idea of matching cities. International organizations with frequent and widespread access could begin to create a roster for both "buyers" and "sellers" to make that learning market more effective. Diagnostics tools need to be refined to help cities get to know their own learning needs. Programs of city visits are brought up again in the next section.

Overseas Development Assistance (ODA)—technical assistance

Capacity-building programs tailored to country needs are organized on a regional or country basis and sometimes, but not always, complement efforts by the development banks. Capacity building and training are offered in more than a dozen areas, including the core areas of planning, shelter, tenure and finance. Many new topics have been added as institutions emerge or morph. For instance, Cities Alliance brought a new emphasis on upgrading and city-development strategies, which both became mission-driven agendas in training and capacity building. Almost no attention is given systematically to how urban institutions get strengthened and innovate in the long term, or how they learn, manage knowledge, and put ideas to work in cities.

ODA financial assistance

The great bulk of capacity building and technical assistance (at least in monetary volume) is carried along by lending or credits provided by international financial institutions (IFIs). Capacity building is secondary to the primary objective of implementing projects financed by loans and credits. Despite policy rhetoric to the contrary, investments in infrastructure—and often a preoccupation with implementing projects—crowd out attention to capacity and institution building.

Most development banks have a capacity-building arm (for instance, Asian Development Bank Institute, Inter-American Development Bank Institute, WBI). The urban focus of IFIs has widened and narrowed many times in the past several decades, as we saw in Chapter 2. At one time, cities were only the places of infrastructure investment. Some years later they were central to the creation of an investment climate for job creation. Improving policy and professional skill, and, more recently, professionalization of management, has been an enduring issue through most of these variations.

Whatever the focus, finances for stand-alone capacity building as in the WBI are woefully out of proportion to demonstrated need. Budgets for WBI urban programs have been small (around US$500,000 annually) and therefore heavily dependent on leveraging with partners and increasingly on distance learning. For instance, WBI's partnership with Monterrey Tech in Mexico has mutual advantages. WBI content enriches Monterrey Tech. With the broadcast power of Monterrey Tech, WBI reaches up to several orders of magnitude more participants than it could on its own. By forcing a dependence on virtual learning, WBI dramatically increases the reach of course offerings, but dilutes the impact of learning and misses the essence of building a learning environment.

New roles for development agencies

The growing shadow economy of exchange reveals a looming opportunity cost for international development agencies that have a mandate for capacity building. The shadow economy suggests the viability of alternative or parallel learning mechanisms. A large number of cities in the North and the South—and a growing number of knowledge agents, the specialized agencies and NGOs—have gained considerable experience in structuring and transferring knowledge to other cities. Development agencies might well find that their comparative advantage lies less in direct provision of knowledge and more in the licensing and management of high-performing cities as knowledge agents.

The means of finance for this learning strategy already exist. Most investment lending (and some adjustment loans) from the World Bank and sister organizations includes technical assistance or capacity components that typically amount to around 10 percent of loan value. It may be cost effective for the banks to concentrate on structuring and regulating a market for urban learning and to develop knowledge-management expertise in cities. These are activities for which loan funds could be used by borrowers to purchase knowledge from cities like those proactive learners that already possess it. Rather than international organizations concentrating knowledge and best practice, then sending it on a round trip back to cities, they could be leveraging their expertise by regulating a market that is already in bloom.

In this scenario, international organizations, with help from associations, could be setting criteria for licensed vendors, cities and LUKAS, and others, holding them to high and monitored standards, and letting loan funds finance the knowledge acquisition. Selected, proven and willing cities could deliver the capacity building. Of course cities supplying the expertise would have to meet performance criteria, be monitored, and retain certification—all functions that IFIs could provide or manage.

National and international partners

All of the proactive learners discussed in this book reshuffled the relationship between and among principal actors—public, private, civic and academic. Each of the cases found ways to engage key groups in a collective effort, putting individual objectives aside in the interests of the community as whole. For strategic restructuring, the public sector is important but far from sufficient, and new tools and techniques are needed to help cities acquire the skills of alliance building. Many programs to encourage and develop leadership are already in operation, for example, academies of management and leadership in the US. But few, if any, focus on alliance building for purposes of expanding the intelligence functions of cities. Fewer still in emerging nations offer a place of learning for community and civic leaders, including but not confined to elected leadership.

A quasi-academic setting allows the leadership elite time to escape daily pressures, observe successful practices and study the fatal flaws of failed efforts, and also to spend quality time building relationships with natural partners. Such a "space" could be created locally (a nearby retreat) or regionally. Recent leadership programs such as DARE (Decision, Actions, Results), crafted by the

WBI and offered in the Lee Kuan Yew School of Public Policy in the National University of Singapore, are getting closer to addressing collective learning.

City leaders are rarely able to devote more than a few days to these purposes. Occasional longer encounters would allow exposure of local communities to other groups from cohort cities with similar aspirations. The proposition would be costly, but global and regional financing from public and private sources may be available, especially when private industry sees enlightened self-interest is at play (and proper arm's-length arrangements are put into place to avoid conflicts of interest).

Box 11.2 *Learning cycles for cities—hypothetical program*

What would be the nature and scope of a learning program for a hypothetical city that wishes to achieve sustainable learning? Typical but carefully selected components can be packaged into a long-term program useful for many purposes. The core idea of the cycle of learning is twofold. First, to establish and reaffirm the nature of the problem in the city, recognize that the city will be engaged in a long-term effort, and accept that the aim is to achieve a more sustainable development pathway. Second, the cycle helps to integrate learning internally, among the major players in a given city, and externally, with counterpart peers from other cities. The program would need to be agreed in advance and managed as part of any project. Four typical learning activities might be included.

1   Conferences and seminars (knowledge exchange on policy and vision): More formal, structured meetings are suited to explore approaches to planning and planning frameworks—for instance, regional planning; institutional coordination; planning theory; and analytical tools, like surveys and forecasting—areas of work that are either abstract or as yet not widely practiced in the city.

2   City tours and visits: These are suited to areas of work for which frameworks are understood and for which practical and hands-on experiences are possible to observe, for instance, treatment of transport corridors, redevelopment zones, cultural heritage in the built environment, and living heritage, as well as land use controls. Visiting on-site and peer-to-peer learning is important because visits allow participants—planners, businesspeople, neighborhood activists and technicians—to see first hand the approaches and techniques used in world-class cities and, as we saw in Seattle, to interact with each other, to build a sense of togetherness and team spirit.

3   City studios for working groups: These events would bring international experts for stays in the city of sufficient duration to allow practical work and achieve specific solutions to specific problems, such as site designs, neighborhood plans, small-scale transportation solutions, and land use. They could be followed by project-specific learning integrated into work programs. (It might also be possible, and is certainly desirable, to link these projects with training institutions as a way to modernize graduate programs and provide credit for on-the-job planners toward eventual further qualifications.) As with the study tours, technical issues should be balanced with activities to build a sense of cohesiveness among participants from technical, political, and business backgrounds.

4   Technical exchanges of days and weeks (some extended into short courses): Selected analysts engage in technical exchanges to study and gain proficiency in use of analytical tools like surveys, geographical information systems (GIS), simulation, scenario development, and other planning techniques.

A national or regional conference can help to set the stage, validate the objective, and reaffirm the commitment in the city as well as in regional and national centers. This visioning conference would educate and mobilize the public and local and national policy makers about the importance of urban learning and the stakes, as well as the activities of cities in other regions of the world. The idea is to convey a sense of movement and purpose.

A goal-setting and benchmarking exercise would follow and set the stage for an international city tour to study the best examples of practice in a given field. Parallel working groups within each pilot city would then set about the work on policy and practice toward implementing key steps to achieve the goals.

In year two, work groups would have encounters with world or regional experts working on the same or similar subjects. Each city would then review its goals and benchmarks and toward the end of year three present its progress in each area to a regional or international conference, along with peer cities. Parallel work groups would continue to make progress in year four and beyond. Further technical workshops or clinics would help to solve specific problems. A small national conference would complete the cycle in year five.

This hypothetical learning sequence is intended to illustrate both the stages and the various mechanisms of learning. Each of the key institutions in a city would be included in the design and implementation of the multi-year and multi-city program. Each would also be exposed to peers—both other pilots and a wider range of cities where programs or best practice have been developed. In addition, local or regional educational institutions would also be included, especially those that offer postgraduate degrees in public urban policy, environmental and urban planning, urban design, transport planning, economics, land use planning and other sub-specialties.

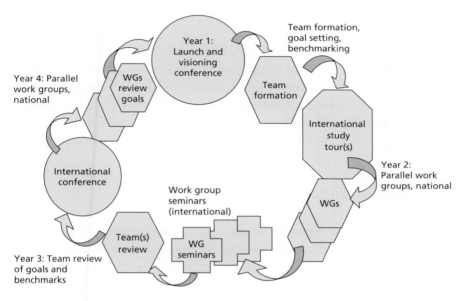

Figure 11.1 Hypothetical sequence of events for city learning and exchange

City readiness to learn

Whether or not a pre-packaged program like the one just described is to be undertaken, cities should know whether they are ready to engage in learning. At least two factors are critical. First, the motivation for learning must be plainly visible and sustainable. Cities that can show a record of effort—of past actions, committed resources, diagnostics, pending trouble over economic base or natural calamity—would fit this criterion. Second, community stakeholders beyond elected officials must be engaged. This criterion is essential not just to bridge the political term of office of elected officials but also to develop a sense of common purpose.

Some literature, including some of my own work (Campbell and Fuhr, 2004), marks the importance of individual leaders, especially in adopting innovation. Yet none of the cases covered in the book suggests that an outstanding visionary leader or champion is indispensable in learning. Outstanding leaders can accomplish great things. A well-respected leader can get the ball rolling in learning. But individuals are not sufficient to carry the weight of a long-term program in urban learning. Not only should leadership be a collective noun, leadership elites should also be widely based in the community and exhibit features of shared values and interests. Nothing showed this more clearly than the city clouds of trust in the cases of Chapter 6, where linkages of trust revealed hidden actors who were otherwise not necessarily community leaders, and certainly not elected heads of local government.

Perhaps the most important quality of leadership is the ability to see across the many variegated and often contentious groups in a city and not lose sight of the common ground that learning can represent for many of them. Great skill is needed to manage networks in situations where, as Crosby puts it, "no one is in charge" (Crosby and Bryson, 2005: Chapter one), but which have a coordinating influence on the many networks that make up city learning machinery.

Selected areas for research

Development institutions and knowledge brokers—for instance, NGOs, the EU, regional associations and universities—are increasingly focused on documenting and extracting lessons and synthesizing best practice, and then gauging the factors of cost and outcomes of city learning. Several key topics are singled out here for further work.

Efficiency of learning

A market for information exchange forms and keeps operating if participants are getting benefit from it. Cities reduce the costs and the risks of innovation and reform by seeing what has worked elsewhere and gauging whether it will work in their own circumstances. In this way, learning cuts the costs of information. But are there more efficient ways to exchange information?

A first step is to conduct comparative analysis of cities engaging in various kinds of knowledge exchange, horizontal visits or other types, including those suggested in Chapter 4, to evaluate value added in both content of knowledge and in formation of innovative milieu. Chapter 8 opened the way with a post hoc look at participants in Seattle's study missions. Evidence does indicate that tighter bonds are formed, but the survey did not cover enough about content of knowledge. Future work needs to understand a baseline of traveler knowledge and outcomes in terms of immediate learning as well as longer-term application. Comparative work could then explore variables—of cities themselves or the categories of knowledge they seek—that shape or determine outcomes.

Evaluation experience in the World Bank Institute attempts to gauge outcomes of different modalities of learning by survey of individual participants from many different agencies (Liu *et al.*, 2006). The WBI organizes thousands of learning events each year in regional, national and local forums. Only about 60 events per year are aimed at officials from municipal governments. Of these, a small handful (e.g., some core courses) is organized for specific cities or regions. Most learning events involve high-level policy makers as well as middle-level practitioners, and evaluations are performed regularly. Periodically, in-depth follow-up studies are also conducted.

Findings from these reviews indicate that, in general, and not referring specifically to cities or city groups, the most effective learning in strategic areas and approaches to problems, as in the case of our type-one and type-two cities, is when action planning of some kind is performed and when higher-level personnel are involved. Reviews for specific countries reaffirm these points and also indicate the importance of a series of events and of engaging the client partner in the design of the events. One central question is whether and how these hands-on exercises—i.e., action planning or team efforts—have been or can be extended into a wider circle in a specific city, and whether, when sustained in a consistent way, they lead to the creation of an innovative milieu.

Virtual learning

We know that the power of the web for signaling alerts and making connections is unparalleled. But can it function to create or support an innovative milieu? Knowledge economies make widespread use of virtual connectivity and there is little doubt that connecting across the web adds to the productivity of information exchange. But does it yield an innovative climate for the interpersonal exchange of values and the formation of trust? This and other related questions can be answered empirically and deserve to be the subject of serious tests. Distance learning, journalism, blogs, electronic bulletin boards and web pages are useful; many are meeting a market test. But often they are tools of the first order, not the third order, of learning. Personal, face-to-face connection is the type that has the best chance of carrying a place beyond smart cities.

Clouds of trust

Analytical tools of social network analysis are well suited to explore the degree of connectedness of practitioner or manager groups in cities. The case evidence introduced in Part III barely scratches the surface, but it is enough to beg the question. To what extent can measures of coherence in networks of city leaders be used to evaluate city leadership, to identify gaps in communication, to serve as a guide to remedy fractured communities and to predict outcomes? These and other research questions—for instance, comparative analysis, both horizontally across cities and longitudinally within a city over time—are easily subject to exploration and verification.

Outcomes of lessons

The cases in this book have only scratched the surface of the learning process, particularly as regards outcomes. Further, we may have been scratching in the wrong places. More careful documentation about learning experiences—gauging some of the trajectory of learning, monitoring the process, for instance of validation, absorption and application—would throw more light on how learning works in loosely organized systems like cities. What can be said about timetables? Do typical shortcuts and detours appear? Many lessons have been learned repeatedly but in separate circumstances, and tracking "policy migration" as Kevin Ward and colleagues have done would help to gain insight on typical conditions and reactions (Ward, 2006).

In addition to a focus on policy in changing places, we also need to look at changing policy holding the place constant. This requires a longer-term perspective on how learning in a specific place plays out over time. Documentation of the twists and turns in the learning path would help to understand where typical problems arise and how to remedy them. For instance, the experience in Curitiba showed how IPPUC adapted its mission to suit the changing political climate. As more populist administrations shifted the focus of investment from infrastructure to social programs, IPPUC began to emphasize its data-management tools, a robust GIS system and extensive neighborhood archive on social and economic conditions. IPPUC survived many changes of this kind. Can we learn other lessons from its successes?

The new urban age: cities getting to know themselves

The pace of exchange for learning and many other aspects seems to be accelerating. Organizational tissue consisting of city-to-city relationships—national associations and international confederations—has grown quickly in the past few decades. This book has focused on learning exchange in policy and practice of the day-to-day business of cities. In recent decades, the agenda of concerns has been expanding—poverty, urban spread, metropolitan governance, environmental sustainability, climate change, corruption and violence.

We can surmise from the cases studies that as cities embark on a pathway to structured learning, they get to know themselves. Many cities are already past the dawn of recognition that the protective cloak of trade restrictions is gone and not likely to return. They are exposed to new pressures to distinguish themselves from neighbors and competitors. They are beginning to take steps to distinguish themselves with slogans, brands, business plans, and reform. No example is better than Bilbao positioning itself as the center of city learning, or Singapore as the go-to source for talent and managerial expertise in Asian urban affairs.

As self-recognition takes hold in the wider world, cities may be expected to see their mutual interests more clearly. The process is not a trivial matter because of the many moving parts in political and social forces in cities. As collective leadership in cities gets more broadly engaged with itself, they come to see the commonalities in contradictions as well as the dormant synergies waiting to be put into motion. Ten years ago, I was struck by the "aha" experience in a room full of mayors. At the closing session on problems of cities, one of the mayors declared, "I see that I am not alone." His discovery was acknowledged and welcomed by his peers with a round of applause. A similar insight underpins initiatives in cities like Bilbao and Singapore to deploy a determined strategy to be hubs of learning and policy advice.

These emerging initiatives may be the bellwethers of the most important and lasting products of moving beyond smart cities. As the city-urbanist movement presses forward, cities turn more inward, reflecting on their growing self-awareness and their new role in global affairs. Our learning perspective has shown cities engaging each other, exchanging ideas, examining policies, and finding good practices. The problems are often common, and the solutions protean. The hunting and gathering of ideas is also spawning institutional layers nationally, regionally and globally to facilitate the exchange, as cities find it convenient to band together for both learning and self-interest. The accretion process may be leading to an entirely new urban age in which cities begin to exercise their common knowledge and common muscle in urban and global development.

References

Campbell, T. and H. Fuhr (2004). *Leadership and innovation in subnational government. Case studies from Latin America* (WBI Development Series), World Bank Institute, Washington, DC.

Crosby, B. C. and J. M. Bryson (2005). *Leadership for the common good: tackling public problems in a shared-power world*, Jossey-Bass, New York.

Czarniawska, B. (2002). *A tale of three cities—or the glocalization of city management*, Oxford University Press, Oxford, UK.

Dobbs, R., S. Smit, J. Remes, J. Manyika, C. Roxburgh, and A. Restrepo (2011). *Urban world: Mapping the economic power of cities*, McKinsey & Company, 49pp.

Liu, C., S. Jha and T. Yang (2006) "What influences the outcomes of WBI's learning programs —evidence from WBIEG's evaluations," *World Bank Institute Evaluation Series EG06-17*, p. 37.

Marris, P. (1974). *Loss and change*, Pantheon, New York.

Sivaramakrishnan, K. (2011). *Re-visioning Indian cities. The urban renewal mission*, Sage, New Delhi.

Van de Ven, A. H. and T. J. Hargrave (2004). "Social, technical, and institutional change: a literature review and synthesis," in M. S. Poole and A. H. Van de Ven (eds), *Handbook of organizational change and innovation*, Oxford University Press, New York, pp. 259–303.

Ward, K. (2006). "'Policies in motion,' urban management and state restructuring: the trans-local expansion of business improvement districts," *International Journal of Urban and Regional Research*, 30, pp. 54–75.

Appendix 1 Features of learning by type

Four main features are important in each type of learning. First is the purpose of learning. One key question is whether the city, understood in a very broad sense, agrees on a problem. Second is the nature of the entity responsible for learning. At a minimum, it is important to understand whether an entity, an agent, has been identified and the agent and mandate are suited for the job. Is it climate change, disaster preparedness, strategic planning? These have distinctly different requirements in technical, managerial and political terms.

Third is the learning style, i.e., the mechanism of learning. This refers to the extent to which the city or its agency is active in pursuing knowledge or is in a passive, receptive mode where knowledge and information flows depend on forces outside the city. Fourth is whether policies are in place to sustain the learning process and whether these are buttressed by their own capacity building. Each of these aspects is reviewed for the five types of cases in Chapter 4.

Table A1.1 Summary features of learning types

Feature of learning	Type 1 and 2—cities and agencies	Type 3—binary pairing	Type 4—clusters	Type 5—networks
1. Why learn?				
Purpose	Crisis resolution, economic transformation, competitiveness	Specific policy issues, best practice techniques	Norms and standards of practice in class of issues (e.g. heritage, reform)	Issues of standard best practice in municipal government

Table A1.1 continued

Feature of learning	Type 1 and 2—cities and agencies	Type 3— binary pairing	Type 4— clusters	Type 5— networks
Subject and focus	Approaches and strategies, benchmarks, elite awareness	Improvement in management, budgeting, procurement, etc.	Conventions, standards, techniques within class of subjects	Varies widely; typical problems of local governments
2. Agency				
Mandate	Specifically defined, long-term strategy	Contiguous with local government	Extends or enhances typical municipal mandate	Contiguous with local government mandate
Leadership (individual/ collective)	Strong, collective	Strong, less collective	Strong, moderately collective	Moderate and variable
Formal/ informal, action plan	Mixed, yes	Mostly formal, yes	Formal, varies	Formal, no
Community engagement	Yes	Limited	Varies	Limited
3. Learning modalities				
Active/passive, source of learning	Active, imports and outbound	Active, imports and outbound	Mixed, mostly imports	Passive, mostly imports
Regularity, term, follow-up	Regular, long term, yes	Regular, short term, no	Varies, medium term, varies	Irregular, short term, no
Core group size, level, and bonding	Large, high, strong	Moderate, medium to high, medium	Varies, moderate, medium	Varies, varies, varies

Feature of learning	Type 1 and 2—cities and agencies	Type 3—binary pairing	Type 4—clusters	Type 5—networks
4. Capacity-building				
Sustained policy guidance	Substantial	Moderate	Moderate	Little
Investment in learning	Substantial	Moderate	Moderate	Little

Appendix 2 List of surveyed cities

City	Pop. (million)	Proactive 1 = yes 2 = no 0 = DK	Reforms 1 = many 2 = some 3 = few
Amman	2.8	1	1
Athens, US	0.5	2	1
Atlanta, US	0.5	0	1
Bangkok	6.3	1	1
Barcelona	1.6	1	1
Berlin	4.2	1	2
Bogota	8.6	2	1
Brussels Region	1.8	1	2
Buenos Aires, DF	2.5	1	2
Cebu City	0.9	2	1
Charlotte	0.71	1	1
Colombo	0.65	2	2
Da Nang	3.5	1	1
Dakar Region	1.1	2	2
Dubai	1	0	1
Hanoi	0.7	2	3
Honolulu	0.75	1	2
Hyderabad	10	2	1
Incheon	2.5	2	2
Istanbul	8	1	2
Istanbul Metro	12.5	2	1

Kathmandu	0.671	1	2
Kobe	1.5	2	3
Madrid	3.3	1	1
Manila City	2.5	1	1
Masbate	0.05	2	3
Mashhad	2.4	1	2
Melbourne	3.9	1	3
Mexico, DF	10	2	2
Mexico Metro	13	2	1
Naga City	0.1	1	2
Paris Region	11.6	1	1
Pateros	0.075	2	3
Phnom Penh	1.4	2	1
Portland	0.87	2	1
Salt Lake City	0.5	2	1
San Salvador	1.5	1	1
Santa Cruz, Bolivia	1.5	2	1
Seattle	0.7	2	1
Seoul Metro	23.9	1	2
Stockholm City	0.8	2	1
Stockholm Metro	1.9	2	3
Surabaya	3	1	3
Tabriz	1.4	2	3
Tehran	12.7	2	3
Turin	0.58	2	1
Toronto	5.5	1	1
Ulaanbaatar	1.1	1	3

Note: Some cities provided incomplete data, others submitted redundant responses. For these reasons the total number of respondents to the survey (53) does not always equal the number presented in tables and figures.

Appendix 3 **Field method**

Data gathering followed a roughly similar procedure in each of the case study cities. Nominations of persons to be interviewed were made by a panel representing public, private and civic leaders and observers, each of whom were associated with a particular project or issue in the city, for instance, a strategic plan, land use issue, or local economic development. In each case, the nomination criteria included: (a) persons who have a reputation for civic-mindedness; (b) had played a visible role in public decision-making, whether representing themselves or their place of work or affiliation.

From the nominations, I selected nominees more or less randomly from each of three domains: public sector; private enterprise; and civic, including neighborhood groups, NGOs and universities. The core group in each city consisted of about 20 persons. Most selected persons appeared on more than one list of nominators.

Face-to-face interviews were conducted following a semi-structured format. Most interviews lasted between 60 and 90 minutes; one lasted more than four hours. Topics covered the interviewee's role in the community; his or her perspective on innovation and change as represented by a specific project or reform undertaken by the city; the sources of good ideas and innovations in relation to that change; and names of others whom the interviewee regards as (a) trustworthy and (b) active like himself or herself. "Sources" in the tables refer to interviewees; "references" refer to those persons named by interviewees.

Appendix 4 Timeline of IPPUC in Curitiba

1943	Agache Plan created
1965	IPPUC created
1966	Master Plan approved
1967	Creation of pedestrian mall in city center
1972	Law extends IPPUC remit to include continuous planning
1977	IPPUC helps to coordinate interdepartmental procedures
1978	Integrated transport network devised; World Bank agreement on loan signed by mayor
1978–1982	Neighborhood bus terminals created
1981	Management system developed to track public works
1982	Change of political administration
1983	IPPUC downgraded to municipal department; objectives shifted to social concerns
1985	IPPUC participates in the national census for the city; transportation vouchers introduced
1987	Further personnel reforms; technicians begin to leave
1988	IPPUC becomes advisory arm of the office of mayor
1989	Lerner elected to office of mayor
1992	Curitiba Resolution, one of the founding documents for Agenda 21 of the UN Habitat meeting in Rio de Janeiro
1996–1997	Revitalization of the historic quarter
2000	Intensification of public participation and linking city to citizen
2003	Protection of Heritage Assets
2005	Climate Change

Appendix 5 IPPUC organization chart

Figure A5.1 IPPUC organization chart

Index